SCREAM THERAPY

A Punk Journey through Mental Health

Jason Schreurs

FLEX YOUR HEAD PRESS

ISBN 978-1-7389-2140-9

First edition

10 9 8 7 6 5 4 3 2 1

Typeset in Futura, Cormorant Garamond,
and Letter Gothic by Ella Collier.

Printed and bound in Canada at Island Blue Print on 100% sustainable
recycled fibre with biogas as the main energy source.

FLEX
YOUR
HEAD
PRESS

5776 Willow Ave.
qathet Regional District
Canada
V8A 4P7

flexyourheadpress.com

Flex Your Head Press gratefully and respectfully
acknowledges that the land on which it operates is on the
traditional territory of the Tla'amin Nation.

For Adam, Gared, and all the punks who have passed.

Punk rock was born out of the struggle to
better people's mental health.
It was a reaction to the world we lived in.
It gave me hope.
It gave me the ability to survive.

–Justin Pearson, Three One G Records

"Punk rock saved my life."

My face leaked tears when I first heard those words come out of someone else's mouth. It happened during my very first interview for this book and the *Scream Therapy* podcast. My tears were happy tears—tears of validation. The kind of tears you let run down your face without wiping them away. Because you want them there. I wanted them there.

Punk rock saved my life, too.

As a youth, somewhere in my gut I knew a safe place was out there where I could be me. In the punk scene, I found my chosen family. Our throats screamed raw; sinew and muscle tossed around with wild abandon. Embodied bodies in unison; individuality as a common cause.

Punk rock isn't a music genre; it's a way of being. For as many years as I've been alive, gritty, outspoken, inspiring bands have led the charge for mental wellness. The punk scene has created a shelter with a "welcome punks" sign on its front doors, and those who make themselves at home find solace.

Punk attracts folks of all ages. I'm 50 years old now, and I'm listening to Minor Threat, a band I first heard 35 years ago. "I Don't Wanna Hear It" is blasting so loud in my earbuds my wife Megan can hear it from across our living room.

One in four people have a mental health condition at some point in their lives, according to the World Health Organization, yet society often looks down its nose at them as if flicking a flea off a dog's back. I've chosen to depathologize language in this book. I believe we don't need anyone telling us we're disordered, ill, diseased, or any other term that stigmatizes us and holds us down. Despite my personal preference, my intention is to make these pages welcoming, not be a language cop.

As a cis white male punk who lives under a roof, has centralized heating, is not currently at-risk, and has never been overtly discriminated against for living with my mental health conditions, I've never felt demeaned or criminalized, and I've never been involuntarily hospitalized. That's not the case for countless marginalized and at-risk punks. Living in Canada—land of universal health care—as a person below the poverty line, I still have access to services that countless people, such as those in the indigenous, BIPOC, and LBGTQ+ communities, sadly do not. And I don't have to fear for my health and safety every single day.

Society labels people who don't, or won't, conform to its standards as troublemakers at best, criminals at worst. It ostracizes people with mental health conditions, and they can have a hell of a time finding any place that will truly accept them. Even more so if they're drawn to punk's "noise" (read: loud) and "danger" (read: cathartic). People's lives are forever changed when they find the punk scene. Or when the punk scene finds them.

Punk and mental health have always been connected. Songs about personal struggle have been shouted into dented microphones and launched out of beat-up instruments since the genre's formation in the mid-'70s. Pioneers such as the Ramones, X-Ray Spex, Hüsker Dü, the Slits, Minutemen, and Circle Jerks challenged conventions, carved out a do-it-yourself ethos for punk scenes worldwide, and tackled the taboo subject of mental health without shame.

Los Angeles punk/hardcore forebearers Black Flag sang about depression and alienation. Henry Rollins grunted and growled onstage with a piercing look that people described as animalistic. I always saw him as rageful yet hopeful. His unnerving glare told me he was processing serious shit and living to tell us about it. Influential Venice Beach skate-punks Suicidal Tendencies had a name that said it all. When I was 13 and listened to Mike Muir yelling at his mom (he wasn't crazy, all he wanted was a Pepsi, just one Pepsi) in the song "Institutionalized," I could sense something much darker was lurking beneath his humour. It took me more than three decades to face it within myself.

The effect punk has on those who embrace it—as it embraces them—is immeasurable. Take it from me. Punk rescued me from rotting in a mill town and pulled me toward the city where underground bands played their hearts out in unlicensed show spaces with sweat dripping down the walls. It expanded my limited perception of the world. In my small town, I had to pretend to fit in. In the city, going to shows with other outcasts in black t-shirts and ripped jeans was downright communal. Screaming at my new friends, them screaming back—call and response, punk style. We were a bunch of magnificent weirdos who flew the freak flag, declaring our truths from rooftops like the Hot Water Music song. We still are.

Without apology, I live life my way. I listen to music most people call noise—come over to my house and bring earplugs—and I speak out against injustice with the knowledge gained from unapologetic punk rock. Since I was a pre-teen, music has lifted me from intolerable moods. It's made me smile and muster a "fuck yeah" when life felt unliveable. Albums by Fugazi, Bikini Kill, Propagandhi, Sleater-Kinney, White Lung, and so many more have helped me accept setbacks, dodge obstacles, embrace emotions, and find stability.

On October 12, 2018, I made an emergency trip to the hospital where a psychiatrist gave me a diagnosis of bipolar, a foreign word I barely recognized. As a lifelong punk, I was a storied veteran. As a person in a mental health crisis, I was a hapless rookie. Since my diagnosis, other punks—musicians, mental health professionals, advocates, and activists—have shared their lived experiences with me, and through theirs I pieced together my own.

"Punk rock saved my life."

Members of the scene who I interviewed for this book and the *Scream Therapy* podcast repeat this mantra again and again, and it's hardly a coincidence. From its unflinching inception, punk rock—for me, for us—has always been scream therapy.

SHOW 0
CRACE MOUNTAIN
NANAIMO, BC
SATURDAY, JUNE 30, 2018

You're staggering on the highway shoulder, headbanging to wake yourself up. You've never been so exhausted. You crawl back into your red Toyota Corolla—the one with two missing hubcaps—slide your tongue along your swollen lips and ease the car into drive like you're cutting wires on a detonator. Five minutes down the road, staying awake is unbearable, excruciating. Your eyelids surrender to the weight as if they're tied to bricks. The car quakes, your eyes jolt open, and you see yourself veering toward the median. You swerve back into your lane. You thank rumble strips for saving your life.

You're the leader of an improv band called Punk Jams. Two hours prior to your near-death experience, you're readying yourself to play the final slot at Sinker Fest, a house-show festival in Nanaimo, BC. Set time is an unfathomable 2 am at a shithole called Crace Mountain. Crace, as it's known, is the ideal venue for Punk Jams' brand of improv skronk noise. It's a dirty, gross, stinking converted basement space with broken sound equipment. Drunken punks litter the backyard.

Punk Jams is heavy on the noise, almost non-existent on the melody. Each night, you haphazardly assemble different musicians to wreak chaos. As the ringleader for a demented punk rock circus, you've found an outlet to channel your neuroses, and with it comes jaw-throttling performances. To add to your fucked-up mystique, you've been carting around garbage bags full of Salvation Army rejects and makeshift masks.

The Crace show is the tour's final gig. Inexplicably, you've booked Punk Jams to play four shows in the past 48 hours. Your tank is so close to empty it hurts, but you dig deep, just like you always do. You find a grimy bathroom upstairs and fiddle with the broken lock, then give up. You rustle through your bags and throw some choice costume pieces onto a sink counter that's orange with mildew. In the mirror, you see angry red marks circling your neck. As you take a swig from a half-empty coconut water someone left on the counter, cold glass in your hand, a spooky twinge shudders you into a flashback. Your feet all cut up, spilling blood at a house show in Nanaimo last year.

It's okay. Nothing bad's gonna happen this time.

Strapping yourself into mismatched clothes three sizes too small with a shredded lace scarf tied around your eyes, you look like a punk rock circus clown who smash-and-grabbed a Value Village. A Punk Jams doomy guitar riff erupts, and you fly down the stairs and charge toward the noise emanating from tonight's bandmates—*your people*. Overflowing with rage and joy, you unleash a bridge jumper's scream. The band churns out an uncompromising dirge, the backdrop to your ear-piercing shrieks for.... Understanding? Justice? Help? Punk Jams is pure expression and emotional release, a desperate form of therapy. A way to protect yourself from yourself.

Halfway through the second "song," all 20 minutes of it, your vocal cords are burning alive. You grab another coconut water off a guitar amp, and the bottle slips in your sweat-drenched hands. Using your ripped crop top, tonight's upper garment, you can't find a grip, so you hand the bottle to a guy in the front row and make wild, bottle-opening gestures. The guy grins at you, shrugs, and smashes the bottle on the concrete floor.

What the...? Your brain sends you an urgent message. *Don't fall in that glass.*

Within moments, you slip on the beer-soaked floor and land hands-down in the sharp, wet mess. Jagged chunks stick in your right palm, and it gushes red. You don't miss a drumbeat, barking nonsensical ramblings while picking glass out of your hand. You rip off your crop top and reveal dark, swollen bruises and deep scratches—shrapnel from previous shows—and tie the shirt around your spurting hand to slow the bleeding. You wipe blood down the front of the bottle smasher's t-shirt for revenge, leaving a palm-shaped, crimson smear. You stumble toward your drummer and collapse near the kick drum. The final bass-drum hit pounds your skull.

Fifteen minutes down the highway, you pull the Corolla over again, and you're back standing on the shoulder. Shaking, deep breathing. A semi-truck rushes by at 140 kms an hour, threatening to blow your wavering body off the shoulder and into the ditch. You're dishevelled, holding up your right hand wrapped in a crop top with an ominous, rust-coloured stain soaking through it. You're sucking in and huffing out, nearing hyperventilation, and the last five days of bedlam rush back. Then, goddamned clarity.

You can't keep doing this. You're killing yourself.

After that June 30 show at Crace Mountain, I would go on to spend nine more gloriously destructive days in August sacrificing my body—*your body*—in the name of Punk Jams. Standing on the highway's edge that night, half alive and melded into one with a whirling dervish I came to know as the Punk Screamer, I had no idea then what I know now.

You weren't killing yourself. You were saving me.

MONSTERS

The lily pads gently ride ripples on the lake's surface, masquerading as floating innocence, clutching the rowboat, holding it still. Their little slits look like Pac-Man's mouth. I'm a Pac-Man ghost and he's coming to eat me. I scrunch my eyes and wish I could magically transport back to shore. I peek between my fingers, and the lily pads are creeping around the boat now, overcrowding it, climbing up the sides. Stems circling my wrists, tying me down, arms, legs, hands, and feet. The summer heat sears me.

"Never look directly into the sun," adults tell me.

"Never talk to strangers," they say, pupils blazing.

I want to go back to shore. Please bring me back to shore.

He drags me from the rowboat's edge and pushes me face down in the bottom, his hot breath moving up my naked shoulder blades, hissing into my ears.

Skip.

In the woods behind the trailer park. Tummy down on the forest floor. Dry pine needles scratch my bare arms, legs, groin, and chest. The ground is like a burlap-sack with thumb tacks punched through it. I'm yanked up from the pine needles. I'm bent over, wiping a sticky mess with my hands—dripping off my bum, down the back of my legs. They're circling me and leering. A dirty BO smell. Their laughs and taunts, calling me bad names.

I'm only six... or maybe seven.

These are my memories of being sexually abused on an afternoon, or possibly two, at the lakeside trailer park where my mom and I lived.

Black swallows the rest—before, during, after, and in between. What else happens in that boat and in that forest? Are they separate memories from separate times? No matter how hard I've tried to answer these questions over the past 45 years, certain memories need to be redacted.

In the years that follow, I began a search to dull my trauma's jagged edges. I need to find something to soothe and distract me—maybe even heal me—and it becomes my lifelong pursuit. With the trailer park left behind, I discover a kind of therapy I could have never imagined.

Hard, fast, and loud.

Close the closet door so tightly
You don't know who might be in there
These monsters are real
These are monsters I can feel
Heavens to Betsy - "Monsters"

"A 12-year-old kid doesn't need to get punched in the head by an adult."

Justin Pearson exhales and a nervous laugh sneaks out as we share a sketchy Skype connection for a *Scream Therapy* podcast interview—just two late-40s punks talking about our trauma. Violence was a recurring theme in Justin's early life, and it didn't begin or end when he crossed paths with his mom's new boyfriend, Frank.

"Yeah, he physically abused me, but it could've been worse," Justin says. "It can always be worse. So, I never complained about it."

Justin and I share a kinship, downplaying our abuse to focus on the less fortunate. He and I have big hearts, and putting others before ourselves is the punk thing to do. Yes, Frank beat the shit out of Justin. Yes, Frank beat his dog. Yes, Frank pulled a gun on him. It could've been worse. Friends that Justin and I know in the scene have had it worse. That doesn't sit quite right for me though, and I sense it might not for Justin either. He tells me he wants to make it clear that he's not discrediting his own experiences, then shifts into hyperdrive and names his trauma in a flurry.

"It still sucked to have a dude beat me up or who liked to beat my mom up. And I'd come home and be, like, 'Mom, why is your arm broken? Oh, Frank did that to your arm. Oh, and that's cool, we're still gonna live with this guy?'"

Around this time, Justin found the San Diego punk/hardcore scene, and it accepted him into the fold. The friendships he made and music he discovered helped form his identity. He aligned himself with an array of people dealing with their own trauma and mental health struggles and made meaningful, life-long connections. Justin's roots have settled in the punk scene's safer space for more than 35 years. He's screamed and played bass in a string of bands, including Struggle, Swing Kids, Retox, Dead Cross, and the Locust, most of which sound like a blender chucked into a food processor. Justin also founded Three One G Records, which has released what he calls "absurd music" since 1994.

Justin admits he was a bit of a dick growing up (yeah, join the club) and is quick to add that any kid embracing punk's rebellion should be, but he also had a tragic reason to be a mouthy, troubled teen. In October 1987, two men robbed and murdered Justin's dad in his driveway in Phoenix, Arizona. In a staccato rhythm, he launches into a story he's recounted hundreds of times. It happened on the night before Halloween. His father had gotten a new job and went to the bar after a meeting. A heavy drinker, he had a few too many and hit on a young woman who was with the two men. A fight broke out and bar staff threw them all out.

"Then these two dudes followed my dad home and beat him and robbed him in our driveway," Justin says. "One of the guys hit him on the head with a crowbar, and a brain aneurysm exploded. That was the technical cause of the death. He died in the driveway and my mom found him. It was pretty fucking weird."

Justin takes a much-needed pause, and his words hang. A gulp lodges in my throat, and I'm triggered back to 1995 when my estranged father—who I never knew—was in a hospital in Victoria, dying. Someone who didn't appreciate his tone had punched him off a barstool at one of his watering holes. When he hit the ground, an aneurysm burst in his head. The similarities of Justin's and my dad's stories are eerie, and we exchange the sighs of fatherless sons. The last time I saw my dad I wasn't much more than a year old. Justin spent 12 years with his—an abusive alcoholic who would look right through him and zero in on another target.

"My dad was abusive only to my mom. He wasn't abusive to me. I mean, he didn't care about me, so I was ignored." Justin lets the sting of paternal neglect slip off his tongue. "After he was killed, my mom met Frank pretty quick, and we moved from Arizona to California to live with him. And he was abusive to me and her. Then it was a new level."

Since an early age, Justin has had chronic migraines that make him puke uncontrollably and require immediate bedrest. "I was always leaving school because I was throwing up everywhere and being just super fucked up," he says. This sounds too familiar. I tell Justin my youngest son has the same affliction with the same symptoms, and we shake off another spooky coincidence. As his migraines worsened, Justin connected them to stress and trauma and has worked hard to manage them. Believe it or not, howling and screeching into a microphone is part of Justin's treatment plan—a way to deal with his shit.

I know punk musicians who talk about dissociation. I've often heard the phrase "I go somewhere else" used to describe the heightened focus that triggers muscle memory and leads someone into a subconscious, unleashed creative space. Justin finds the sweet spot at the thrash-zone epicentre. Onstage, he goes into beast mode—an unadulterated, pure-body release as soon as he hears the first snare-drum hit.

"It's almost like a gunshot. It's, *boom*, there's the race! It helps me transcend somewhere else. I don't become fully aware and rational until I'm done," Justin says.

I've seen singers' pupils roll back. Guitarists hurling their bodies and instruments at each other. Drummers destroying their kits mid-set, pinned under a disaster of cymbal stands and floor toms. I've watched with equal parts worry and fascination as punks self-harm onstage with zero self-awareness. And I've seen Justin, veins in his neck bulging, eyes bugging, spitting trauma all over the stage.

"What do you think?" I hesitate before asking Justin the second part of my question. "Are you channelling your trauma?" He dives into his answer. "Man, I don't wanna say I'm channelling my trauma. I think I'm channelling everything. Fuck man, just standing there, whatever is happening in my mind, or beyond my mind, it feels like when my parents beat each other up, and I'd have to grab my dog and hide behind the couch, so we didn't get hurt. It kind of felt like..." He makes the growling noises of a snarling beast and I understand. I've felt the same need to force my innards out of my mouth. "I look at pictures or videos of myself from shows," Justin says, "and I think, 'Fuck, you look pretty fucked up right there." He shoots me a toothy grin. "Screaming is this intense, I'm-gonna-stab-you-in-the-neck type shit, you know?"

He puts a pause on the violent imagery to clarify that his pent-up rage boils over into pure joy, and the two feed off each other. Justin says most people he's yelling at during his shows understand and appreciate his outbursts.

"We're performing to people that are like-minded, loving, smart people who I want to relate to and connect to, so I don't really want to attack them," he says. "It's all part of the music and communicating beyond words."

It's impossible to say how many people gravitate toward the punk scene to either confront or distract themselves from trauma. Throw a guitar pick into the crowd at a show, and it's bound to bounce off people who use punk's energy for exactly those reasons. While the ratio of punks who have severe trauma versus those who don't isn't much higher than the rest of society, the intensity of the music is a form of exposure therapy where survivors can confront their trauma in a controlled environment.

Understanding the effects of traumatic events on someone's mental health, and their healing process, is like pinpointing a drummer's signature style. Everyone has their own way to bash on a kit, and despite what type or level of trauma, there's no right or wrong way to do it. Trying to slap a rationalization or definition onto someone's trauma is detrimental to someone's experience and can be harmful. The medical world considers the Diagnostic and Statistical Manual of Mental Disorders (DSM) the be-all, end-all publication for the classification of mental health conditions, but critics say it overpathologizes emotional behaviour and isn't particularly trauma-informed.

One of my dear friends lives with dissociative identity. People living with this condition have suffered severe and repeated abuse and switch between one or more alternate personalities as a protection mechanism.

Everyone living with mental health conditions has their own individualized experience to tell, and I'm afraid of minimizing my friend's experiences by using blanket language from the DSM. I do know, with absolute certainty, that my friend is a constant inspiration and has taught me more about their condition than I could ever learn from a book compiled by psychiatrists. Moral of the story: listen and learn from folks with lived experience.

Punks have been known to choose Stephen Dansiger as a trauma therapist based on a single line in his website bio: "Dr. Steve played CBGB and Max's Kansas City in the late '70s."

Stephen jokes with me about the intersection of his upbringing and client base while wearing a button-up shirt I suspect has a punk shirt underneath. Although he's what I'd call a "decorated" health professional, not many of his colleagues or patients are aware, deep down, or maybe not so deep down, he's a decorated punk rocker as well.

Stephen spent his teenage years in the Long Island suburbs, less than two hours by metro to the infamous New York live music venues. By age 16, he found himself in the late '70s New York punk scene's sweet spot. The city's pedigree included Johnny Thunders and the Heartbreakers, Television, Suicide, and Patti Smith. Stephen estimates he saw the Ramones play 20 times. On September 21, 1979, he stared, jaw agape, as the Clash bass player Paul Simonon heaved his bass guitar over his head like a battle axe and smashed it on the Palladium Concert Hall's stage, an image immortalized on the band's *London Calling* album cover. As I said, Stephen's decorated.

Now based in California, Stephen's a family psychologist with a doctorate in clinical psychology. He developed a protocol combining reprocessing therapy and Buddhist mindfulness that's now used in trauma and addiction treatment centres across the US.

As is the case with most people, Stephen has his own trauma to work through. His older cousin, the person teenaged Stephen looked up to most, was hit by a drunk driver while walking home with some friends one night.

Stephen has no recollection of his mom breaking the news, and the trauma from his cousin's death led to depression, migraines, and drug and alcohol misuse that landed him in recovery in his mid-20s. He tells me without hesitation that the punk scene saved his life, words that always affirm my own experience.

"How did it save my life?" He lets the question hang between us in a shared knowing and looks over his square-ish-rimmed glasses. "It saved my life by helping me work through my trauma to the extent that I was able to during those days. And then when I went back to the scene as a recovering person, I realized I loved the music even more. Punk became part of my post-traumatic growth-resiliency program. I could really just be in joy in the music." Wait for it.... "So, yes, 100 percent, punk saved me."

Stephen is also a master therapist and trainer in eye movement desensitization and reprocessing (EMDR), a psychotherapy developed by American psychologist and educator Francine Shapiro. Using EMDR, therapists ask patients to recall traumatic incidents using bilateral stimulation, such as side-to-side eye movements, to come to adaptive resolutions. "We're faced with these traumas that have brought us to maladaptive processing, and we find what we need to survive. For some, it's punk rock; for some, it's alcohol and drugs; for some, it's dissociation; and for some, it's as simple as reading books. It could go any direction."

A singer writhes on the floor, screeching bloody fucking murder, while a bass player and drummer lock in so tight it's as if they're hearing each other's thoughts. A guitarist jumps in the air, kicks over an amp, and dives into the crowd. (Guitar solo orgasm faces are thankfully rare in punk.) Many punk musicians, as well as members of the audience, describe "going to another place" with the music to purge their inner demons. They often perform as opposite or different versions of how they present in their everyday lives. The reason for this dichotomy, according to Stephen, is we all dissociate to different degrees.

"When I hear people talking about that effect of dissociating, it can be the music or the performing that helps them to get out of themselves, like really out of themselves, to the point where they're like another part of themselves, or what you might call a persona," he says. "For others, it's more like they're just in a really, really cool flow state. They're in mindfulness."

Stephen's voice tends to sit in a higher register, and he's more excitable than the average mental health professional, talking with his hands in an almost worrying frequency. Although he'd cause a multi-car pileup directing traffic, his helicopter-blade gestures help me understand how trauma works and ways to process it. This is what I glean from Stephen's fast-fingered explanation: I picture a filing cabinet with my traumas inside, except the files are messy and out of order. They can skip past-present-past-present, and I need therapeutic resources to sort through them. Like aspiring toward a meticulous record collection, I can begin to organize and categorize the traumas in my filing cabinet. Punk is one piece of a treatment plan to get my files in order.

"I look at punk rock as being one of the many internal or external resources that a person might have," Stephen says. "Some people can work their trauma out and have it released and stay that way. They can have a positive result from punk that's sustainable. For other folks, the punk scene is a great place to work some stuff out, but then it comes back again. So where do you go from there? Where you go is mutual help groups, or treatment, or therapy."

Amygdala. The walnut-sized piece of the brain's limbic system. It acts as an alarm bell to signal danger, real or perceived, and puts the body into a fight, flight, or freeze response. For those who have experienced what's referred to as "capital T" trauma, such as severe abuse or neglect, an internal alarm bell can ring (*danger!*), or errant guitar feedback can shock the system (*squueeeaaall!*). Between fight, flight, or freeze, punks often choose to fight. This doesn't have to be a dust-up with white-power skinheads in a venue parking lot. It could be managing a mental health condition. It could be fighting each day to survive. Amygdala. It would make an amazing band name.

It's Halloween weekend, October 2016, and I'm at Fest in Gainesville, Florida (of course). Everyone who's close to me knows I'm a diehard, decade-long veteran of the annual punk festival because I'm always talking about it. On day one of this particular Fest, I'm watching Amygdala (ahem, amazing band name), one of the most rabid groups I've laid witness to. The San Antonio, Texas, band's fury is unbelievable, and I thrash along, injected with an endorphin boost. I look up from my headbangs and herky-jerk dance moves and lead wailer Bianca Cruz' performance tweaks major solidarity in me. She's crouching and rocking back and forth in anguish, purging memories of her childhood sexual abuse, vocal cords nearly rupturing. Jumping on the spot like she's pounding her trauma into dust under her feet, she's dismantling and reconstructing her amygdala's alarm bell.

Punks at her shows hold space for Bianca, and carved-out safety like this begets empowerment. Safer spaces create an environment to address topics that are fucking hard to talk about within the punk scene, never mind outside it. As I watch Bianca shiver and spasm, double fisting her microphone to shriek even harder, a realization slams me in face. I don't ever have to bury my childhood sexual abuse. I take a cleansing breath and headbang even harder.

Bianca lives with borderline personality, a mental health condition in which people suffer extreme emotions, usually flipping between love and hate, and traumatic flashbacks, dysregulating their moods for days or even weeks. Triggers lurk behind every exchange and experience, waiting to pull those living with borderline into dangerous states.

Onstage, the cyclone cacophony of Amygdala's punk metal mayhem coupled with Bianca's blood-curdling screams brings her to constructive tears. I bear witness from the front row and I, in turn, let tears drip down my face and onto my dingy Against Me! shirt. By the end of Amygdala's set, I'm like a dog wrestling a chew toy, and my neck is stiff for the rest of Fest. My shirt is a wasteland of spit from screaming along, so I upgrade to an Amygdala shirt.

"I might remember you from that show," Bianca says on a dicey video call from San Antonio. She has an unexpectedly calm voice for the person I saw yelling her face off at Fest, and I'm shocked that my dance moves from six years ago stuck with her. Bianca says she rarely forgets people she meets on tour, especially the ones that are having transformative experiences in the front row. She doesn't downplay the therapeutic affects her music has on people at Amygdala's shows.

"Me crying, showing these emotions, is really important. I feel it's my duty to be the person who talks about what we don't want to talk about. Or scream about," Bianca says. "Even people who aren't into punk rock, when they see Amygdala and what I'm doing, they receive it really well, and they say we need more stuff like this—people screaming about the things they're going through."

Can folks use punk as a qualitative tool to process trauma? I'm convinced they can. Trauma dissipates with therapy, creative expression, and physical activity. Punk combines all three. For me, punk is both the sword and shield I use to fight my daily battles. For Justin Pearson, it's a way to confront childhood abuse memories in a community he's loved—that's loved him—since he was a teen. Dr. Stephen says, in his expert opinion, yes, 100 percent, punk helps process traumatic events, and he's seen it first-hand. And for Bianca, tears are a positive release, cueing her audiences to release their own.

"People come up to me after shows and they're crying, but they tell me it's a good cry. They tell me they're glad I'm doing this." Bianca's voice cracks. "It feels good to know I'm not alone in the struggle." Being in a band gives Bianca the opportunity to tour and create what she calls a "self-healing journey" through music and lyrics.

Self-healing journey. What a perfect way to describe life as a punk.

SHOW 1
CAMPBELL RIVER, BC
EAGLES HALL
WEDNESDAY, AUGUST 8, 2018

You've been obsessing for days over how to cram everything you want to bring on tour into your Toyota Corolla. Most bands use a cargo van to load their gear and merch into the back, then squish the band members into the front. You're beginning the Punk Jams tour alone, and you're using a different setup altogether. As always, you'll have to scramble to find band members to play improv punk noise with you, otherwise it would be a solo tour, and an ugly one at that. Recruitment usually goes like this: book the show, hope your recruits don't ghost on you the night of, and poach members of other bands on the bill, if necessary. On constant worry alert, you slept an hour tops last night, fretting over logistics and whether the Corolla can bear the load of music gear, boxes of merch, and garbage bags crammed full of costumes.

Will everything fit? Please make it fit.

An omniscient narrator would describe Punk Jams as a bizarre, ill-founded fantasy. But it does have an origin story. The improv band with no steady members except you has gained momentum for two years since mutating from the subconscious place where you concoct your wildness. How did Punk

Jams come to be? The idea came to you at an ungodly hour while staring at your bedroom ceiling in a frenzied state of frantic idea building. You'd been in bands before, but never one like this was going to be. You craved unpredictability. Chaos. Danger. This time, nothing would stop you from sacrificing your body in punk's name and pouring your innards out for everyone to see. If that meant finding a new band each night to supply the soundtrack for your emotional surrender then, fuck, you'd damn well make it happen.

You put out a call for anyone interested in jamming to congregate in your dingy, poster-plastered basement. Soundproofing consisted of old carpets and enough egg cartons for a small-scale organic farm. None of it did anything to dampen the sound. The first Punk Jams instalment featured you and two other quasi-musicians willing to give hearing loss a try. While you tooled around on a destroyed guitar doubling as a percussion instrument, your friend shouted into a wonky effects pedal. To complete the trio, some guy lost to improv-punk history showed up to bang the drums. Curious on-listeners would have said it sounded like feral cats fighting in a wind tunnel.

Freaks and geeks came out of the woodwork. And the house shook. The same few punks kept coming back, loose jams got tighter, and Punk Jams decided to play its debut show in the same basement it was birthed in. Before long, you and the "band" were playing out-of-town shows. You even talked John Wright of legendary Victoria band Nomeansno into graciously pummelling the drum kit for a few local shows, an odd pairing with a scruffy guy who played mandolin through a distorted guitar amp. As the jams climaxed, the sheer volume transported you to a punk rock promised land, but it wasn't all paradise. Your erratic behaviour included near-serious injury. At one show you climbed the venue's speakers, pounded on undeserving ceiling tiles, flung your microphone into the crowd, and fell off, right arm folded underneath. You remember the soundperson running over and steadying the speakers as you toppled off. And the daggered pain in your arm.

Your costume concoctions, which you threw together in venue bathrooms, became increasingly outlandish. One of them, fashioned out of reflective space blankets, made you look like a silver Stay Puft Marshmallow Man. Sometimes you pulled back the reins and wondered, *are you taking this too far?*

Two years after that first basement jam, you booked a nine-show tour, the longest ever for Punk Jams, and with you as the only constant member again. Its itinerary will span Vancouver Island with Victoria weirdo punk/new wave band Crashing Into Things and legendary Vancouver band DOA joining for the last four shows. You weren't sure how you got DOA to agree to the shows, and you were careful not to jinx it, shrugging aside any uncertainties. The August 2018 Punk Jams tour would storm through Campbell River, Cumberland, Cortes Island, Gabriola Island, Nanaimo, Duncan, Quadra Island, Port Alberni, and Ucluelet, in that order. The Island route was as erratic as patches sewn to a crusty punk's leather jacket.

It's 6 am, and you're packing the Corolla to the gills with the gear and merch you've been meticulously organizing in the basement for weeks. You've checked and rechecked everything, but you can't stop obsessing.

You forgot something. I know you did.

You fend off a barrage of tour what-ifs so you can focus on the surmountable worries. To arrive from point A to point B, your anxiety will need to take a breather. Not to say you haven't been stuck in a quicksand mindfuck for months about the tour's bigger questions. You still don't know who will be joining you in Punk Jams. If it ends up being just you and someone who's played *Guitar Hero* a couple times, so be it. You want the full-deal band though—a force of nature that will, with sheer sound, propel you around the venue causing havoc. You fire off messages to anyone who might be interested in joining along the way.

You've somehow squeezed everything into the car. They call it *Tetris*-ing, named after the '80s puzzle video game, and this is your finest *Tetris* to date. You run back to the basement to do an "idiot check," a term you'll become all too familiar with on this tour. You pass the test; you're not an idiot. You manoeuvre yourself into the driver's seat, and the Corolla is so cram-packed the steering wheel is crushing your knees. In the rear-view mirror, you can't see anything past the music gear and merch stacked to the roof. You try adjusting the mirror and lock eyes with yourself. You haven't even played a show yet, and your grin is wide and wild. The Corolla crawls along, and the rumble of passing trucks shake it, the weight of all the gear and your questionable judgement dragging it down the highway.

You've been fretting for weeks about the tour's first show in Campbell River.

This is going to be a complete disaster. See, you're an idiot.

Your negative self-talk isn't far off. The capacity at the Eagles Hall is 150 people, and you have no idea if anyone is going to show up. It's a bad omen when locals tell you Campbell River hasn't had a punk show in five years. The town has no bulletin boards and local shops aren't interested in putting up posters for the gig. This town isn't sleepy; it's comatose. This is shaping up to be a failed experiment in booking a small-town show, but your consolation prize is having a crack team of noisemakers to fuel your antics. Tonight's Punk Jams line-up features two guitarists poached from tourmates Crashing Into Things. Its members will become regular jammers on the tour, and they're always an easy out for nights when other improv-ers dry up. On bass is Cam a.k.a. Little Pharmer, a self-proclaimed "pharm-punker." On drums is octopus-armed recruit Keith, who lives in the area and previously annihilated the skins for '90s noise rock band Superconductor, a Vancouver monstrosity that had at least four guitarists and two bassists. Like an earlier-era version of Punk Jams, but with actual songs.

Show time. You're inside a garbage can that you found in the corner of the hall. Someone is pushing you around in it, you're not sure who. You can't see past the rugby headgear that you picked up for 50 cents at a local thrift shop. Your voice echoes in the trash bin and creates eerier yowls than your usual ones. Your ears throb, so you signal the pusher for your grand exit and bail out. On the way up, you trip over your costume, which looks like a bomb went off at a garage sale.

Glaring fluorescent bulbs and general malaise is the Eagles Hall's ambience as 15 people watch the spectacle called Punk Jams. Half are shaking their heads; the others are laughing. Your costume is silly and terrifying at the same time. Under the headgear, a pair of extra-small camouflage underwear stretches over your face to match the dark blue pair down below, pulled so tight over your heart-covered pyjamas they have your crotch in a chokehold. Top it off with a pink "No Bullying Day" t-shirt. You're not going to let the show be an AM-radio-style bummer. You pound the hardwood floor, arching your back to let out the howl of a wolf desperate to find the moon. You swing the microphone into the ground with an ear-busting pop, and it makes harsh feedback.

You have this fascination with tape. All kinds. Duct, painter's, Gorilla, masking—any tape you can get your hands on, really. You're under the delusion that tape is a sticky rope that can pull you to safety. You wrap half a roll of packing tape around your torso, hand the end of the roll to someone else in the audience who's brave enough to creep close to the garbage can, and you jump back in. You signal the kind soul to pull you and, amazingly, the tape holds. You're whipped around the hall, a snarling dog in a cage holding an extra-long microphone cord in its paws. You and your new handler circle the hall twice before the tape snaps and the garbage can goes down on its side. You slide out of the can, birthed from black plastic, and lay on the hardwood floor, bashing your forehead against age-old, freshly waxed pine. You're pitching a fit, stuck in the packing tape mess like a rat in a glue trap. You wriggle loose, spring up, and lock your scream with the band's latest monolith riff from the netherworld. The can puller has had enough of this nonsense and walks off.

As the Punk Jams mess ends, you don't hear applause from the 15 people in the hall, just their polite exit. You flee to the bathroom to strip off your ripped-up, sweat-soaked fashion faux-pas and hide in a stall where you begin your disrobing ritual while chattering to yourself in tongues. Shedding your costumes after a show is a final, shuddering purge. Once you shove your soiled gear back into the garbage bags, your demeanour switches. You throw the bag over your shoulder, a punk rock Santa Claus with a bag of pungent presents, and calmly walk back out to the hall. Your friends Kristian and Sarah approach you, and you suspect they took part in the garbage can incidents. You ask them sarcastically if they still want to be your friends, and their exuberance confuses you.

"Of course we do," Kristian says. "That was fucking awesome!"

Reality sets in. The hall costs $250 to rent. At $10 a head, with only 15 people, you're short $100. It's not a responsible way to start a nine-show tour, but you refuse to admit defeat. You take a breath, spin on your heels, and walk into the decrepit Eagles Hall bar with insufficient funds in hand. You approach the bar with a hesitation you'd never show onstage and muster authority.

"Hi. Can we negotiate the hall payment?"

The grizzled hall manager eyes you like you're a raccoon in his woodshed.

"Hall rental is $250..."

You yank out your best Droopy the Dog impression and lay it on thick. The manager rustles up a morsel of pity.

"Okay, look, how much can you pay me?"

You slide the $150 to him across the bar in your still-perspiring mitt and prepare to plead for mercy. The manager sighs, shakes his head, and stuffs the crumpled, soggy bills into the cash register.

One show down, eight to go.

OCCUPY MY BRAIN?

Before punk, there was heavy metal.

My friend Jerad's older brother Sam zeroes in on me. I'm fresh meat. He grabs me by the scruff and pulls me into his room, shoving an eerie looking album into my hands.

"Ready to have your mind blown?"

I'm terrified. I've never talked to Sam before, just heard him screaming at his mom and slamming his door whenever we get close to his room. He's usually just a swish of golden, greasy hair with an unforgiving scowl. And I'm thinking Jerad's mom has some kind of mental problem because the only time she comes out from her bedroom is to yell at us. She and Jerad's brother fight a lot, like, a lot, and I'm always anxious when I go over to their house. Today, Sam is on a hellbent mission to recruit a new heavy metal convert. Me.

"It's the heaviest album ever," he boasts, pushing an LP at me, his upper lip tweaking in a devilish curl. I'm given the ceremonial honour of putting the record on the turntable, and I slip it from its magical cardboard sheath. On the front, a creepy witch with a puke-green face walks through what looks like a haunted field near a haunted farmhouse. I shiver, toss the album cover on Sam's bed, and focus on the task at hand. Ever so gently, I lower the needle to the vinyl. Its spinning blackness hypnotizes me and my hands tremble. *Don't scratch it... don't scratch it... don't scratch it.* A self-preservation prayer. The needle caresses wax, the soft kiss of a baby dragon, and Sam nods his approval. I hear the crackling grooves in the vinyl and anticipate something I can never prepare for. The static grows louder and louder as Sam turns the volume knob up to what seems like an impossible level. Ominous thunder and church bells. Rain splatters off the haunted farmhouse's rooftop. An enormous guitar riff threatens to seize and cement my heart. A demon chants.

What is this that stands before me?
Figure in black which points at me
Turn 'round quick and start to run
Find out I'm the chosen one
Oh nooooooooooo!

I'm listening to Black Sabbath for the first time, and this moment will change everything. This is heavy metal, the gateway to punk rock, and it roots itself in me. Metal whispers, *it's okay, don't be scared. I'll show you the darkness, and I'll protect you from it.*

Weekends are a chance to do stupid shit like drink Lucky Lager in the bush beside the mall and shoplift heavy metal cassettes from Big K Music. A brazen 12-year-old, I'm about to graduate from Black Sabbath to something incomprehensibly louder and heavier.

"I know a pawn shop that has a bunch of tapes for 25 cents each," my best friend Tory boasts after school one Friday, and that's a price we can afford. The pawn shop is in a ramshackle building below Knight News, a corner store where we steal an unreasonable amount of comic books when its orders come in. When the store goes out of business years later, I'm convinced it's our fault.

We poke our heads into the pawn shop like pimply groundhogs, and the shopkeeper grunts his disapproval and waves us in anyway. A musty smell wafts from the dusty shelves as we flip through the cassettes and search for anything that looks remotely heavy metal. Conway Twitty, Neil Diamond, Nana Mouskouri, Barbara Streisand... fuck, these tapes suck. Black Sabbath is my favourite band, the heaviest on earth (in my opinion). Tory prefers Iron Maiden, the heaviest on earth (in his opinion). We're convinced no other bands compare, but it doesn't deter us from the hunt. I fish through the tapes with no covers as a last-ditch effort and pull one out with a name I know is meant for us. Metallica, *Ride the Lightning*. "Creeping Death," "Trapped Under Ice," "For Whom the Bell Tolls." Judging by the song titles, this could be the real deal. No tape cover? Ten cents? Sold.

Back at Tory's house, we fumble the tape into his boombox and push play on side A. The acoustic guitar fake-out at the beginning of "Fight Fire with Fire" fills his bedroom. Some Harley-Davidson-type dude starts bellowing at us through what sounds like blown speakers. Guitar riffs crash like a multi-semi-truck pileup, and the bass and drums are like a sinking ship in reverse. This isn't even music, and it's the best shit we've ever heard. Teen angst turned up to 11.

Metallica, along with Slayer, is a forebearer of thrash metal—an uncompromising, dangerous wall of ferocity. Thrash metal allows me permission to confront an internal darkness I don't understand. It becomes my confidante through middle school as I navigate humiliating girlfriend scenarios and petty crime for the sake of petty crime. Then, tragedy. I'm 14 when my mom, pregnant and bed-ridden in a Vancouver hospital, gives birth to quadruplets. My sister weighs just over a pound when she's born. Her three siblings die. My two brothers are gone within days, and my other sister after eight excruciating months confined to an incubator and hooked up to breathing tubes. It's a loss so deep even Tom Araya from Slayer's throat-searing scream at the beginning of "Angel of Death" can't soothe me. So, I find another outlet to cope with my family's grief and try to avoid the sadness saturating my mom's eyes.

Today is ceremonial; sacrificial. I jog up the hill near my house holding my unscathed Powell Peralta Tommy Guerrero skateboard. Rated on a scale of one to 10, I'd say the hill I'm climbing is at least an eight. Halfway up, I look down and petrify on the spot. *Right here. That's high enough.* I turn around, cringe at the slope, slam my board on the ground, put my right foot on the grip tape, and plant my left one on the pavement. *Here we go. One, two, three. Shit.* I force myself to lift my left foot—no turning back. This demon hill is my initiation to skateboarding, and a makeshift hospital bed is only my driveway away.

Before I can learn my first ollie, I join a misfit skateboard crew. I'm stoked. Squealing wheels on pavement and the loud pops of ollies and kickflips spark my neurons in the same way thrash metal guitar riffs do. At the end of a skate session one day, an older skater hands me two life-changing cassette tapes with the words "skate punk" scrawled on their cases. *Thrasher Skate Rock Volume 2* and *Thrasher Skate Rock Volume 3*—titles forever burned into my memory. Until then, my closest brush with punk rock is thrash metal bands like Anthrax and Megadeth, influenced by punk's speed and power. Skate punk is different. It's pulsing, chaotic, messy, and dangerous, just like skateboarding. The Accused, Corrosion of Conformity, and Septic Death have screamers that make Metallica's James Hetfield sound like a '50s crooner in comparison. I dub my new friend's *Skate Rock* tapes, play them until they wear out, and order new copies over the phone from Smooth Transitions, a skate shop in North Vancouver whose staff will soon know me by voice.

The older skater, my punk gatekeeper, is Blaine. He takes me on as a fledgling underling in the crew that includes his younger brother. They reek of cigarettes and need a bath. Like the trucks on his skateboard, Blaine has an aluminium shell. I'm constantly trying to catch up to his mess of curly, mop top hair as he grinds curbs and disappears around corners searching for the perfect concrete bank to bust out a Boneless One. He teases me and bastardizes my last name (*Shu-wear-is*, not even close), but he also doses me with my daily punk rock. On my deathbed, I'll owe Blaine for introducing an underground punk community that taught me... me.

I spend every free moment improving my skating. Landing my first kick-flip and touching down on the board requires the same grounding techniques I learn from my therapists later in life. *Focus with intention. Breathe. What does it feel like to have your board under your feet?* It feels fucking awesome.

I walk to school with my flame-covered skate deck tucked in my arm and a canary yellow Sony Sports Walkman clipped to my waistband, its door-flap clamped tight, cassette tape spinning inside. I add to the experience by shoving the latest Stephen King book in my face and perfecting the art of reading about a possessed, murderous car without a normal car running me over. I must look like a freak reading a book in my the Exploited "Punk's Not Dead" shirt with an oversized Walkman clipped to my jeans, but I couldn't give a fuck. I know who I am now. This morning's tape choice is Suicidal Tendencies' first album—a pure skate-punk classic.

I'm a suicidal failure
I gotta have some help
I've got suicidal tendencies
But I can't kill myself
For the walk home, it's Black Flag's mind-melting *Damaged.*
Depression's got a hold of me
Depression, I gotta break free
Depression's got a hold on me
Depression's gonna kill me

Songs like Suicidal Tendencies' "Suicidal Failure" and Black Flag's "Depression" ooze shock-value cool and give me a rush of "are they actually saying that?" They also leave breadcrumbs for me to circle back to later. On the surface, punk songs are a "fuck you" to parents, teachers, and preppies. I feed on the blazing bursts and their antiauthoritarian lyrics, and they connect pathways in my hungry brain. Cranking tunes is my ritual when I wake up and before I fall asleep. With headphones fused to my ears, my parents never question my late-night binges.

As my skateboarding improves, thoughts of landing new tricks are all-consuming, and I obsessively watch the latest skate videos on repeat. As I power-slide into sleep each night, the tricks loop onto the back of my eyelids. Every day, excitement and pain join me for the sketchy ride—nasty road rash, goose-egged hips, tweaked ankles, and cement-slapped palms. I always bounce back up, bloody, and not broken. With each trick and bail, my endorphins flare while bands cheer from the side lines. Dead Kennedys,

Dirty Rotten Imbeciles, Agnostic Front, and Excel blare from my Sony ghetto blaster, the same bright yellow as my Walkman.

The more I skate, the closer I roll toward trouble. My small town is rife with drugs and alcohol, and it becomes a serious issue for some of the outcast skaters I hang with. Partying isn't for me; it's the punk and skateboarding I'm here for. Sitting on a curb outside Circle K for our lunchtime slushie break, the guys in my skate crew share in the camaraderie of being freaks and outcasts. I fit right in.

As has become our after-dinner routine, we drag a launch ramp out in front of Blaine and his brother's house. The lingering sun shines a fading pathway for our favourite grab tricks. Nose, Tail, Frontside, Backside, Airwalk, Japan, Method, Stalefish...Catching air is a flash of freedom we clutch onto as looming darkness marks the end to another skate day. Blaine's mom yells out the window at us to, "Go home, dammit," and muscle memory allows us one more launch into the shadows before we pack it in.

We all know their mom is sick. To make matters worse, Blaine and his brother are estranged from their dad. Same old story. And then their mom dies from an autoimmune disease, and I have no idea what to say to them. I've never even heard the words "autoimmune disease" before, and there's no such thing as the Internet to look it up. The brothers seem like they're in shock and party harder than anyone else in our skate crew. I'm too nervous to ask if they're okay.

So, we skate. On summer nights, sweaty and stoked, we scour our sleepy town for new skate spots, avoiding hockey players in jacked-up trucks and uppity seniors wagging their fingers. We push back at anyone who tells us we can't skate, and we stake our claim. We don't run from burly security guards, we run at burly security guards. We don't turn our boombox down in strip-mall parking lots, we turn it up. We scoff at our curfews and stop skating whenever the hell we want. Busybodies in town tell us to wear helmets, we don't have any. When a muscle-headed hockey jock clotheslines me off my board in mid-grind one night, my crew doesn't hesitate to chase him off using their skateboards as weapons.

We all find what we need—a chosen family. Epic skate sessions soothe the brothers' grief, but they fray and deteriorate. Hushed talk of drinking and drug binges are more than rumour, and I notice the day-after results. Sporting bloodshot eyes and greasy, tousled hair, the brothers skate one step slower and can't land signature tricks. Blaine doesn't have any interest in following the rules at his uncle's house and comes to live with my family. He sleeps on the Hide-a-Bed in our rumpus room and leaves messes of potato chip bags and empty Coke cans. Before long, my mom finds mice nesting in the bed.

"I think it's time for Blaine to move out," she loud-whispers before school, already crushed by the prospect of breaking the news to him and holding that burden. "We'd let him stay longer, but it just seems like he's going through more than we can handle right now."

My own emotional struggles are an unknown force and nightmares crash my system—held down in bed, a clammy hand over my mouth and nose, suffocating me. Other nights, I'm wired, burning through my VHS skate videos and punk cassettes and dodging sleep. Skateboarding and punk are my lifeline. Day and night, they're all I think about. On rainy days, I'm moody and lonely. I glare out my bedroom window, willing the pavement to dry with Wasted Youth's "Good Day for a Hanging" my pissed-off cell mate.

I worry about Blaine after he leaves our house. How does he cope after he hangs up his board at the end of a skate day? What's going to happen to him when I leave this stinking town behind? I never slow down enough to find out.

I often wonder if I found punk rock or if punk rock found me. When Blaine handed me those *Thrasher Skate Rock* tapes, he must have had a hunch they could alter my path, but he couldn't have known the impact they would have on my life trajectory.

As high school grad approaches, I realize the high I get from punk is better than anything my druggie friends and I experiment with. The noise and chaos intoxicate me, and I crave them constantly. Rapid-fire lyrics somehow calm my racing thoughts and become life-altering morality lessons. I sit on my bed late at night and look through my alphabetized cassettes, tracing my fingers along their spines. Nomeansno, Nuclear Assault, Overkill, Poison Idea... an all-you-can-thrash buffet. Within the plastic casings lies miniature magnetic tape, holding sounds that overwhelm my pleasure centres, spooling from one reel to the other.

Punk also connects me to the outside world. I begrudge my secluded hometown because I know so much is out there beyond it. The kids at school like me well enough, but I still don't fit in, and not in a nerd-sitting-in-the-corner way. My oversized, technicolour skate clothes, my British-Columbia-by-way-of-Cali slang, and my penchant for cranking punk and metal from my Chevy Sprint in the school parking lot doesn't jive with 99 percent of Powell River's youth. The proud outcasts in the bands I listen to spark my identity, so I write to them, carrying out my clandestine letter-penning during English Lit—the class where Mr. Schmunk (we call him Schmuck, for obvious reasons) tells us to open to page 463 of *the Canterbury Tales*, puts his feet up on his desk, and reads *Patriot Games*.

Hey Puke,

I think your band rules! I'm writing from Powell River. It's a shitty place. Up north!! Ha ha. I wanna order the Stop Killing Me cassette. I put $5 in here. Your band fuckin rules! Your last tape Not a Pretty Sight rules!!! I'm coming to the big city after I graduate and I can't wait to leave this fuckin town. It's fuckin lonely here and I hate it. None of these fuckers understand me and I feel like a freak. We only have five punks in the whole town. What a joke! Like you said, Not a Pretty Sight!!! Ha ha.

I hope you write back,

Jason

Punks like Puke Cleaver, singer of Vancouver band Death Sentence, are heroes to me, and I don't expect a response. To my shock, Puke writes back.

Jason!

Thanks for your letter and your order. Here's the tape and I threw in some stickers. You're coming to Vancouver? The scene here is rad. It's fuckin awesome, actually! I know what you mean, I feel like a freak most of the time, too. Maybe being a freak is a good thing!!! Hahahaha. Fuckin rights!

Write me anytime,

Puke

It's the only letter Puke and I exchange before I leave Powell River after graduation. In 1997, Puke Cleaver, real name Pete Keller, died from a heroin overdose, eight years after we exchanged letters. A reliable source tells me he once nailed his ball sack to a park bench on a dare. R.I.P. Puke.

The bus lets me and my hometown-best-friend-turned-Vancouver-roommate Bill off at the Cambrian Hall on Main Street for our first all-ages show. He sports a half-shaved head, and I counter with an undercut mullet. I'm jittery; worried my first punk show will be anticlimactic, but I'm dead wrong. Under fluorescent lights, a staple of all-ages shows, I stand near the stage with boggled eyes and a hanging mouth. The muscle-bound, blue-mohawked vocalist of Toronto band Bunchafuckinggoofs is smashing a TV with a sledgehammer and shouting about fucking the government. One of Bunchafuckinggoofs' guitarists wears a Jason Voorhees hockey mask and is bludgeoning his guitar.

I catch an errant fist from the guy next to me. My new friend grabs me, shakes life into me, yells "punk rock!" in my face, and tosses me into the mosh pit. I crash into Punk Rock Andy, an anxiety-ridden guy seven years my senior wearing a denim jacket with more studs than fabric. He's a friend for life as soon as I catch him stage diving, and he returns the favour on my first ever crowd surf. Held up by a throng of misfits—my new people—I relent. I'm carried around like Jesus, but punk rock is my true deity. I'm let down and a burly dude in a Circle Jerks t-shirt promptly body checks me to the floor. I spring up, he boosts me onstage like nothing happened, and I scoot around the band for my debut stage dive. No one is ready to catch me. Rookie mistake. I soar from the stage, imagine I'm being body slammed by Andre the Giant, crash to the floor, and pop up like a snotty Whack-a-Mole. My elbow and hip start to swell, and the big-city scene licks my wounds. The small-town punk in me morphs.

At these formative shows, Andy pries me off the floor more times than I can count, and so do the others. We smash together, land on our asses, and hike each other up again and again. Mosh pits, crowd surfing, and stage dives—punk rituals—beat my body into tenderized meat, and it's tough to tell where one bruise ends and the next one begins. I stagger home, damaged and thrumming with excitement.

If a glam rocker were watching us from the balcony, they wouldn't understand that this is our therapy, our way of belonging. It's the place I had been searching for since childhood, and I go to as many all-ages shows as I can.

I've found my home.

All day long I think of things
But nothing seems to satisfy
Think I'll lose my mind
If I don't find something to pacify
Can you help me, occupy my brain?
Black Sabbath - "Paranoid"

He tells me it was like a scene out of a bad movie. Listening to Brian McTernan's commanding voice lilt as he recalls the day that he would give anything to forget, I nod with what I hope is enough empathy.

"My mom and I had breakfast before we went to the hospital," Brian begins, "and I felt great, and then I walked through a door and my mom stayed, and the door closed behind me. It was, like, 'Wait. What the fuck is going on?' And I just disappeared from the world." Brian says it was incredibly traumatic to have his doctor and parents admit him into an adult psych ward as a teen. His parents never told anyone, and he still wonders if they were ashamed of themselves for putting him in the hospital—maybe ashamed of him too.

Brian lives with depression, has done so his whole life, and began therapy in Grade 2. It wasn't long before the powers-that-be pegged him as a problem child, then a problem teen, then a high-school delinquent. They decided he needed to be dealt with, even if his lashing out, picking fights, vandalizing, and being on the wrong side of the law pointed to a volatile household where both of his parents lived with mental health conditions. His Baltimore, Maryland Catholic school asked him to leave in Grade 6, and then his public school expelled him, leaving his parents to explore other options. Brian's family doctor had been monitoring his behaviour and suggested he be hospitalized in an adult ward. The wrinkles on my forehead lift. I've never heard of a doctor locking up a troubled teen with adults, maybe because I was born, raised, and live in Canada where even the mental health establishment is polite. (Ever seen the Canadian mosh pit meme? Canuck punks slam dancing and saying, "Sorry. Sorry. Sorry. Sorry.") Despite Brian being from a more, let's say, totalitarian country, we agree the doctor had a colossal overreaction, a failed quick fix with detrimental results.

"I had no visitors, no anything. It was a fucked-up place. Some of the stuff... It was very traumatizing." Brian says group therapy was particularly disturbing. Is the barb in his voice directed at the doctor, his parents, himself, or a combination of the three?

After his insurance ran out, the hospital released Brian and his parents found another school that would take him. There, he met a group of teen punks to hang with. If he could be in an environment where he belonged, he thought everything would be okay again. As is the case with most young punks, Brian stumbled upon refuge via his elders. These types of wise and weathered gurus are often several years older and willing to take wide-eyed youth under their torn jean jackets. In my case, it was Blaine, the mop-top skateboarder two years older than me who saw a punk twinkle in my eyes. Before Brian's parents and doctor hospitalized him, his punk mentor was his older brother who showed him the goofy 1986 punk dramatization *Suburbia* on VHS. Oh, and a jolly anti-fascist skinhead guy mocking Brian's Sex Pistols *Never Mind the Bullocks* t-shirt from across the street one day after school.

"This guy walked out of a house six or seven houses down, and he just yells, 'Sex Pistols are Bollocks!' I'm like, 'What?!'" Brian chuckles at the formative memory. "He comes out and asks me what I listen to and tells me I'm not listening to the good stuff." Soon enough, Brian and his older brother started hanging out with the happy harasser—obviously. The skinhead guy played them harsher British D-beat hardcore/punk bands like Discharge and GBH, which were a bit too intense for Brian and his brother's younger ears. The guy became fixated on finding bands the McTernan brothers would love. During one of their hangouts, the well-meaning skinhead put on an album by Las Vegas melodic punk band 7 Seconds, and there it was—Brian's revelatory moment. "Holy shit! It was fast. It was melodic. And I could understand the words." He tells me he knows the songs on 1984's *The Crew* and 1985's *Walk Together, Rock Together* note-for-note. "That was the beginning of the next 35 years of my life."

In my case, I was quick to leave home after high school because I craved the inclusion of a big-city scene. For Brian, leaving his parents' house for a more stable environment allowed him to focus on turning his pain into positivity. Brian poured all he had into screaming in bands and organizing shows. At age 16, he booked a West Coast tour for Ashes, his first serious band. At 17, he went to Europe with Battery, the straight edge hardcore band his name became synonymous with for the next eight years. Between tours, Brian moved to Boston when he was 18 and set up one of the most popular recording studios of the '90s and '00s. He named it Salad Days after the final release by the life-changing '80s hardcore band Minor Threat. If we had more time, Brian and I could bond over the profound effect the influential Washington, DC, punk/hardcore band has had on us. Brian recorded more than 200 releases at Salad Days over three decades, including albums by Converge, Strike Anywhere, Cave In, and Snapcase.

But depression creeped back into his life after opening the studio. He buried his internal turmoil and poured everything into the music, surrounding himself with a support network of bands like Gainesville, Florida's Hot Water Music—unwavering rays of positivity with members that would do anything for him. It was the most amazing time of his life, but he kept his struggles hidden, stifling his inner doubt and emotional pain.

"I was one of the most sought-after record producers for bands all over the world, and I felt like a failure." Brian digs deep for the right words to make sense of that time. "The thing about depression is it's not fucking reasonable. It doesn't make sense." Years later, Brian's nervous system refused to hold back his depression any longer. He'd done all he could to block it out and finally he ran out of options. After selling the recording studio and taking a cushy job as a project manager, he was drinking way too much, not being present for his wife and daughter, and missing the punk scene more than he ever imagined. "I remember my wife saying to me, 'You need to be doing music. You need to be writing.' I had to force myself to think about my issues and acknowledge them and not let them grow and become corrosive." One evening, Brian picked up a guitar in his basement. Less than 10 minutes later, he had the first song he'd written in 20 years. I picture his song as a battering ram, bashing the pain trapped inside. "I can't express to you the weight that came off my shoulders." Brian sighs and tells me singing and songwriting for his new melodic hardcore band Be Well is his daily therapy. Returning to the scene re-grounded him in a place where connections and friendships had always given him purpose and a way to contribute.

"I don't know that I've ever felt so much gratitude as I feel toward punk and hardcore," he says. "It gave me a family and an avenue to find myself at multiple times in my life when I needed a community to hear me, and see me, and appreciate not only my strengths, but my weaknesses." Brian chokes up and pretends to clear his throat. I do the same. His words could be mine.

Without Rodney Mullen, we wouldn't have modern-day skateboarding. Rodney's groundbreaking style inspired tricks the top pros have used as their foundation. I mean, the guy invented the kickflip.

Rodney struggled with depression and was mostly mute when he was young. Teachers pegged him as autistic, a label that followed him through his life, although doctors never diagnosed him. In his 2004 autobiography, *The Mutt: How to Skateboard and Not Kill Yourself*, Rodney recalls how, as a scrawny, weird kid, the insular skateboard community accepted him.

"By being a hardcore skater in the 1980s, you were already a social reject..." Rodney writes. "Skaters had their own look, their own slang, their own way of looking at the world... We were considered the bottom feeders by society, constantly chased by cops and security guards, harassed by pedestrians, and mocked by non-skaters everywhere. That persecution from the outside helped us bond."

Skateboarders and punks banded together in the '80s and '90s due to their reputations as outsiders and hellraisers. They accepted each other, bonded over in-your-face fashion and music, and reclaimed the insults hurled at them. For early skateboarders, the outside world shunned their lifestyle until the infamous X Games launched in 1995 and busted skateboarding wide open. Soon, it became co-opted, but skate punks stayed underground where their idiosyncrasies and street smarts belonged.

As a youth, I would slash curbs on my scratched-up board with my filthy skull-print pant legs dragging along the concrete, BL'AST!'s "Out of Alignment" part of the soundtrack to my teen resistance. I brawled with thugs who knocked me off my board, pinned me down, and yelled in my face, "Head case!" At the time, skateboarding was the ultimate expression of rebellion. We were rabble-rousers finding comfort through congregation, our damaged goods salvaged by simply being part of something.

In the article "The Importance of Community and Mental Health," Stephanie Gilbert of the National Alliance of Mental Illness explains how finding community is critical to a person's mental health, especially those who are already isolated, alienated, and lonely. According to NAMI, the most beneficial aspects of a community are belonging, support, and purpose. At its height in the mid- to late-'80s, skate punk was both a skateboarding subculture and underground music subgenre, and it raised the ire of authority figures and schoolmates. In *Bones Brigade: An Autobiography,* legendary Powell Peralta skateboarder and musician Tommy Guerrero, the namesake of my first skateboard, says the skate community was a life preserver for him.

"Every faction in school gave me grief. It didn't matter, the cool kids, the stoners, the jocks. I was like, 'Fuck... fuck you, man.'" In the film, Tommy rubs his thumbs with his index fingers, conjuring the magic of his youth. "Skateboarding was the only thing I could find sanctuary in—a sense of peace."

Skateboarding and punk rock were once interchangeable, and both have continued as creative reprieves from those fuckers that beat Tommy and so many of us down. I often daydream about unearthing my old board, recruiting a "mature" skate crew, and mangling my middle-aged body to the soundtrack of Black Flag's "Rise Above." If I made it out alive, my sprained ankles and bruised hips would be worthy sacrifices to the skate-punk gods.

When he enters our Zoom room with a "ding," I expect Lee Willingham to dodge me, like I'm going to reach through the screen, grab him by the lapels, and huck him into a virtual mosh pit.

I offer a warm smile, he returns the gesture, and we delve into each other's musical worlds. Lee comes from a classical music background and, with his feathered grey hair and sturdy chin, has the look of an esteemed choral conductor. He's been an Associate Professor at Wilfrid Laurier University in Waterloo, Ontario since 2004. I'm familiar with Laurier in a peripheral sense, only because CKMS, its radio station, airs the *Scream Therapy* podcast. Lee has spent his recent academic years focusing on the relationship between music and community, authoring the 2017 book *Engaging in Community Music*. In many ways, punk rock and classical music are opposites in sonic missions and attitudes, but Lee is quick to point out that all music scenes benefit from communal creativity. Unfortunately, people often peg classical musicians as snobby perfectionists, he says.

"In classical music, our primary goal was to get rid of mistakes and make the music sound great, often at the expense of the musician. It's a potentially soul-destroying process." Lee sounds alarmed at his own severity. "What we've found in community music is the opposite. It's a soul-expanding process where we privilege the experiences, the maturity, the aspirations of the people we're working with, and hey, you know what? The music sounds better too."

Lee's quip leads him to pause and reflect. He had spent decades teaching music theory that puts virtuosity over musicians' wellness. It led him to a new outlook in which healthy artistic collaborations are more important than collective proficiency. This, in turn, creates a supportive scene within the classical music community, he says, much in the same way it does in punk.

"It could be the energy of the music itself that draws people into punk," Lee ponders, "but it could be they sense some like-minded people in that group with similar needs, similar yearnings, similar aspirations, maybe similar challenges." Lee's on a roll, and although we come from opposite musical backgrounds and different genres, the key piece we share is community. Punks don't have to be locking eyes in the mosh pit to know they're in the same communal zone. They bond over playing music, but also by organizing benefit shows, publishing zines, and being politically active.

"Communities are not made up of people that are all alike. They're typically made up of very diverse populations that have some kind of common connection, passion, and identity," Lee says. "So, the punk movement attracted all sorts of people, I would gather. They didn't all look the same, they weren't the same age or the same demographic, but something about the vitality of the music gave them hope, gave them identity, maybe got them on the right path toward a more productive life."

I distinctly remember walking up to the doors of my first show, forking over $5 and offering the back of my hand for the volunteer doorperson to stamp it, electric jitters turning the inked X on my skin into squiggly lightning bolts. Inside the hall was a hurricane of bad-asses with Manic-Panic-dyed hair and studded jackets who were warm, caring, generous people who I was swiftly convinced would do anything for me. As Jenna Pup from Philadelphia grind band the HIRS Collective explained to me during a *Scream Therapy* podcast interview, punk is like a "never ending support group." Jenna said finding the queer-punk scene in Philly helped her figure out her queerness and transness. Through glassy eyes she told me, "Punk is doing something I believe in, and something I love, with the people I love, and for the people I love." Using Jenna's conviction as a conduit, I ask Lee to pinpoint why music communities have such an ability to draw people together and bond them for life. He throws the answer back at me in the form of a question.

"Yeah, there's some magic there, right?"

Right.

Of all the people who have uttered the five magic words, "Punk rock saved my life," Neal Page is the most convincing. From the moment he opens his mouth to say it, I'm sold. Travelling East Coast to West Coast using computer magic, his voice takes a pregnant pause before his declaration—a declaration of countless people I've talked to—and his voice reaches a premature crescendo. "I would not be on this planet without this community, no way. I would be dead. That's a fact."

Neal's the guitarist/vocalist of Baltimore bouncy pop punk band Panic Problem. He lives in the same city as producer and Be Well vocalist Brian

McTernan. They've likely been to the same shows. Neal's favourite part of the day is when he dumps his work clothes in the laundry basket, throws on his Strike Anywhere long-sleeve t-shirt, and makes a beeline to his record collection.

"Everyone has their moments of self-doubt and dark times, but you put on that music, or you go to that punk show, and you can let all of your baggage go." Neal's dedication gleams in his piercing blue eyes. "There's a lighthouse, there's a beacon, and it's called punk rock."

Neal lives with attention deficit hyperactivity and generalized anxiety. He rattles off his symptoms: delusions of grandeur, volatile mood swings, dark thoughts, and out-of-control hyperactivity, to name a few. He will hyper focus on one thing, then his mind will drift away as quickly as his fingers cruise down his guitar's fretboard. Sometimes it's the other way around; drift away, then hyper focus. In public places, he finds it difficult to listen to other people's voices while focusing on what they're saying at the same time. He describes "one fateful day" when he was driving north of Baltimore on his way to hot yoga (not a typical punk hangout) and barely avoided rear-ending a minivan near a Target (also not a punk hotspot).

"I can't remember if I was lost in thought, or if something caught my attention, but my mind was in 50 million places." He shudders at the worst-case scenario. "My wife was about to have our first kid, and it dawned on me that I was at a point in my life where this could actually negatively impact other people. That's when I decided to seek treatment."

Neal's doctor told him comorbid diagnoses of attention deficit hyperactivity and generalized anxiety can result in a crushing handshake. Nearly a third of those living with mental health conditions have more than one, according to a study published in the Journal of Medical Internet Research. As Neal began to accept his challenges and find a healthier path, he was able to harness his energy in constructive ways. For one, he could follow through with his plans, including more involvement in the punk community, the only place he's ever felt welcome. Without it, he says he would be a perpetual outsider.

"This community is the only place that I fit in. I experience that on a daily basis. Daily. Basis." His rhythmic pauses lull me as if we're performing symbiosis across the continent. "Most of my life is pretending. I have a professional life where I pretend. In terms of being a whole person, there's no place for people like ourselves where you're truly allowed to find a voice. And find rest. And breathe. And find clarity. There's no other place like punk rock. I would challenge anyone to show me. And it's been that way, effectively, since day one."

Listening to Neal's voice find cadence, I wonder about the statement "punk saved my life," one I've often used myself. Is it literal or figurative? As I trudged aimlessly through suicidal ideation after my bipolar diagnosis, two friends I met at Fest in Florida reached out to me through Messenger and temporarily righted my course. At that moment, their simple message meant everything.

                                    Miss you, love you buddy.

Had I not found the punk scene, would I have rotted away in my mill town listening to Lynyrd Skynyrd? Without a place where I could truly be me—a place where I could lose myself in welcome bliss, but even better, find myself in it, I'd be living a life of constant unease. Discovering punk can alter paths that might have ended in misery, but sometimes finding salvation is as simple as listening to Slant 6 or Operation Ivy just to get through the fucking day.

SHOW 2
CUMBERLAND, BC
MASONIC LODGE NO. 26
THURSDAY, AUGUST 9, 2018

Sweat dribbles down your back, over the curve of your tailbone, pooling in your ass crack. Your pores won't stop leaking. Scrambling behind the merch table for a towel, you're coated in your own juices. A woman in a Crass tank top rushes up and shouts in your face.

"That show was amazing!"

She's one of the few who recognize you out of costume. Only keeners know the primal fiend onstage in long underwear is also the mild-mannered guy standing behind the records and t-shirts. Crass woman has questions.

"What was the second song called? What were you screaming? Was it, 'Punk is the saviour?'"

You stare at her like a deer heard a gunshot. How are you going to explain that Punk Jams doesn't have "songs," that it's all improv, including the lyrics—that those words you shout can escape your mouth and never come back? You're oblivious to anything you do during certain shows—what you said, what you wore, how your "band" sounded, what reckless behaviour you engaged in. And this was one of those shows. It's like you weren't even there.

"The songs are made up on the spot," you blurt, surprised at your honesty.

"Um, what do you mean?"

"We're an improv band," you say. "We don't have songs. We just make shit up."

Her brow furrows, and her face lights up.

"No fucking way! That's so cool. You guys made up those songs?"

"Uh, kinda," you say cautiously. "I put together a new band every night."

You shove your shaky, still-sweaty paws into your pockets.

"That's unreal. So, what were you singing about on the second song?"

All you can do is shrug.

"Yeah, sorry," you say. "I have no idea."

Earlier in the day, you're greeted by Henry, the show's promoter. Within moments of meeting him, you know Henry is a kindred spirit—another jovial weirdo. Henry has a one-person project called JAL that's half Lady Gaga, half extra-terrestrial dance party. Henry/JAL wears high heels and ripped fishnet stockings, prancing around in a creepy alien mask while cooing and wailing at the audience. It's one of the weirdest musical acts you've seen, and you feel a kinship. Walking down Cumberland's main drag with Henry is like walking down Hollywood Boulevard with Axl Rose. "Hey Henry!" "How's it going Henry?" "Where have you been, Henry?!" Henry's Cumberland is a hip little town; Portland compressed into one block. Keep Cumberland Weird. It has a nice ring to it.

By Henry's account, tonight's show is a relative success compared to last night's dud in Campbell River. Henry tells you the decent-sized crowd included four right-at-home eccentrics who danced around as if they were listening to a surf band, not what sounded like someone sledgehammering a bonfire. During the more bulldozer-ish parts of Punk Jams' set, he said a handful of miscreants kicked off a five-person mosh pit. This is what you live for, had you only remembered it.

A small group of audience members stick around after the punishment to absorb the after-essence. Others skirt to the exit for a smoke break before the next band. Out of costume, you emerge from your toilet-stall changing room and wander outside to tame your sweat monster. Without your masks, you're skittish and self-conscious. A traditional-looking, middle-aged white man with ruffled, light brown hair hiding grey streaks. Not too tall, not too short. No visible scars. Despite your straight-laced appearance, your post-show paranoia kicks in.

What did you do? Oh god, they all hate you now.

A group of punks smoking near a bus bench fall silent when you walk by. Anxiety tingles in your chest, and your mind skips to a false narrative that even in a scene that's always celebrated your weirdness, you're a pariah. You lean against the wall around the corner and breathe.

One, two, three, four, hold... one, two, three, four, hold....

You walk past the bench again, and everyone smiles at you this time. One young woman with a shaved head gives you a thumbs up.

"Dude, that last band was fucking awesome!"

Inside, another audience member has approached you at the merch table after your set. This time it's a guy in a NOFX shirt.

"I'm glad you liked it," you say.

"That singer guy's insane! What a freak! Did you see him crawling around on the floor? I'm surprised he didn't get his head stomped." NOFX guy chuckles nervously. "Dude, is he around? I'd love to meet him. Seriously, that was one of the best shows I've ever seen."

You think fast on your swollen feet. "Yeah, I'm not sure where he's at right now," you say, "but I'm really glad you liked it." It's too complicated to tell NOFX guy you're the freak who just finished rubbing his crotch against the stage. To shine a spotlight on your blacked-out exorcisms could illuminate images and words you don't want to remember. Until tomorrow night's show, you lock the door that you force open to regurgitate your pain.

SADNESS COMES HOME

We're two grown men, huddled around a computer screen like pre-teens drooling over a Super Nintendo on Christmas morning. My best friend Greg and I are entering data into a painstaking punk rock encyclopaedia in the form of a 368-page Word 98 doc in 10-point font. This ramshackle collection of minutiae we're furiously compiling is to be *Generation Gap: Victoria, BC's All-Ages Hardcore/Punk Scene, 1990-2000*, a comprehensive guidebook documenting what we're convinced are the best 10 years of our lives. We're already halfway through 1999 and our self-imposed deadline is clawing at the door. The book must be in people's hands by the end of the decade it's covering. It just has to be.

Greg and I also run the largest punk rock mail-order/distro in Western Canada. We're spending hours a day, seven days a week, packing up orders, while also booking all-ages shows, and now this book project. These are ways of giving back to the scene that helped shape our personal and political lives—the real-world education we never found at school. We don't make any money for our efforts; wouldn't dream of it. Our projects are not-for-profit because making money off the scene is sacrilege to us. Every dollar we make we put back in. If we let capitalism monetize punk rock, what we love so much loses its meaning and is sucked into the system it denounces. Two of our favourite bands are I Spy (*this music saved my life, so I'll be dead and fucking gone, before it's bought and old, just like appliances and cars*) and Propagandhi (*anyone remember when we used to believe, that music was a sacred place, and not some fucking bank machine?*). Furious, ass-kicking songs like "Appliances and Cars" and "Rock for Sustainable Capitalism" validate our raised middle fingers. These lyrics bite back.

When we're not working shifts at a tele-survey company and commuting with a co-worker named Bruno, who tells us he's been in prison and slips in and out of a French Canadian accent, we're plunking away on the epic Word doc listing bands' album and song titles, band members, show promoters, zines, and so much more. We don't understand how time-consuming the project is until we're drowning in dusty demo tapes with barely legible liner notes. We come to realize that only Victoria punk scene diehards would want to read such a thing.

Why are we doing this?

My obsession with punk rock dominates my life. I have a wife and one-year-old son and a new job as assistant editor at Camosun College's student newspaper. To squeeze my self-imposed duties into the day, I stay up after my family goes to bed, filling orders for punks around the world and obsessing over the book project. Working into the wee hours, I become an expert in not waking my sleeping beauties with the obnoxious sound of packing tape scraping off its roll and, trust me, that shit is hard. Day after day, week after week, Greg and I process new stock, haul records around to sell at all-ages shows, half of which we promote ourselves, and input information into the never-ending computer file of lost memories. It's punk rock Groundhog Day.

We miss our Y2K book deadline (although our computers don't implode) and interest in the Victoria all-ages scene fizzles into the early '00s when punks begin to defect to the pub scene. We try to resuscitate the life force that superseded dingy dive bars and fashion-forward haircuts, but all around us bands are peddling homogenized rock packaged as punk to ex-straight-edge kids hacking cigarette butts on patios of shit-can pubs, cheap beers clutched in the same fists they used to pound skyward.

Young adulthood blends into full adulthood. Greg and I have "real-life" responsibilities now, like paying the bills and, in my case, being a husband and dad. We decide to do the logical thing, phase out the mail-order/distro, and abandon the book project. (Years later, I find the files in a forgotten folder and, consuming an entire holiday break, post the obsessive scene listings as a WordPress blog.) We just don't have the energy to be punk rock stewards anymore, so we hatched a plan.

Hundreds of records, 'zines, and books adorn the Pandora Project's community centre gymnasium. This is the infamous all-ages show where we set up our wares one last time and put up a sign saying, "Free punk rock, first-come first-served." Bright-eyed punks charge toward our tables like anarchists on Black Bloc Friday. They clamour over complimentary rebellion, victorious, thrusting the records and zines toward the gym's roof in a universal "fuck yeah!" Paraphernalia is flying everywhere like cartoon dust clouds. Gifting records and zines is a source of pride for us. We want to reassure these punks that they aren't alone in the world—that the music and its messages will guide them and keep them safe. We hope they'll find therapy in the vinyl grooves and 'zine pages.

By now, Greg and I are burnt out and bitter about how many people are turning to the bar scene. Bands write songs about sex, drugs, and rock 'n' roll to match their surroundings, and we aren't willing to adapt. I'm worried the kind of punk that fuelled my youth and taught me to be a better person will skip generations, predicted by our would-be book's title, *Generation Gap*. One of our legendary-status albums, Propagandhi's *Less Talk, More Rock*, features the slogans "pro-feminist, animal-friendly, gay-positive, anti-fascist" on its back cover. Will the next generation care, or will they be too busy drinking tall cans in the alley behind the bar, fake IDs at the ready? Through disillusioned lenses, we see ambivalent drunk-punks wearing beer goggles. We write them off and assume they're too busy drinking their lives away in the local watering hole to appreciate punk's true ethos. Faced with the perpetuation of pervasive alcohol culture, we have nothing left to contribute to this warped scene. We've already given enough, so we give up and get out.

I sink into depression, unable to replace the energy and inspiration of screaming along to bands pouring their hearts out at Food Not Bombs benefits. Greg and I do our best to avoid shows for more than a year. In dark mode, I burrow myself into the scenes that originally inspired me like Dischord Records' DC punk/hardcore scene, Ebullition Records' emo-hardcore crew in Goleta, CA, and the Kill Rock Stars riot punks in Olympia.

Will punk ever be the same?

Now a full-time husband, dad, and newspaper editor, I settle into my 30s. I buy into the idea that growing up means burying my inner punk as an internal wagging finger nags me to "grow up" and let go of this so-called youth culture scene. But another factor is in play. I'm also a freelance music journalist and late-night writing is my new obsession. With time freed up from my previous all-consuming activities, writing and editing music articles swallows the sacred hours of 8 pm to 3 am when my emotionally neglected wife and our now-four kids are asleep.

"Get to bed!" Every evening around 7:30, I bark orders at my gang of children, settle them down with bedtime stories, and pray they will soon become unconscious so I can escape. Headphones cranked, I hole up at my computer and let the words fly out, spewing out an in-the-zone barrage of record reviews and band features that I submit to my appreciative editors. They say I'm "quick" and "clean," which I translate to mean "manic perfectionist."

I can do it all.

After pulling four- to five-hour sleeps for months, it never dawns on me that this constant activity is a coping mechanism for my wavering mental health. I'm doing anything to avoid what lays dormant. I've fused myself to punk since junior high, and it's clear how being cut off from the scene is exposing my vulnerabilities. I have no community, no connection. Solitary confinement, even with headphones, a keyboard, and a steady supply of new albums from record labels, is still solitary confinement. My dedication to the scene all those years had been protecting me from swirling down the toilet bowl that my life could easily become. And lately, when I sit down to write, my stomach has been rumbling like the low E string on a bass guitar. On the horizon, a real shitstorm.

I'm spinning, swaying, sprinting, stomping, punching the grass, and pulling out handfuls, screaming along to the nearly indecipherable lyrics in my head-phones as loud as I can at 4 am on Victoria's empty suburban streets. My life is falling apart and I'm euphoric. Drunk on alcohol and high on mania, I jive and dive, booming my feet to the ground with each bass drum kick. Emotional pain is puppeting my drunken solo mosh as slash-and-burn punk amplifies my distorted thoughts.

I could just end this now.

Converge's furious "Sadness Comes Home," with its serrated riffs and unrelenting piledrive, saves me from stage diving into traffic. This flailing, one-person dance party borders on a psychotic episode.

I've heard the word "psycho" in horror movies, but the foreign concept of psychosis, that this could be something more than five drinks too many, doesn't cross my mind as I stumble up to the front door of my house. My empty house. Not away-for-the-weekend empty. Empty empty. *You go first*, I mumble to myself, hand tremouring on the doorknob. I don't like going first.

After months of relentless haggling, I've convinced my ex-wife that we need to leave Victoria and move back to Powell River. While I stay behind to work and sell the house, her and the kids go early so they can start school in September. By this point, my marriage is in rough shape, and the move hasn't done its deterioration any favours.

My erratic behaviour escalates from afar and messy phone arguments become the rule. The radio silence that follows each call is enough for my ex-wife to suspect the worst, and she's right. I hang the anvil of our marriage from the rotting back porch by a threadbare rope. I don't understand why I sabotage myself and shove away the ones I love.

Punk shows resume their role as my safety zone, and I go to as many as I can. Walls of noise calm me, loosen my pent-up innards, and let hope ease out. No one can hurt me here. But when the last band of the night finishes, I always end up alone in the shell of my former familial home, a final resting place for my weary head. I speed along the days until I can see my kids again, sneaking into movie theatres and ducking the cleaning staff between afternoon screenings. I occupy corporate bookstores, let their too-comfortable-to-be-true lounge chairs swallow me up, and read books cover to cover until closing time.

Living in a suburban McMansion in Powell River, my family's back together, and I'm commuting to Victoria and back every other weekend. It doesn't take long for my ex-wife and I to hurl ourselves headlong into a soul-wrenching separation. Within months, after disastrous visits home and bitter ultimatums, we're signing a separation agreement. A year later: divorced. One house becomes two, and the kids seesaw between them.

A rare, purely happy memory with my kids during this time comes when Cruiser shows up. Cruiser is a jolly "bikepacker" who pedals the world, his long ponytail flowing behind him. He's in Victoria to make money before his next epic trip, and he rides to Powell River to spend the weekend with us. Cruiser will do anything for a friend. He's saved me more than once over the years, so asking him to watch the kids while I make dinner is like asking a drummer to play an AC/DC beat. Easy, breezy. Cruiser goes into the garage with the kids to get up to... whatever. I'm exhausted, I don't care. I'm fine with Cruiser corrupting their kid-sized brains with Satanic death metal, his soundtrack of choice, if that's what it takes. I come in to ring the dinner bell, and I'm delighted to see Cruiser and the kids circling the pool table on their bikes like a mini racetrack. They're having such a blast, so I smile and head back in the house. Dinner can wait. I pop back a bit later and, sure enough, death metal is belching from the garage stereo, and everywhere I look are grins. Much to the kids' chagrin, Cruiser's weekend visit zooms by and we relinquish him and his bike to the great unknown. If I recall, his next destination was South America.

The week-on, week-off schedule with the kids is parental ping-pong. The commute to Victoria and my mental deterioration wear me down, and my insomnia makes it impossible to plan our days properly. The next time their mom drops them off, I propose the only game I can muster. "It's called garage mosh. It's like the game you played with Cruiser, but we run around in circles and do tricks instead of riding our bikes." Their faces light up. I put on Converge, this time the herky-jerky "Lonewolves," not the lurch and hammer of Victoria's late-night "Sadness Comes Home," and we bolt into what's affectionately known as a circle pit. Running around the pool table, I lap my youngest and pick him up for a ride, put him back down; then my daughter, pick her up, spin her around, and place her down at the back of the line; catch my older son, lift him over my shoulder and deposit him behind his sister. They're giggling and shrieking. This garage circle pit could go on for hours, but we're pooped in 10 minutes. With weekly practice, we learn to build our mosh endurance, aspiring to tirelessness.

I tighten the grip on my tears and turn into my ex-wife's driveway, struggling to find the best words to keep myself in my kids' thoughts for another week.

"Bye you guys... love you."

It will have to do.

I watch them scramble up the driveway—not my driveway—and their mom greets them at the front door—not my front door. My eyes dribble like a pin-pricked garden hose.

Parked around the corner, my entire body trembles, and the hose bursts. I fumble for my phone, connect it to the car stereo, and push play on one of my spiked coats of armour. Converge's "Sadness Comes Home" is a turbine massage for my skull.

I gather my broken shards and drive home, dreading the McMansion's emptiness. Going in through the garage, I sit on the steps, stare at the pool table, wish for the comforting chaos of our mini circle pit, and a shroud drops over me.

I scramble for projects to keep myself occupied and count the days before my sons and daughter are back. Listening to and writing about punk rock carries me through, the tunes on over- drive, my fingers locked to my keyboard. The parenting yo-yo repeats for months— euphoria when they're with me, grief when they're not.

One by one, the kids decide they can't handle my erratic moods and bouncing between houses, and they move in with their mom. Their scheduled visits slowly seize like ungreased gears.

From a distance, I strive to be a stable presence in my kids' lives, like the garage mosh game and its familiar, mach-10 soundtrack. Our circle pit was one of our happy places. In a loud frenzy of running, playing, and laughing, I was able to stay present with them. Converge's auditory chaos still grounds me to this day. I often picture singer Jacob Bannon speed-screaming in my face—encouraging me to be the father I always knew I could be.

There's no such thing as good enough
For arctic eyes and hard-earned rust
I've grown tired of counting odds
To somehow make things even
When sadness always comes home
Converge - "Sadness Comes Home"

Punk's not all circle pits and high-fives. Onstage intensity can lead to self-harm. Desperate song lyrics might be cries for help. All-night afterparties can fuel substance misuse. What percentage of punks have thrashed bodies, erratic behaviours, unstable lives... How many of them juggle inevitable timebombs? During my decades in the scene, it's been difficult to figure out which punks I've seen onstage (and offstage) are exhibiting warning signs of mental health issues. With flailing limbs and throats screamed raw, punk is synonymous with wild abandon. It begs the question: when does lack of inhibitions end and undiagnosed mental health issues begin?

The Music Industry Research Association reported alarming numbers in a 2018 study documenting the link between musicians and mental health. The report revealed musicians were twice as likely to have depression symptoms than non-musicians. Musicians who had suicidal thoughts were almost quadruple the general population. These numbers don't consider those that go undiagnosed or untreated due to lack of services, stigma, and other factors. Oftentimes people's symptoms go undetected, even by themselves.

Artists are sensitive to the outside world and driven by a need for creative expression to address difficult emotions. In the 1993 book *Touched with Fire: Manic-Depressive Illness and the Artistic Temperament*, American psychologist and author Kay Redfield Jamison examined the relationship between mental health conditions and artistic creativity. According to Jamison, who lives with bipolar, those with wild artistic temperaments are probably living with mood dysregulation, such as unipolar or bipolar depression. Buzz Osbourne, guitarist/vocalist for legendary metal/punk band Melvins, told me during a *Scream Therapy* podcast interview he agrees with Jamison. With more than 40 years' experience in the underground scene, Buzz has befriended thousands of musicians, most notably fallen Nirvana frontperson Kurt Cobain. "The ones that were the best musicians always had some kind of issue, mentally," Buzz said in his signature baritone bursts. "They put so much time into being that good they let other areas of their life suffer. But you put a guitar in their hands, or put them behind the drums, and they couldn't be beat."

Although punk bands often face a lack of financial backing, gruelling tours, and discrimination for playing music that mainstream society considers rambunctious noise, their members have a better chance at mental health thanks to freedom of expression within a nourishing community that encourages self-advocacy. But does the beneficial cancel out the detrimental?

Swedish music industry up-starter Johan Svarnberg and his team at Record Union were taken aback by the connection between mental health issues and independent musicians. The independent record distributor undertook a 2019 study called the 73 Percent. What it found was that out of 1,500 independent musicians surveyed, 73 percent had experienced anxiety or depression related to playing and promoting their music. In the study's wake, Svanberg's team developed the Wellness Starter Pack for musicians, a progressive approach to mental health he calls "prehab." From his office in Stockholm, a five-minute drive from the palace where the Swedish royal family hang out, Johan tells me he's laboured over a chicken and egg argument. The chicken: are musicians' mental health issues exacerbated by lifestyles that include financial hardship, pressure to succeed, excessive travel, sleep deprivation, poor diet, drinking and drugging, and other unhealthy activities? The egg: Do these kinds of lifestyles hatch mental health issues? My money's on the chicken. No, wait... the egg? Johan has a more measured response. "Probably both."

Licensed psychologist Blythe TwoSisters usually sports a purple mohawk. It's an individuality beacon and nod to her upbringing, a Bat-Signal for those looking for a different type of therapy. Blythe's current look—a short, cropped cut and crimson lipstick—isn't as stark as her normal, flashy, spiky-headed up-do. Current hairstyle aside, her holistic mental health approach has never wavered. In her mid-40s, Blythe models her decades-long work in the Houston, Texas mental health community after the punk rock ethos in her toolbox.

As a teen in Houston's all-ages music scene, Blythe took on a maternal role with the punks and skateboarders in her circle, often driving them home after shows. Relocating from the Florida skate and surf scene, she didn't fit in with Houston's "NASA astronaut kids," so she sought out the local scene and started taking photos at shows. "I just liked the people… they were rowdy." Her tattooed eyebrows twitch, and she lets loose a nostalgia-wrapped chuckle. "I didn't go to prom. I went to a punk concert instead."

In her private practice, Tabula Rasa Psychology, Blythe uses the moniker Punk Rock Psych Doc as an "I see you" for marginalized folks needing complementary care. Traced to the writings of Aristotle, the Tabula Rasa theory's main tenet is that knowledge comes from experience and perception instead of built-in mental content from birth. In a perfect world, those with mental health issues would have a doctor like Blythe who understands that without empathy for and understanding of one's history and views, therapeutic results are limited. I wish I'd found someone using Blythe's approach to help me during all those years that I just thought I was a total fuckup, completely unaware of what was going on. I wish I'd found someone like her before I went into crisis.

"I want people to come to me and know I will see them as they are," she says. "In the therapy world, a lot of people won't disclose that they're poly, into kink, queer, or even disclose their substance use because they're afraid of being judged. And I'm, like, 'Come as you are…' I'm so far removed from the average therapeutic environment. We're not going to do the work saying, 'Oohhh, how does that make you feeeeel?' Ugh." She leans to one side then turns and shoves the other side with both arms. "I want people to know, I'm your doctor. I don't give a fuck. We're going to cuss a lot. You can look how you want, and you can dress how you want."

Blythe says she observes coping behaviours in her clients to spot warning signs of mental crisis. If her clients don't follow agreed-upon action plans between sessions, it's clear they aren't coping well. She becomes progressively concerned when patients appear to be "buying time with their nervous system" and start to have suicidal ideation.

"When patients tell me they just wanna run away. I ask, 'Okay, where are you going?' Or they say, 'I just don't want to wake up tomorrow.' There's a spectrum of suicidality, like, 'I just want the suffering to stop. It would be great if I woke up tomorrow and all of this has gone away,' versus, 'I'm outta here. This sucks. I'm done.'"

Four years ago, my long-time friend died by suicide 20 minutes from my house, and I grappled with his decision. Still do. Blythe tells me she respects freedom of choice in all aspects of life, including death. "Part of my punk rock mentality is I will tell people if they don't want to be in physical form anymore, that is their choice," she says. "However, I want to talk about it, and talk about it, and talk about it. So, that's not something we would decide in one session—that they could tap out." This type of agreement is more effective than the no-suicide contracts that became popular in the early '00s. Blythe and others in the mental health community suggest these "contracts" between doctors and patients can create false confidence. Doctors might use an arrangement on paper to put unfair onus on a patient, sometimes increasing their anguish and desperation and causing a back-against-the-wall situation. "These contracts hold no weight. If someone signs a piece of paper, that doesn't mean anything. What I have people do is look me in my eyes and we'll agree, 'Will you be here next week? Are you going to die between now and next week?' And they'll say, 'Noooo.'" She looks around the Zoom room sheepishly, demonstrating how her patients sometimes react. "And I say, 'I want you to look me right in the eye and tell me that I will see you next week at our appointment,' and they say, 'Okay,' and they have to repeat it to me. That is a contract."

Blythe and her suicidal patients have regular check-ins between appointments. If a patient is convinced that they want to end it, it's time to talk about preparation for dying, but also what steps they're taking to stay alive. "I have a patient who's been suicidal... probably the entire time that I've seen him for three years, and he's still alive. It's a lot of work. A lot of work. If someone's talking about suicide, that tells me that they are deeply un-okay with being in this world. So, I look for ways to make their environment better, if that's even possible."

If you've ever gathered around the lunchroom microwave at a dreary office job, as I unfortunately have, you might have seen a poster for the R U OK? campaign. Launched in Australia by a non-profit suicide prevention organization in 2009, the campaign has gained traction worldwide. The idea is to focus on someone who is having a bad week, or bummer life in general, and ask them if they are okay (sorry, R OK). It's often the person who hangs back during torturous staff meetings, or the one who never makes eye contact with their co-workers as they walk back and forth to their cubicle. "R U OK?" See how clever?

But is it enough to ask a quasi-rhetorical question about someone's wellness? Do we have tools and resources for the difficult answers? I remember being on the receiving end of an R U OK? at my former job. She was the employee; I was the employer. She pointed at the poster on the lunchroom fridge and asked me the infamous question. She could tell my got-it-all-under-control boss facade had been crumbling in recent weeks. Her "R U OK?" planted a seed that I needed to reduce my overtime, find a better work/life balance, unlink my personal and business social media accounts, and stand up from my desk more than twice a day. Did her question and its goofy acronym help me seek mental health treatment or increase the frequency of my counselling appointments? No.

Asking, "R U OK?" is an awkward conversation starter, but we should be taking it one step further, like, "I know a good counsellor..." Granted, I K A G C isn't as catchy, but it offers more opportunities for intervention. We need tasked action plans for addressing mental health issues. This face-value R U OK? shit isn't doing the trick.

This is where mental health advocate Jonny Boucher, founder of Hope for the Day, enters the picture. Jonny came up with a better tagline. "It's OK Not to Be OK." Hope for the Day is a non-profit organization focusing on suicide prevention through education and outreach services, particularly for marginalized folks. Setting up info tables at Chicago's music venues was the humble beginnings for mental health programming called Proactive Prevention that's now used in 50 states, 26 countries, and 17 languages. At least half of Hope for the Day's 16 staff members have strong links to the punk community. Jonny started the non-profit in 2011, a year after his mentor and concert promoter Mike Scanland died by suicide after jumping off his Chicago fifth-floor apartment's balcony. Grieving his friend's suicide, a sad realization slapped Jonny across the face. The number of people in his life that "completed," a term Jonny uses because he says it empowers someone's choice of death, was too much for him to take—a final-straw revelation he knew he had to act on.

"The one common denominator of the people I've lost is no one wanted to talk about it. So, after Mike took his life, I decided that we needed to start talking about it a lot more." Mike was number nine of 16 people Jonny knew who has died by suicide. To address his staggering loss and move forward, Jonny became a suicide-prevention educator. "Our goal at Hope for the Day is empowering the conversations on proactive suicide prevention to simply just meet people where they're at, to let them know it's okay not to be okay."

Blythe TwoSisters is pulling her arms into an air hug and recalling the friendships of her youth. Living with dysfunctional families in abusive homes and struggling with poverty, depression, and suicidal thoughts, her friends were suffering, and she was suffering too. Blythe and her friends created a special bond—one she calls the "glue of punk rock" and the image sticks with me, pardon the eye-roll pun. Blythe has specific questions when she sees her patients struggling. If she could go back to the shows of her youth, she'd ask her friends the same questions.

"For the person that's letting their hair down at shows and getting crazy, what are they doing during the day? Are they going to work? Where do they work? What are they eating? Are they going outside or just sleeping all day until they go to the next show? If someone isn't balancing themselves, they will get sick, whatever sick looks like." Blythe tells me she would use the same approach if someone in a punk band walked into her office today. "I'd ask, 'What do you do when you're not performing, or when you're not on tour?' Same stuff I ask my other patients. 'What are you eating? Are you brushing your teeth? Are you wearing your pyjamas all day? Are you moving your ass?' It's the same treatment, whether you're in a punk rock band or you have 37 kids."

Traumatic events and decades-long build-up of stress can engage and ignite a predisposition to a mental health condition. If a crisis hits, life may never be the same once the warning-signs doors slam shut. "When you have these micro-changes and adaptations to mental illness, you may not notice, and people around you may not notice," says Blythe. The alternating inflection in her voice sounds like she's imitating the dips and dives in her patients' lives. "At one point you're like, 'Whoa, this is not manageable.'"

A tell-tale sign of undiagnosed mental issues is self-medication, and it's prevalent in the punk world. Hard drug and alcohol use was the norm in punk's formative years, particularly in the New York, Los Angeles, and London scenes where many followed a lifestyle that reeked of nihilism. Although gratuitous substance use in the scene has dulled since the late '70s, it hasn't gone away. As an example, alcohol use is still pervasive in the punk scene, and anyone who's seen the amount of drinking inside venues, out in the parking lots, or at afterparties—never mind what goes on behind closed doors—understands what I'm talking about.

I'm an alcoholic who's been sober most of my adult life. My teen drinking binges ended when I was 19, locked in a bathroom and threatening suicide on New Year's Eve. I didn't drink again for 16 years. Alcohol tracked me down later, when my life was falling apart, and consumed me between ages 35 and 41.

Those truly out-of-control drinking years fuelled my compounding stress and undiagnosed mental health issues. I sacrificed my 16-year-long sober, straight edge lifestyle for obsessive next-drink planning as a desperate coping mechanism that kept me afloat until it couldn't anymore. Like a bulging dam, my life would crack, buckle, and burst. Human organs can only handle so much pressure before they shut down. Of all the body's parts, the brain is the most complex, and mine was ready to snap like an over-tuned guitar string.

Blythe's description of what can happen in a crisis like mine is blunt and welcome. As someone who could've used a reality check before my mental health shit the bed, I appreciate her definitiveness.

"Eventually you hit this wall," she says, "and now you're fucked."

Tell me about it.

SHOW 3
CORTES ISLAND
GORGE HALL
FRIDAY, AUGUST 10, 2018

You're staring into a vanity mirror with two missing lightbulbs in a rundown dressing room. You're a punk rock diva. But you're not. But you think you are. You've meticulously laid out your flamboyant costume options for tonight's show—tattered clothing worthy of a decrepit free pile by the side of the road. Somehow, red velvet drapes with random, unfinished lyrics written in Sharpie found their way into your garbage-bag Tickle Trunks. You gently run your fingers over the scrawled words.

Where is the... used to be the... so human... so alone... this is a song we sing together... there is... now we don't know how it goes.

Also found in the dressing-room free pile: a green bungee cord with plastic hooks, not metal, because the one you used to have in your costume arsenal scratched the hell out of you when you turned it into an over-the-shoulder holster.

Hmmm, lots of things to choose from.

You pick up a pair of Red Converse All-Stars, the shoes you wore at your wedding in a different life and rub your palms against their ripped soles like an out-of-practice shoe shiner. The mangled footwear couldn't stand the force of your high-kicks on the last tour and have white Gorilla tape wrapped around foot-sized holes. Soon, they'll be flapping like a mangy dog's tongue.

Cortes Island's Gorge Hall, with its stunning oak wood floors, doesn't deserve the battering it's going to get tonight. You find out that locals built the hall in the early '30s, and you have a rare twinge of restraint.

Maybe you should take it easy tonight?

You knew Cortes was going to be a freaky place with an even freakier music scene. You pictured the small, remote island two ferries away from Vancouver Island having an untainted, small-island, weirdo culture. People from Cortes talk about it with reverence and make it sound like everyone lives in cozy cabins with power generators. You get the impression that locals eat what they kill and kill what they eat. "I'll bring dinner down to the hall," the promoter says. "Do you guys like pulled pork sandwiches?" Your saliva glands shift into overdrive. With the amount of energy that you're burning onstage you should be ingesting a steady intake of raw eggs and bagged almonds.

Pre-show soundchecks are music-nerd rituals you'd rather not be in the building for. Guitarists loosen up their fingers with dextrous soloing, battling feedback while they tool around with amps and pedals. Drummers hit the same beat repeatedly as a sound person fiddles knobs and shouts, "Again," again and again. As the lead screamer, all you need is a functional microphone with a mic cord long enough to reach the crowd. Those other guys and their damn soundchecks?

Shut the hell up. It's time for dinner.

The hall doors open and people file in. Your neck hairs prickle and signal that this show is going to be special. You've been messaging back and forth for months with Gargoyle City's guitar player Emmet about the band's hometown debut. Dozens more people come into the hall, smiling and hugging each other, chattering about the show. With enough people to cover costs, your nerves settle, and your responsible self tries to cram the restlessness of wanting to storm the stage down into your belly.

To distract yourself, you wander around the hall saying hi to everyone. They're unaware that the same pleasant, middle-aged man wearing a grey trucker hat with a "gender is not a genre" sticker on it will soon be scaring them shitless. As you mosey, you come across a beautiful sight. Sitting on a bench are three pre-teen boys wearing punk t-shirts and talking amongst themselves. These aren't the painfully shy kids you're used to seeing at public events. They seem excited; engaged.

"How did you hear about the show?" you ask one of them.

"Our dads told us."

You scan the venue. "Are they here?"

The second kid chimes in. "No, they're at home. They said we should come instead."

Amazing.

"Are you guys fans of punk?"

Third kid: "Yeah! We love the Clash, Dead Kennedys, DOA, Black Flag, Minor Threat..."

What is even happening right now!?

You've never met kids this age that didn't think punk was just uncool music their parents listen to. These are living, breathing youngsters who can rattle off the coolest band names as if they're checking off a Grade 6 English quiz. Then it dawns on you. These kids don't have cell phones. Your eyes dart around the room, and no one seems to be awaiting the next flash or ding. This is blowing your mind. You need to tell someone about your unbelievable discovery and run back to the dressing room. The Gargoyle City guys are tuning their guitars, and the scrawny drummer is hammering away on a practice pad. They sneak glances at the dirty costume choices behind you. A clumpy nervousness hangs in the air. You raise your voice a couple octaves too high.

"Why doesn't anyone have cell phones?"

You had no idea life was possible without a phone welded to your hand.

"There's no cell service," says Emmet from behind his Gibson SG. "Most people don't bother using their phones unless they're at home."

This show is shaping up to be a downright celebration, and it is. During Gargoyle City's set, audience members bust out individualized dance moves. One young woman does a jump, twist, and shake that appears to defy gravity. Gargoyle City, Cortes Island's newest heroes, finish with a cover of the

Stooges' "I Wanna Be Your Dog," and more than 150 humans aged 19 and under sing along. It's as if you've entered another dimension—the punk dimension.

No one fully understands Crashing Into Things' music, and that's what makes your tourmates so incredibly cool. An impossible mashup of Killing Joke and Devo, two groups that couldn't be more different, the Victoria square pegs are super-serious musicians playing a brand of post-punk unlike any other. Tonight, the merry gang of oddities is the perfect precursor for the mayhem to come. By the time Punk Jams hits the stage, most of the youth are all danced out. An older audience moves to the front as you unleash your own joyous jig, wearing a flamboyant ensemble the equivalent of a circus clown's dirty laundry. The bass and guitar sync up as you hit your first unholy wail, jump into the crowd like you're in a punk rock trust game, and—boom—the rest of the show is black.

The next morning you wake up in a loft beside Punk Jammer Little Pharmer, wondering how you got there. Something 'bout a truck swap? Flashes from last night… you, running to the foyer and climbing up on the window frame, taunting the teen mob outside to come back in. Finding a stash of children's toys behind the stage to use as props. Doll with head becomes headless doll. Hobby horse becomes bucking bronco in the mosh pit. You shouting words from kids' picture books become jumbled, secret blasphemies. The show's highlight, retold to you by Pharmer, was scaling the hall's towering fireplace, as your ankles can attest. The crowd cringing at your unsuccessful attempts until you managed to scramble to the top and go airborne with a synchronized scream. Life and limb, life and limb.

Time on Cortes is over, and you're already nostalgic. On the ferry, you can't stop obsessing over the show. That's how it should be—a punk scene kumbaya utopia. Then another memory from last night returns in a face spasm as if your own ghost passes through you. Utopia has a shelf life.

You're sitting at a table outside a dilapidated RV, the makeshift hangout for a group of way-past-drunk punks that you met at the show. You're about to have a crucial conversation, but not an ideal one at 3 am after a show on a remote island.

A woman pulls you aside and confides in you the trauma she lives with because of one of the dark sides of punk rock—the dark side of humanity, really. She explains how she related to what you were screaming during the show, even though you don't remember what that was, and is comfortable talking to you because she knows you understand. She tells you she was just discovering the underground scene in Victoria when a notorious punk musician sexually assaulted her. When other scene members harboured him, she left Victoria because she wasn't safe. Years later, it happened again. This time a sexual predator had infiltrated the Vancouver Island punk scene via Quebec. She eventually found Cortes Island, a place to feel safer in a fucked-up world.

Listening to the woman's story pokes a branding iron in your liver. You can't imagine what she's gone through, and all you can do is listen and support her, even though your blood-boiled instincts tell you to go on a vigilante mission. See, you've been having flashbacks threatening to reveal what you never want to remember. Overwhelming emotions. Anger, sadness, fear— your regulars. A heaviness can take you over in a blink. Huddled and nodding at the woman's story, it's not a heaviness you feel. It's studded, black rage.

NERVOUS BREAKDOWN

It's the first time I've talked to Mike about what happened—how my addiction to self-validation on the internet, and the hypervigilance entwined with it, hurled me into crisis mode. Beads of cold sweat form on my forehead and upper lip as I brace myself, knowing we'll be reliving my unravelling.

"It was tough watching you break down on social media. I felt very protective of you," Mike says. "A lot of people said, 'Oh, Jason Schreurs, what the fuck's his problem? He's just being an asshole calling a bunch of people out and freaking out on them.'" Mike's face warms. "But I knew there was way more to it, and I tried defending you."

On the patterned white light behind my eyelids, a blinking "what's on your mind?" Facebook prompt taunts me. My fingers twitch at the chance to fill the status box with something. Anything. Memories materialize from fog. From an omniscient view, I watch my youngest son and I riding the Vancouver Skytrain on a trip to the big city. Me, glued to my phone. Later that night, awake in bed at our hotel with my phone hovering over my face, neck muscles taut, waiting for someone, anyone, to pay attention to me. The amount of time I spend on my phone, as life passes me by, is disgusting. Endless wormholes on a touchscreen enable my incessant, supercharged desire for people to like me. I can't find contentment in real life and the people who care about me the most. I'd rather have that Facebook hit.

Mike is unphased by my extended silence and picks up where he left off. "Then you deleted Facebook. I'd see people a couple of months later who would go, 'Oh, ha ha, where's Jason Schreurs? He used to be the social justice police,' and I was like, 'Just so you know, Jason has been really struggling.'"

Shame hits my nostrils like smelling salts, and I squirm in my chair. My negative self-talk accelerates to an auctioneer's pace. *Do people remember the stupid shit I said on Facebook? Did everyone think I was a fuckup? Oh god, what did I post? What a fucking idiot.*

"It was pretty intense what was going on with you there. You were manic on Facebook. It was pretty obvious." Mike doesn't soften his blows. Maybe he thinks time has re-toughened my skin. "Rape, sexual assault—that's what you were focused on."

Several years earlier, in another life, I'm riddled with indecision over quitting my job editing the student newspaper in Victoria and settling in Powell River with my new wife Megan. I rack my brain for a meaningful job in Powell River and put unreasonable pressure on myself to become an upstanding member of society, whatever that means. The more I think about conforming, the more life jabs my ribs. I've seen punks hold respected positions in their communities—city counsellors, visual artists, educators, filmmakers, and mental health professionals. That could be me too.

I want the freedom to be creative and the opportunity to make a positive contribution to my community, a job where I don't have to cave under the pressure to work, eat, sleep, and repeat. I don't want to work for "the man," I need employment with a punk/life balance. I take a job as editor of Powell River's corporate-owned community newspaper and tell myself it's a sacrifice for my family, money I'll use to pay child and spousal support. The president promotes me to publisher/editor, a position with long hours, all-consuming responsibility, and a job description I wrote myself. Financial figures are a constant concern and managing 20 staff members causes me intense pressure. Having never worked in a corporate environment before, I'm out of my element and conflicted. Aspects of the job go against my ethics of fairness, respect, and accountability. I fend off the company president as he pushes for downsizing, automation, and outsourcing, and I try to run a community-driven business under a dollar-driven employer.

Each morning before work, I flip through my time-honoured t-shirt collection and wish I could wear Propagandhi instead of Gap. The irony of scoring two-dollar designer shirts at the thrift store while making more money than I ever have, and probably ever will, isn't lost on me. Will my employees notice the magenta sheen on my Calvin Klein button-up has dulled? Pressed polyester is my workplace costume, and 100-percent cotton black t-shirts are my evening and weekend wear. At Monday morning meetings, I'm an undercover punk in business attire. By noon, I'm leaning over my desk with my head in my hands.

Two years into the job, I'm at a Powell River Chamber of Commerce function dressed in my clown clothes. Black shoes, wrinkle-free pants, leather belt, purple dress shirt... clown clothes. I'm a guppy ready to fend off a capitalist shark frenzy in a room full of schmoozing business schmoes, and I'd rather be anywhere else. I spot a friend of a friend and exhale. He's new to town and looks just as uncomfortable in his own clown clothes. A credible source tells me he's a punk and that we should talk shop. I walk over and offer an icebreaker.

"I feel so out of place here," I say, stretching my shirt away from my chest, almost popping off its buttons, and letting it slap back. I float a question past him. "Do you ever come to these things and think you'd rather be at a punk show?" His face softens and he smirks. "All the time," he says. My knotted stomach relaxes a bit.

Underneath all the job stress, punk's freedom and rebellion call me. In the weeks to come, I obsess over ways to stay involved in the scene despite my full-time career in community media. In bed, I ruminate for hours and try to shove punk-in-the-sky thoughts away and return to "real-life" problems. I find time to promote a show here and there, but work stress sucks out all the joy.

I need to let one of my employees go for poor job performance, and it's killing me. I've never had to fire anyone before, and I'm not cut out for this.

My morning baths are marathons as I try to soak off the what-should-I-dos and come no closer to an answer. I stew in the water until it's tepid, wishing I would sink through the bottom of the tub and a robot would replace me. Corporate HQ directs me to terminate the employee.

Terminate?

The next morning, I slide a pink slip across her desk, and my heart plummets. I battle the guilt for weeks. I start to lose my temper and micromanage my employees—a horrible boss on the exterior and a warm and squishy hot mess inside. My first year on the job I won the Chamber of Commerce's "Employer of the Year" award. By year two, I'm creating all the makings of a toxic workplace. Pressure at work comes from all angles, and the office becomes a minefield. I bring stress bombs home from work, and my bathtub is the bunker where I cower. My family doctor prescribes me an antidepressant. It doesn't do anything.

Scheming at four a.m. Pervasive thoughts keep me in a second-guess holding pattern. I'm second guessing my second guesses. After sweating through my sheets every night for weeks, I hand in my resignation at the newspaper and begin my yet-to-be-decided next chapter. A pressure valve releases. My family is concerned but supportive when I tell them I'm leaving my job, as families tend to be about life-changing decisions. Unbeknownst to them, I'm spinning word-magic, making shit up on the fly, trying to convince them I've planned my next steps with diligence. At a dinner party with friends, I grit my teeth and announce my decision to leave my job with as much gusto as I can muster. Cue the puzzled faces and annoying questions. "But wasn't it your dream job?" "Why would you leave?" "What are you going to do now?" I can't spell out my deep need to re-immerse myself in the punk community. My reasons are gleaming crystals in my head, my explanations stumbling messes from my mouth. Being a punk is an integral part of my identity, and I need to focus on that again. I just can't verbalize why.

Unphased, I'm on a mission to be a punk rock maven. Before I clean out my desk at the newspaper office, I'm already booking tours for bands and launching a music production company. Small Town Revolution, named for small-town punks like me, will be an impetus for people everywhere to create their own scenes. Really, it's just a cool logo and a website address "under construction" with no concrete rollout, owned by a guy (that's me) with a runaway Facebook addiction. Other ideas that sleep deficiency tricks my exhausted brain into include running a record label, organizing a music festival, doing promotions for bands, opening a record store/ramen joint (my best idea in hindsight), and becoming a tour manager, a tour booker, or even a touring musician—this coming from a guy who can barely hold a tune or play a guitar. I'm convinced these grandiose plans will solder my role in the punk scene.

For weeks, I only sleep a couple hours a night. The more sleep deprived I get, the more wired, knees shaking and feet tapping constantly, like I'm playing blast beats. I'm the first person to show up at a party and the last one to leave. Appearing drunk while completely sober, I talk at a roadrunner's pace, interrupt conversations, and accuse people of being misogynists and rape sympathizers. With lack of sleep comes irritability, and I take it out on Megan, arguing over mundane topics and deliberately poking at her triggers. I drive a wedge between us, and our couch becomes base camp for my social-media binges while she snores in the other room. I instigate ALL CAPS wars and plow headfirst into the #MeToo movement, posting my own declaration. My sister texts me a screenshot moments later.

What's this about? Mom wants to know.

I start to believe I'm the all-knowing protector of my cyber-connected chain. My mission is to take down everyone on Facebook who makes racist, sexist, homophobic, and transphobic comments. If I need to stay up all night to do it, so be it. Social media posts don't come with trigger warnings, and when a Facebook friend of a Facebook friend posts a rape joke, I come unhinged. I call the guy's boss and demand she fire him, then threaten him on Messenger.

Running on fumes, I spin 360, and depression comes in terrible waves that flatten me. I'm soaked in existential dread (*why am I alive?*) and self-inflicted verbal abuse (*worthless piece of shit*). I cancel my weekly visits with my kids, sleep until noon, and wander the house aimlessly, waiting for someone, anyone, to rescue me. I plead for my doctor to put me on a different antidepressant.

The new meds fuck my world.

Day 19 on an SSRI. I'm in "beast mode" behind the steering wheel. Modern Life Is War's *Witness* is blaring so loud it's shaking the car as I circle town on a rampage. The foreboding rat-a-tat-tat of "Young Man on a Spree" fades in, and I'm no young man, but this is going to be a spree. Someone could've flagged me down, dragged me from the car and onto the street, slapped me around, and said, "Look, you idiot, you're having a reaction to your new medication," and I would have just fended them off, jumped back in the car, and returned to Modern Life Is War, the soundtrack to my internal firestorm.

Childhood sexual abuse memories slurp and slop around inside me. I'm filling in the blacked-out scenes locked in my mental filing cabinet since I was a kid. Glitching out, I see one of my abusers sitting in the passenger seat, leering at me. I flick my fingers to shake off images I've shielded myself from for decades. It dawns on me that my 10-year-old son has been doing the same finger-flicking for months.

No.

My snarling beast flies into an unbridled rage, and I'm smashing the dashboard with my fist. My pained howls cut through the music. My screams, guttural. My delusions, unshakable.

Are they abusing him too?

I make frantic pit stops. The apartments where the people I'm convinced are abusing my son live now, RCMP Victim Services, a lawyer's office, the lakeside trailer park where I was sexually abused when I was six... or maybe seven. I pull over to call my mom, my aunt, my sister, my ex-wife, dumping my suspicions on them in paranoid flurries.

"Put me on the next ferry because I'm going to kill them," I tell my aunt. Or was it my mom? My abusers and the people I think are abusing my son have melded into one. Nothing makes sense anymore. Everything is hellfire. My go-to calming agent, the punk grenading from the stereo, isn't working. My face muscles blip and my jaw twists.

The guys who raped me are out there raping other people.

I'm in danger.

My son's in danger.

My rapists need to be stopped.

I'm gonna find them and rip their guts out.

This is my psychosis.

I'm about to have a nervous breakdown
My head really hurts
If I don't find a way out of here
I'm gonna go berserk
Black Flag - "Nervous Breakdown"

When Kelsey, who prefers not to use her last name, disappeared on the first night of Riot Fest 2019, her friends freaked out. The popular festival takes place each September in Chicago, and this was Kelsey's third Riot Fest, a two-hour flight from her home in Toronto for three days of bands, beers, and buds. Every year, I see the line-up and have pangs of regret that I can't afford the trip.

During Jawbreaker's headlining set that night, Kelsey's friends saw her and her fire-truck-red hair bobbing up front, stage right, rocking out with a Pabst Blue Ribbon king can in each fist as the final chorus of "Kiss the Bottle" rang out in Douglass Park.

I kissed the bottle

I should have been kissing you

You wake up to an empty night

With tears for two

Suddenly, no Kelsey. Her friends scoured the outdoor venue and surrounding pubs. They searched the streets. They texted everyone they knew at the festival and posted SOSs to social media.

> Has anyone seen Kelsey? Last seen at the Jawbreaker set front right of stage.

> We're searching for her. This is serious. Please DM if you've seen her.

For the next 12 hours, Kelsey was a ghost.

A 10-minute ambulance ride away from the outdoor stage, in the emergency room at Northwestern Memorial Hospital in downtown Chicago, two orderlies and a nurse restrained Kelsey, forced her into a hospital bed, and pumped her with sedatives and anti-anxiety meds. All she could think about as she nodded off was being back in her Toronto apartment with her husband, three-year-old daughter, and two tortoiseshell cats.

"I was screaming that I wanted my daughter. It felt like I was breaking in half and the world was ending," she tells me. "I hate talking about it. It's so embarrassing."

With years of hindsight, Kelsey has no idea how she got to the hospital or who called the ambulance, but she understands more about the path that led to her mental health crisis. She bites her bottom lip until it's white and tells me how she'd been "super stressed" before travelling to Riot Fest. Her employer was making her work unreasonable hours as a clerical assistant at a computer software developer. She was a model employee, but the job became too much to handle, and her family life suffered. Then the panic attacks began. I tell her I can relate. I used to be convinced my chest was caving in every morning on the way to my uber-stressful newspaper job.

Leading up to Riot Fest, Kelsey was boozing more than usual, and she started binge drinking as soon as she arrived at the festival.

"You know how people talk about going on a bender? This was a bender on rocket fuel," she says. Kelsey has lived with generalized anxiety for years, but what happened at Riot Fest was a whole new level. "At the hotel, I was having panicky feelings, and my chest felt really tight. I forced myself to go out and see the bands. As soon as I got to the outdoor venue, I started chugging beers. I would finish a drink, and someone would hand me another one. I was buying beers for the people all around me. It was totally out of control. I checked my bank balance when I got home, and I had spent almost $300 that first night."

Around 4 am the night Kelsey went missing, just when her friends were considering abduction as a legitimate possibility, someone responded to their Facebook post.

I have your friend's phone. DM me and I'll drop it off.

These small acts of kindness are commonplace at punk festivals. One time, I lost my phone at Fest in downtown Gainesville, Florida, and before I even noticed it was gone, the person who found it had already messaged my roommate.

Swimming in a booze and anxiety stew in a strange hospital bed, the last thing on Kelsey's mind was her phone. Now that her friends had it, but still no Kelsey, they were even more worried. What was worse, a phone without its owner, or an owner without her phone? Scanning for any memories of what happened between Jawbreaker's set and the hospital, Kelsey gives up and drops her chin to her sternum.

"I was so inside my own head. I had no idea my phone was gone, to be honest." She says she does remember being doped up in a hospital bed for hours—"I'd say five or six"—before she saw a doctor. "She told me my anxiety and the binge drinking had put my system into crisis mode. She said anxiety gets worse as the alcohol wears off. I guess that's why they kept me for so long." Kelsey screws up her nose and shakes her head. "When I got home, I started telling people I had a nervous breakdown." She ended up missing days two and three of Riot Fest, including the long-awaited reunion of the quintessential Olympia, WA, riot grrrl band that's one of her all-time favourites. "Bikini Kill hadn't played in, like, 20 years, and I was stuck at home in bed. It was so shitty."

Kelsey was in trouble before she arrived at Riot Fest. When people enter a state of crisis, symptoms can go undetected for weeks or months before a full-on breakdown. Health professionals suggest developing a pre-emptive safety plan. Easier said than done. My own mental health breakdown blindsided me after I had been stuffing painful emotions down my gullet for decades. No one flagged me as mentally unwell, so asking me to create a crisis plan, just in case, would be like asking me to buy an all-access pass to Riot Fest without knowing it's a 33-hour drive from my house.

Extreme stress and trauma from as far back as early childhood can bring on a mental health crisis. It could manifest as struggling to function at home, work, and social situations and result in depression and anxiety, extreme mood swings, severe lack of concentration, and significant changes in sleep habits. Kelsey's friends were with her, on and off, during the first night of Riot

Fest. Her binge drinking was blatant, which must have seemed out of character, but in an environment where booze and endorphins flow freely, were they to assume she was in crisis? They could have pulled her aside and screamed, "Are you okay?" over the amazing racket, but she was escalating too fast.

"My friends in the punk scene have supported me so much after that night at Riot Fest, and they've never made me feel bad for what I went through," Kelsey says. "After my breakdown, a couple of my closest punk friends called me and said they'd do anything for me. I told them, 'Same here.'"

Since 2010, Steven Gray has been shouting about his lifelong struggles with anxiety and manic behaviour in his Gainesville, Florida melodic-punk band Dikembe. Watching Steven's band do a shiver-inducing cover of Fugazi's "Cashout" featuring his strained, impassioned vocals was a highlight for me while watching Fest at Home, an online version of the cancelled Fest 19.

Steven tells me during an early morning *Scream Therapy* podcast interview that his life changed in 2015 when a panic attack he describes to me as "world-ending" clobbered him. Years of therapy had put Steven in a stable place after the attack, then another mental health crisis came out of nowhere and brought him to his knees. It was the sudden passing of his mom, and it absolutely crushed him. Our video call connects his sadness to my empathy, but I don't have the heart to ask him how she died.

In my case, a crisis reared up when a misprescribed antidepressant ignited decades of stress and mental instability. My personal hell came from a tiny pill with a name I couldn't pronounce. In Steven's case, it wasn't medication that broke him. It was shock, devastation, and grief. He cocks his head to the side, a bit out of his Zoom frame, and swings back in, his bushy beard lining his clavicle. He laments the years he'd spent in therapy—how they didn't prepare him for tragedy.

"I was, like, 'What a fuckup.' It just completely levelled my whole view on the world, everything I had worked towards. It had me examining my entire life... again." Steven says the word "again" like he's spitting out poison. "It felt like a reset button, and it wasn't fair. It had me in the most manic state I've ever been in my whole life."

Steven faced a decision that wrenched him between his family and his band. Dikembe already had a West Coast tour planned, including a stop at 924 Gilman Street, the legendary Berkeley, CA, all-ages venue which bred bands such as Operation Ivy, Green Day, Jawbreaker, and Neurosis. Just weeks after his mom died, Steven opted to go on the tour, and it was unhealthy from the starting line. Trying to distract himself from his mom's death, being on the road was a huge trigger. He drank too much, ate shitty food, and didn't sleep enough. As grief hooked in, the constant stimulation of the tour overwhelmed him.

"I remember being outside Gilman where the side entrance is. A lot of people were walking up and down that street, and I remember crashing so hard and having the worst depressive episode of that tour—in the street, just crying." He could barely finish the shows, he tells me in his deep, gravelly voice. I'm not an expert on Florida accents, but he's got one. When the band returned to Gainesville, Steven went to therapy for a brief time, then gave up. "I was, like, this doesn't work, nothing works, everything is fucked." He and his band members were cautious about going into the studio to record their fourth album, *Muck*, but putting his creative energy into a new album ended up being the stabilizer Steven needed, and it empowered him to seek professional help again. Steven found a new therapist he clicked with, and in a moment of pure serendipity, the guy gifted him a guitar. Steven tries to contain his years-old excitement and squirms in his seat. "He straight-up gave me a Resonator and said to me, 'I'm not going to use it, you have it.'"

A mental health crisis isn't a solitary breakdown or one-off lowest point. Crisis can return after traumatic life events and during times of unmanageable stress. In Steven's case, it walloped him when he least expected it. Now he keeps a close eye on his symptoms as he continues to grieve for his mom. "It's sort of like a person in a room waiting with a boxing glove, hiding behind something, and at any moment they pop out and say, 'Remember this?' Wham! And then you're back at square one. It's a knockdown roller coaster."

Ellen Forney and I are trying to decide what term we prefer to use—"crisis" or "breakdown." Ellen's a Seattle-based artist and health coach best known for her graphic nonfiction books, *Marbles: Mania, Depression, Michelangelo, and Me,* and *Rock Steady: Brilliant Advice from My Bipolar Life.* I've learned a ton from mental-health memoirs, but I will stand by my proclamation that Ellen's books taught me more about mental health than any others I've read. Plus, they're hilarious.

In the background of her Zoom frame, I can see pencils in a rainbow of colours and brushes in various thicknesses that she's jammed into plastic holders. Her impressive looking workstation includes a bonafide drafting table. My desk (a converted dining room table) in my office (a converted dining room) sports half-dead pens, chicken-scratched notebooks, and a stack of library books waiting for me to return them. I digress. Does Ellen say "crisis" or "breakdown."

"Ummm..." She messes her silver-streaked hair, and the lines on her forehead tip me off that this is a tough question. She chucks it back at me like a dodgeball. "What do you think?" I've never verbalized this before, but I give it a go. "At first, I called it a breakdown," I tell her. "I could picture myself breaking in half, falling apart. Now the word 'crisis' feels more accurate because a crisis is an urgent, scary situation, whereas a breakdown just feels like something's crumbling and there's no hope." I take a grounding breath. Navigating this language is vindicating and gives me confidence, and not just because I worked the word "whereas" into our conversation.

Ellen lights up when she hears my preference for "crisis." "I think so too. Some people might say, 'Oh, it's just semantics, breakdown and crisis mean the same thing,' but it makes a huge difference. It's like the difference between a garbageman and sanitation worker." I snicker and tell her I've referred to a janitor I know as a "sanitation engineer." Ellen switches to a serious face that clashes with her funky faux-fur vest. "Seriously though, it works counter to your healing to think of yourself as broken, as opposed to, 'Okay here's something I need to figure out. How can I get beyond this?'"

By this point, I hope it's clear that punk isn't just a music-based subculture. It's a way of life in which we can claim our power. Ellen's living it. She received a bipolar diagnosis in 1998, right before her 30th birthday. In her private health-coach practice, named Rock Steady after her second book, she uses the goofy acronym SMEDMERTS to teach the importance of having routine and using coping tools to avoid crisis.

"The best way to deal with a crisis is to not get into a crisis," she offers. "That sounds obvious, but it's not easy, and that's my aim for what to work on with a client." Ellen says she has been in crisis twice in her life—two bouts of full-fledged mania and the inevitable depression that followed. In the second round, her mania, more extreme than ever, lasted five months before she nose-dove into a year-and-a-half depressive episode. Manic episodes last, on average, two to four months, while depressive episodes can put someone living with bipolar in a misery chokehold for eight months or longer, according to Harvard Medical School. Without treatment, episodes can become more frequent and last longer.

"That's something I hope to never, ever repeat, or even get a taste of, frankly," Ellen says.

Thanks in large part to SMEDMERTS, she hasn't had a severe mood episode in more than 20 years. The first time I turned a page in *Rock Steady* to see the lop-eared SMEDMERTS mascot and its ridiculous, sideways grin, I happy-laughed, reared up off the couch, and almost dumped kombucha down my front.

The nine tenets of SMEDMERTS are:

Sleep.

Meds.

Eat.

Doctor.

Mindfulness.

Exercise.

Routine.

Tools.

Support system.

Ellen tells me she considered adding an F for faith and I joke that SMEDMERTSF doesn't sound as good. Snarkiness aside, I'm awestruck at how an acronym and its mascot, no matter how silly, can alter someone's mental health plan. Just follow the SMEDMERTS trail to wellness? Could it be that simple? It's taken me almost four years to grasp the tools on Ellen's list, and it required a drastic change in lifestyle, maintaining a stable routine, and slowing the fuck down. For a guy who thought mindfulness was a scam sold in grocery store magazine racks, I learned to do breathing exercises while listening to punk rock to ground myself. Not many people can crank Pig Destroyer to 10 and enter a zen state.

The word "blindsided" keeps coming up while Ellen and I talk about our mental health crises. Full disclosure: it's almost always from my mouth. As misprescribed meds jacked me up in 2018, I had no idea I was in crisis as I drove around town hellbent on spilling my childhood abusers' blood. "Blindsided" is the most fitting word for what happened when psychosis hit me. Ellen waits patiently for me to finish and reflects on her own manic ride and eventual depressive crash. "It's really traumatic and how can you not be blindsided, you know? It's really intense and it always feels like... should we sing it together?"

I'm not sure where she's going with this, and I play along with an anticipatory nod. I hope we'll sing "Second Skin" by the Gits, one of Ellen's favourite songs. ("It's loud enough to hurt a little," she told me in an email.) Instead, she half-emotes lyrics from dinosaur rock band Foreigner's "Feels Like the First Time." I've heard this song by accident before. Predictably, I miss her cue.

It feels like the first tiiiime... it feels like the very first time.

It's not "Second Skin," but it will have to do.

SHOW 4
GABRIOLA ISLAND, BC
SKOL PUB
SATURDAY, AUGUST 11, 2018

Blood will spill on the dance floor, and that's okay, hardly anyone is here to dance. It's day four on the nine-day Punk Jams tour, and you walk into the Skol Pub as a metaphoric pile of flaming turds, irritable and sleep-deprived. The drive from Cortes Island to Gabriola Island would have been just over four hours if it weren't for the ocean and ferries, which doubled the trip's length. This tour schedule is starting to catch up with you.

The pub is dead. Five uninterested Gabriola Islanders sit on the deck. A weathered barfly, an obvious fixture here, points at a sign above the bar. Ice cold Lucky, on special, $3.50. "Notha wunna them," he slurs. Someone has the radio dialled to classic rock and that shameful '80s tune by Loverboy comes on. "Lovin' Every Minute of It." You make a fart face. It's the same song you bounded down the street to drunk one New Year's Eve, boombox raised above your head, yelling the goofy chorus to the heavens, and scaring the neighbours into 2013.

Lovin' every minute of it? Come on.

During load-in, you're distracted by shit music you secretly like and slice your knee on Little Pharmer's patented metal stomp box, open a considerable gash and leave button-sized blood droplets on the bar floor.

Oh shit.

The pub manager runs over, and rather than telling you to get the fuck out of her bar, she pries open a first aid kit the size of your face. She unrolls gauze with the care one of your childhood babysitters gave you—maybe just a little too much care? Your babysitter's face and your new nurse's warp together. *It's okay. It's not her. Or is it?* Glitch. Could be a facial recognition error—you've been having those lately. The manager wipes away the dark stream running down your calf with a bar rag, swaddles your knee in gauze, and stares at it like the wound will coagulate on the spot. Your mind skips. *Isn't there a death metal band called Coagulate?* Mind blip—you've been having those lately too.

Without hesitation, Little Pharmer fires up his notorious pharm-punk, a weirdo punk, folk, country, grunge, hip-hop combo. Sitting on a stool and thumping on his stomp box to an empty room, he punishes his guitar while yelling about compost and organic produce. Pharmer has had enough of playing to no one and drags his one-person-band onto the patio to serenade the five don't-give-no-fuck Islanders. He somehow manages to win the patio crew over by the set's end, but their stand-off-ish looks make it clear they've had enough noise for one night.

It's time. Confrontation. Your targets? The now-liquored wannabe hipsters sitting on the patio in this shitty pub on this shitty island with its big-money vibe, every fourth driveway leading to a mega-home. Your blood percolates. Pressure builds in your stomach. Gabriola is so far removed from the amazing all-ages show the night before in Cortes. This show isn't even in the same stratosphere.

Where the fuck is everyone? It's time to show these patio fuckers what punk is.

You take out electric hair clippers, plug them in beside the stage, flip the switch, toss one of your garbage bags full of costumes over your shoulder, and slink to the changing room, a washroom stall that smells like a disgruntled patron has smeared feces on the walls. You rewrap your knee with the crimson, stained gauze and draw a big, black X on it to signify how you hate bar shows, which brings you back to the pervasive thought that's hounded you since you got off the ferry.

Why did you book this show? What the fuck are you doing here?

Swelling guitars caterwaul into the bathroom. You wrestle into a Santa-red snuggly with its bum flap hanging open, fashion a superhero cape using ripped-up fabric, and wrap a grubby scarf so tight around your face it makes your cheeks throb. Your hair sticks out the top of another head-to-toe fashion disaster as you strut out of the washroom and down an imaginary catwalk toward tonight's Punk Jams band. You're a mangy supermodel, stained ensemble trailing behind you, falling off piece by piece.

The hair clippers bounce around on the floor like a wasp battling a fly zapper, and you stumble toward them. Squinting through the scarf, you grab a bar stool and head to the deck. The five patio dwellers snap their heads towards your demonic, feral howl. You climb the stool, wobbling precariously, legs shuddering, and bring the clippers down on your scalp. *Zzzzt.* A chunk of hair drops through the patio's wooden slats. A dual-guitar exorcism erupts from inside and you screech even louder. *Zzzzt.* Another chunk. Two onlookers on the patio laugh, another two of them look appalled, and the last one scoots into the bar through a side entrance. The set goes by in a blur, and it's time to pick up the pieces.

That was the performance of your life.

Show after show, the same delusions, the same unadulterated bliss, the same absolute fucking mayhem. During load-out, you envision tonight's show swirling down the shit-stained toilet in the pub's shit-walled washroom stall. Deep in your bowels stir turds of excitement.

You're going to annihilate Nanaimo tomorrow.

ALL THROUGH A LIFE

When they hunt me down, I'm still pulsing with psychosis. My sister, a psych nurse, fast-tracks me to a psychiatrist. The whoosh of the hospital doors behind me sounds like a skateboard whizzing by on smooth pavement, speed-wobbling my electric head.

"I'm getting out of here someday, right?"

My joke doesn't land with Megan and my mom. Their faces look as if I'm going to bolt into the forest behind the hospital. I'm led into the waiting room where I squirm in an ass-numbing chair and juggle a hornet's nest of racing thoughts. I'm clenching my phone so tight it's a wonder the screen doesn't crack. The psychiatrist calls me into her office, and it takes less than 15 minutes. No tests, no family history, no checklist, no debrief, no soft landing.

"Jason, you have bipolar disorder."

I don't understand; I'm not well versed in these words. I ask questions and can't comprehend the answers. My entourage is in the office now, and I look over at their blood-drained faces. My support system. My team. Family. Safe people. We have more questions for the psychiatrist. My mom has the first one: "Are you sure?"

"I have seen thousands of patients," says the psychiatrist, "and I have no doubt this is bipolar. It's the people who are depressed that we have a hard time diagnosing. When they're manic like Jason is, it's very easy to determine." The psychiatrist turns her focus to me. Her flawless makeup and impeccably smoothed hair accentuate the no-bullshit look of a doctor with a framed degree from Dalhousie University on her wall. I zero in on her name in gothic font and away from the intensity on her face. "I'm going to prescribe you a mood stabilizer for the mania," she says, "and an antipsychotic so you can sleep, okay?"

The pounding behind my eye sockets subsides a little as she explains what comes next. Medication and sleep are the most immediate necessities for the long, hard road ahead. My barren lungs beg me to take my first deep belly breath of the past few days' skull-fuckery.

It's my mom's turn to squirm in her chair. The look on her face reminds me of the time a doctor tweezer-ed Cowichan sweater fragments out of the crook of my six-year-old arm. A summer camping trip cut short by hyperactivity, scalding hot chocolate, and a night in the hospital. "It's going to be okay," She said through tears as she pinned my squirming frame down on the emergency room table.

"Jason, can I ask you something?"

She's talking real words. Here. Now.

"Sure, what?" I say.

"Will you give me your phone?"

My 19-day descent into psychosis jumped between reality and an online world that wasn't the real world, but was sort of the real world, but really wasn't. I was convinced I had the power to influence all my 4,854 "friends." I was a holy saviour fighting the assholes who were harassing anyone in my network and a social-justice grim reaper for the ones doing the harassing. Before my mom asked me for my phone, you couldn't pry it from my hands with a crowbar. She can't stop me from using, but she can cut me off at the source. I snap out of my social-media trance, relent, and hand over my cellular drug.

"Okay, you can have it," I say. Now it's my mom who's clenching my phone. A thought sparks—*Am I free?* At home, heaps of medication bring me down from mania, but I'm jonesing to post status updates about my diagnosis. Facebook remains the dark angel on my shoulder, goading me to search for instant gratification in well wishes and "you're so braves!" Like a tantruming child, I beg Megan to give me back my online lifeline, and when she relinquishes, I'm right back to using.

I read online that a psychotic break is like a head injury, and the helmet fits, so I'm stuck wearing it. I collapse into the couch, hit shuffle on my iTunes library (all 2,136 hours) and open the floodgates on loud music to dull my pain. I leave the house for disorientating walks with Megan and her dad, and the music soldiers on in the living room without me, supplying a cacophonous entrance song as I come through the front door. Couch-bound again, blunt-force trauma flattens me.

Medication rescues me from the danger zone, but my moods start ping-ponging in a vicious cycle. Depression suspends me upside down in its torturous compression chamber, but I wriggle loose and bust out like a manic Houdini on steroids, my mind flooded with impossible magic. A week later, I'm depressed again. Two weeks after that, manic. I'm a super-hero, I'm a drowned corpse. I'm a superhero, I'm a drowned corpse.

To a signature soundtrack of punk and metal, my superhero—name and powers to be decided—is back and hatching grandiose, elaborate plans while runaway telephone wires swing toward my cerebral cortex. *I can write a book and do a podcast while I'm recuperating.* I scribble the words "Scream Therapy" in a notebook, then "book" and "podcast," and they sit there for over a year while I pare down a tangled mess of other ideas. *I can open that ramen shop/record store/live venue I've been talking about... I'll buy that bus I was looking at and be the tour manager for Propagandhi... I'll move to Gainesville and help organize Fest.*

The medication isn't keeping my mania and depression at bay, so my psychiatrist ups my dose for the cloud-hopping highs and adds an antide-pressant to the mix for the bottom-scraping lows. Skull-crusher, vice-grip headaches take me down for the count. Meds up, meds down. Old meds, new meds. I'm trapped on a mood-cycling terror ride.

I want to die. *Please let me die.*

My latest delusion: I will turn my life into a Fringe Festival show with me doing spoken word over bastardized soundscapes. The last time I'd done live theatre was 30 years ago in junior high, and I already have this year's Fringe submission guidelines, deadlines, and North American travel plans all mapped out. I'm on what's supposed to be a casual hike with my friend Luke when I launch into him with my on-the-fly elevator pitch: "A punk stage show about mental health and music, and my own story too. It could be really dark and have soundscapes, visuals, and spoken word."

I try hard to recruit him, tossing out the different cities and dates we'd hit on the tour. Elevator pitch line two: "I can do the spoken word, you can do the visuals, and we'll both do the music." In my mind, the show is stage ready. In my peripheral vision, I suspect Luke is shaking his head in a royal "what-the-fuck?" Amidst my chatter and unnecessary details, our hike turns into a bushwhack, and I pester and pester while we trudge our way through thigh-high undergrowth. Finally, Luke offers measured diplomacy. "I'm interested, but let's give this idea some time," he says.

At home, I scribble "Fringe show" in my notebook with three exclamation points after it. Two days later, I scratch it out and replace it with "Small Town Revolution Fest" and make a list of band names to play at my very own music festival in Powell River. Before long, I lose track of my ideas and depression steals my imagination. My head is a monolith on my neck, overflowing with wet cement. I'm a drowned corpse again.

My bipolar diagnosis forces me to sift through a lifetime of memories and question my conscious part in them. Was mania my body-snatcher? Can I explain away all the damage I've done in my life and blame it on bipolar? *It wasn't me. It was bipolar.* I'm overwhelmed with thoughts about how life has cursed me. Shameful memories surface—the hurt I caused others, my failures as a husband, father, and son—and I'm locked onto them like a shitty pop song on repeat. Did I act alone, or is bipolar a long-time accomplice? A dastardly duo? Will bipolar absolve my terrible choices? I inventory my shitty laundry and depression swallows me. I dissect an endlessly looping film reel with random scenes of all the stupid, horrible shit I've done, even the relatively harmless things, like the night I threw a beer bottle at a taxi one of my friends was trying to hail, shattering glass over the hood and ricocheting shards at him. How, on the walk home, I risked my media career by punching and kicking holes in election signs, ripping them from the ground and smashing them over my knee. The next morning, I pictured my smug face on the front page of my own newspaper. "Publisher fired for tampering with provincial election." Sightings like this of Hurricane Jason were commonplace before my diagnosis, from juvenile vandalism to life-altering self-sabotage I can't bring myself to talk about.

Why didn't I see the patterns?

Medication is my stability baseline. Each morning at 9 am, I fumble with pimple-sized white tablets, then shake pastel-orange pills into my tremouring hand and look down at their misshapen mini hearts. To get the right dose, I break the hearts in half, and there's a metaphor in there somewhere. Another medication in my repertoire is miniscule, potent, take-as-needed anti-psychotic pills that knock me out when sleep deprivation rushes me toward mania. My magic med concoction is supposed to stave off the recurring versions of hypomanic and depressed Jason. Sometimes, my mood episodes are too strong and override the pills. Other times, the meds keep the episodes at bay.

As the meds settle in my system over the next year, acceptance becomes another bad-ass tool in my mental health toolbox. My psychiatrist notices before I do (as psychiatrists do). "You're presenting a lot better today," she says at my appointment. "I sense more acceptance in you than before. This is a big step."

Some old guy, I can't recall who, said "knowledge is power." I'll use an alternative version: "Acceptance is power." I learn that acceptance affords me even-handed reflection, and to move forward I had to accept the damage I'd done. What I couldn't change didn't have to own me, and neither did bipolar.

"Coexistence" is a loaded word, the nicer cousin of "codependence." Is living with bipolar a blessing or a curse? The answer, the crux of my diagnosis, is a work in progress. Without bipolar, I doubt I would have immersed myself in punk—its soothing flash and fury that's allowed me to tap into the creativity I crave, whether it's splattering my emotions all over a Word doc, creating pandemonium in the basement loud enough to scare the neighbours, or sitting down with a cup of tea and my PJ Harvey colouring book.

Bipolar, like punk, is an integral part of what makes me who I am.

I'm looking back
And in looking back I hope to get beyond
And start to mend all those days
That they left undone.
Rites of Spring - "All Through a Life"

I facilitate a support group for people living with bipolar, and every Sunday night at 7 pm, we convene to share with and listen to each other. Certain members attend every week like it's a can't-miss punk show, others have never been to a support group before. I've had people tell me, "This is the highlight of my week," and, "I don't know what I'd do without this group." Every time I hit the "End Meeting for All" button on Zoom, marking another week of hopefulness, I tingle with reward. Helping others is my jam.

The bipolar group has more than 300 people on its email list and a revolving cast of 15-20 attend each week. Support groups mirror my experiences in the punk scene. I find other outcasts and freaks (oh, those wonderful terms of endearment) who grow to have deep respect for each other, listening and learning without judgement. Ergo, support groups fit the definition of punk. Unlike the communal yells at gigs, during group meetings I wait for someone to pass me the conch shell before I find my voice, but the message is the same. Thank you for allowing me to be myself.

Many members of the support group cite the beginning of their mental health journey at the point of diagnosis. For them, it's a launch pad for an informed life, a benchmark for a new beginning. It's medical confirmation of what's been disrupting their lives and enables them to look back at their troubled history with more clarity. For others in the group, diagnosis is an acrid pill lodged in their throat. A psychiatrist tells them they have this or that (or more than one this or that) and sends them home with a prescription they might have to refill for life. In the mirror, under blankets, or on an anxiety-inducing trip to the grocery store, once the weight of diagnosis kicks in, it can be a self-depreciating, epic trudge toward understanding the medical system's labels and macheting another path from there.

At the time I was diagnosed, it felt like the game-changing event of my life—a life that an unknown entity had plopped onto my lap like a screeching guitar that needed to be tamed. Fuck, I never even knew what the word "bipolar" really meant before October 12, 2018. So, my journey must have started there. Then I talked to someone with a differing perspective, took time to digest it, and did a 180.

That's allowed, right?

All writers have regrettable moments where they ask someone a question, they wish they could suck back into their mouth and swallow, like the key to a door they never want reopened. Presenting: one of mine. I'm in the middle of a *Scream Therapy* podcast interview with Sascha DuBrul, a mental health activist and founder of Transformative Mental Health Practices in Oakland, California. Between the ages of 18 and 33, bouts of manic psychosis landed Sascha in the hospital four times.

"Well... um," I stammer. "I wanted to get a sense of what your journey looked like from diagnosis until now. In my mind it goes, diagnosis, therapy, and then recovery. In your experience, how did it go from starting your mental health journey after being diagnosed to where you are now?"

"It wasn't like that for me. Not at all," Sascha says...in a mocking tone? I flinch, and my anxiety kicks in. I'm worried I've blown it with this guy that I've been trying to connect with for months. Sascha leans forward and offers me a playful smirk. I exhale. *Thank you for sparing me, punk gods.*

Sascha spent his youth in the late '80s and early '90s hanging out in squats on the Lower East Side of Manhattan. Playing bass with his friends in ska-punk band Choking Victim was a formative revelation, complete with bodies-bouncing-off-walls live shows and pissed-off anthems like "Fucked Reality" and "Hate Yer State." Not long after, Sascha co-founded the Icarus Project, an activist organization and support network that reframed mental health as a social justice issue. Now, as a coach, counsellor, and someone with lived experience of bipolar, he encourages clients to consider different mental health perspectives to take the power back from the mainstream health care world. In other words, applying the spirit of punk rock—rebellion, resistance, and reclamation—to their wellness plans.

"First of all, and this comes from someone who's spent a bunch of time locked up in psych hospitals and is also someone who's worked in the public system," Sascha says, "we do a great disservice if we start with diagnosis, because that assumes diagnosis is, like, 'Oh, this is where the journey started.'" An intensity comes across his face like he's about to speak with his Caps Lock on. "Look, for NO... ONE... EVER... does the journey just start with diagnosis. The journey starts way earlier."

Sascha's words rush through me in a near-peeing sensation. He's naming my nagging uncertainty that my diagnosis was a be-all, end-all event, and how I thought it would spearhead my life going forward. The flashing blue light on my $25 podcast microphone lulls me into a trance and painful memories from scrambled pieces of my past bubble up. Plotting ways to escape a soul-sucking job, my shaking legs banging my desk until my knees are bruised.... Disappearing into my cheap headphones on a Greyhound bus, heading back to a failed marriage... Pine needles on the forest floor, poking tiny holes in my skin while they loom over me.... My psychiatrist's face softening, then hardening, her mouth speaking the alien word—bipolar—that would consume me.... These are snapshots of my journey in no particular order. Is diagnosis part of a non-linear continuum with no beginning, middle, or end? Is it simply a signpost on someone's mental health journey?

Sascha's commanding voice brings me back. "A better question to ask is, 'Okay, I got diagnosed with bipolar when I was 18 years old, but what led up to me getting diagnosed with bipolar, and what's happened since?'"

Sascha's Coles Notes:

He left home and went to college when he was 17.

It was his first time on the West Coast.

It was incredibly stressful.

He was smoking too much marijuana.

He was drinking too much coffee.

Throw in a little acid.

He didn't sleep for a very long time.

He started dreaming while he was awake.

His unconscious process was coming out in his daily reality.

He went back to New York.

He had a vision that the world was going to end.

He thought there was a grand conspiracy.

He was going to play a vital role in a revolution.

He was convinced primetime television was broadcasting him.

On all the channels.

He was having an ecstatic moment.

He had a sense of connection to something much larger than himself.

He was doing what he was put here to do.

It was probably going to lead to his death, but that would be okay.

One day, he thought it was his last day on Earth.

He jumped from a subway platform onto the tracks.

He walked past three stations.

He was taken into custody and put into a psych hospital for three months.

"So, yeah, they diagnosed me bipolar," Sascha says. "What would you do?" We share a quick laugh. But I'm losing focus again. If all of this took place leading up to Sascha's diagnosis, what did the rest of his journey look like, before, after, and in-between? "I could go on, man," he says. "I could just tell you a whole story, but the long and short of it is, I got my shit together, got locked up again, got my shit together, got locked up again...."

It was Philip Yanos who connected me with Sascha DuBrul. Back when this book was just a noisy kernel popping around in my head, I came across an article in *Psychology Today* entitled "Punk Rock and the Dream of Accepting Community." The piece quoted the 1979 anthem "Fuck You" by Vancouver band Subhumans (a middle-finger salute later recorded by fellow Vancouver punk trailblazers DOA).

Philip, a professor of psychology at the City University of New York and author of *Written Off: Mental Health Stigma and the Loss of Human Potential*, co-developed a group-based treatment called Narrative Enhancement and Cognitive Therapy. Its premise is that internalized stigma in individuals with mental health conditions is one of the largest barriers to recovery. Philip and his associates conducted a study citing evidence that almost a third of those with severe mental health conditions have elevated self-stigma that compromises their recovery.

With diagnosis comes stigma: no question. The medical establishment doles out diagnoses that the general populace misunderstands and sends people off into the cruel world with limited coping techniques, therapy options, and resources for support. Society has been known to collectively scrunch its nose at people who are neurodivergent. To complicate matters, drug companies back massive anti-stigma campaigns, selling the message to not be ashamed—*here, just take our pills, and it will all be okay.* Stigma feeds on its own tail.

Growing up in New York City, Philip was a moody teenager with a psychiatrist dad and few friends. Of Greek descent, Philip couldn't live up to what he describes as a macho male stereotype. His social anxiety and persistent depression kept him withdrawn from others, and his parents worried about him. Philip's interest in loud music went beyond picking up a guitar and playing and attending shows in New York's punk hotbed. It gifted him an opportunity to discover his identity.

With the NYC skyline as his Zoom wallpaper, Philip has a bright smile for me. "I did check out some of your podcast episodes, and the recurring theme is 'punk rock saved my life.' I do believe that is true in my case." He looks a bit bashful and runs his fingers through his feathered hair. "Music gave my life meaning, made me feel good, and didn't ask me for anything in return."

Philip tells me the punk/hardcore bands he discovered, like Rites of Spring and Hüsker Dü, spoke to him in deep, personal ways. I nod approval at the band names—he's speaking my language. In his late 40s, Philip listens to more punk than ever, citing '80s Chicago-based hardcore band Articles of Faith as a current favourite. He says the education and acceptance he found in punk as a youth prepared him for his groundbreaking work studying mental health stigma. "Punk became the formative experience of my life," he says. "It was extremely important to me, both because of the community and the fact that I could express myself in a way that I hadn't before. If I'd never found punk, I would have always had this unsatisfied feeling."

Under the stigma umbrella is stigma from society, stigma from one's community, and internalized self-stigma. All three can cause people with mental health conditions to question their worth. Punks with mental health conditions are living in the eye of stigma's perfect storm. As punks, they need to justify why they look and act a certain way and why they listen to "devil's music." As neurodivergent people, they must prove themselves as "functioning" members of society. Nail that perfect job, tie the knot, crank out a couple kids, chase "success," run yourself ragged, retire, die. Maybe an all-inclusive trip to Mexico every three years. Buy into the system or something is wrong with you. Punks tend to avoid these heavily treaded paths, but that's where their strength lies, Philip says.

For me, the most important job is staying healthy to avoid a bipolar relapse. I want—no, need—to focus on creative outlets that make me happy. My priorities are writing, doing the *Scream Therapy* podcast, listening to and playing music, carving out time for walk-and-talks with my loved ones, and my mental health volunteer work. I've stopped giving a fuck about a fancy job. I had one and it crushed me. I won't go back to that kind of life, and I dare anyone to say I'm lesser for it.

"Right, right," says Philip. He's a thoughtful, active listener. "The punk reaction to ostracism is to dig in and be even more strident about it. 'Well, I'm really different,' right?" He clenches his fist and shakes it like a true punk. "The way you view yourself has a very profound impact, and if you can change that, you can also help change people's views. They're going to see you as someone who isn't conforming to their expectations."

Philip lands our conversation on the song which led me to him in the first place. "I know you're from around Vancouver, and one of my favourite bands is DOA, maybe the fastest, tightest band ever. Their cover of 'Fuck You' is probably the definitive one," he says. "What's awesome about that song is the message is, 'You should come join us.'" I'm nodding enthusiastically but keeping one eye on the clock—I don't like keeping busy people like Philip longer than their schedule allows.

We could use one last fist-pump before we say goodbye, so he clenches his and leans in slowly as if he's cracking the stigma code. "Being a punk has a stigmatized status in society, but not one that contains self-stigma, because it's an empowered stigmatized status. Punks may see the world as hostile and may be treated in a hostile manner by the world, but the punk aspect of their identity is one they celebrate. What the punk scene proves is people with lived experience of mental health can feel that it's an empowered identity, and that can make all the difference. And you're not the only one. You're going to find others." Philip has reinforced my opinion that we should have permission to stare stigma in the face and yell "Fuck You" like Subhumans and DOA did.

We agree it's time to end our call, and we should keep in touch. I click "end meeting," but, shit... I realize Philip and I should have listened to "Fuck You" and thrashed around our Zoom room before we said goodbye. Talk about a missed opportunity.

Now that I'm in full bipolar learning mode, I want to soak up knowledge about my diagnosis. Someone in my support group tips me off to a BBC documentary series called *The Secret Life of the Manic Depressive*. In it, English comedian Stephen Fry, who lives with bipolar, asks people if they want their condition "cured" so they can live a "normal life." His interview subjects include pop musician Robbie Williams (ugh), actors Carrie Fisher and Richard Dreyfuss, *Electroboy* author Andy Behrman, and a bunch of less "famous" folks. The majority of the people in the series choose a cure. They want bipolar turfed.

Both choices have merit. In my experience, the question is painful to contemplate, and its answer can change daily. When I'm depressed and want to run away and never come back, please cut this bipolar fucker from my body and throw it into a Slayer mosh pit. But if I'm in the hypomanic zone, like I am today, everything has a thrilling sheen, and I don't ever want it to fade. My fingers thrash the keyboard so fast I hit the delete key every three strokes and still type faster than a stenographer. (Thank you, autocorrect.) Today, the words I write are golden nuggets. Tomorrow, they could be chunks of raw sewage. Today, I'm keeping bipolar; tomorrow, I might be giving it a solid "fuck no." Finding what sits somewhere in the middle would be like ripping out pieces of me, splaying them on a metal table, and picking and poking at them like I'm dissecting a frog in science class. I'm no scientist.

Yes, mental health diagnoses can be a curse. Having to confront the past, experience stigma, risk overmedication and side-effects, and experience pervasive guilt and shame can compound into self-loathing and suicidal ideation. But a diagnosis can also be a blessing. Access to a long-needed mental health team, income assistance and health services, support groups, and treatment and therapy can improve quality of life and help someone stabilize.

So, blessing, curse, or both?

"Curse!"

Alicia Bognanno blurts out her answer and surprises herself. "I don't know why it would be a blessing," the singer/guitarist/songwriter of Bully says, interlocking her hands. "I feel like being overly sensitive can be a blessing and a curse, but mental health stuff? I don't wish it on anybody." Carefully, I suggest a diagnosis could validate people like her and I to be more creative and take risks, and is an opportunity for musicians and other artists to raise awareness about mental health. Like, bipolar power? "I try to be hypersensitive about things like that," Alicia says, "because in the music world, and particularly in the rock world, it can be romanticized... and that's just treading dangerous water, you know what I'm saying?"

Born and raised in Minnesota, Alicia and her band have released five studio albums since 2013. Sometimes-debilitating symptoms such as severe paranoia, depression, and anxiety have derailed Alicia and her music projects in the past. She messes with her bleached hair that's pulled up with a guitar-capo-sized clip and cradles her cheeks in her hands. "My paranoia skyrocketed," she tells me in an extended drawl that buys her a moment to compose herself. She explains how, five years ago, her symptoms reached a fever pitch that affected her personal and professional life. "I started to think people I loved or worked with had ulterior motives when really they just wanted what was best for me. I was paranoid about taking certain shows because I had it in my head that I was going to get booed off stage, which has never happened, and things just all plummeted from there. At that point I said, 'Okay, I need to go and get help.'" A therapist gave Alicia a bipolar diagnosis, and she's been maintaining her mood stability ever since.

I tell her I read a dismissive article in the mainstream press that normalized her mental health condition and suggested that now that she's diagnosed and stable, she's somehow "fixed." Alicia's careful not to slag the journalists who have gushed about her music—like *Pitchfork*, an indie music Bible for hipsters with disposable incomes, which called her signature scream "a resuscitating jolt of protest"—but says the long-form articles overfocus on her emotional struggles.

"Sometimes I don't want to fucking talk about bipolar," she says, "especially if you're in the middle of it and you don't feel good. It's heavy to think about and not something you want to constantly revisit." Having been a journalist for the better part of my 50 years, and as a creative nonfiction writer living with bipolar who specializes in music and mental health, I hope Alicia will give me a pass. "Well, yeah, you're the first person I've talked to that also struggles with bipolar out of the 30 or so interviews I've done about it, and the hardest thing is vocalizing the feelings that you have going on inside of you," she says. "It just feels isolating knowing that even if you're able to, it's not fully making sense to the person you're talking to."

The word "isolating" shakes me into action. I'm cautious to avoid a hard sell, but I'm horrible at soft ones. "You should come to my bipolar support group," I say, biting my tongue a moment too late. Wait... her widening eyes tell me she's into it. "Oh, I should join!" she says. "What do you do to help? I want to go to your support group. I definitely want to do that." The next day she emails me, and I add her to the membership list.

As Alicia continues her nonlinear, post-diagnosis journey, she's welcome to join us on Sunday nights to support other people's experiences and share her own. No one in the group has cracked the bipolar code, but we discuss types of therapy, access to the medical system, the effects of medication, relationships with our loved ones—most of whom will never truly understand us—and what diagnosis means to us. As for the blessing or curse question, from what I've seen as a support group facilitator, the answer is fluid, and with fluidity comes so much potential to learn.

SHOW 5
NANAIMO, BC
THE NANAIMO BAR
SUNDAY, AUGUST 12, 2018

You're scrambling into another thrift store nightmare, lost in your pre-show ritual in the Nanaimo Bar's bathroom stall. Punk Jams is readying its second clobbering of the Harbour City this summer, and this tour is becoming harder on your psyche by the night. You've been puppet-mastering a disgusting side of yourself for five days straight—a side you hide in your regular life.

You fall back on the toilet seat and rock back and forth, hiding a demented Joker smile under your multi-layered mask. First, black lace cinched against your mouth and nose, impeding your breath. Second, a pair of ripped panties digging into your forehead and chin. Over top is a broken ski mask, its jagged edges penetrating the layers of fabric. The sharp plastic pokes at your jawline and snaps you out of your disembodied trance, and you jerk up from the toilet seat.

You're huffing and puffing now, shaking with adrenaline. An internal switch goes off, and you're uncaged. You kick open the bathroom door and stomp down the hallway, spooking the bar staff along the way, ready to unleash a spectacle the audience of less than 20 people won't soon forget. Storming a stage barely big enough to hold your band, you spew garbled, stream-of-consciousness lyrics that pour from your trauma files.

Your latest ragtag band of accomplices grin at each other and feed off your reckless abandon. Lurching into a failed handstand, you smash into one of your guitarists and knock over a microphone stand on the way down. You wrap cords and patch cables around your neck—a makeshift noose—creating an impossible tangle of PVC coils on the floor, then squirm around in the mess like a fish trying to out-flop a wooden whacker. Flailing your arms, you windmill off swaths of ripped, sweaty fabric and expose your bruised and beaten trunk, which you've been pulverizing since the tour began. Gauze hangs from your hands and knees, revealing bloody knuckles and a reopened gash from last night's show on Gabriola Island.

The scant audience is trying to figure out what the hell is going on, equally fascinated and disturbed. They heckle and jeer, and it doesn't faze you because you're a noise messenger, and you're planting a seed. You repeat holy words to yourself.

If you can do it, anyone can. If you can do it, anyone can.

In your mind, you're the living embodiment of punk rock, on the tour of your life.

In your mind, no matter what happens, you won't stop until your punk mission is complete.

In reality, you might crack and never come back.

BRAVE FACES, EVERYONE

Mom's waterbed squishes and sways. She strokes my hair and tells me everything will be okay, that this profound sadness, possibly my first major depressive episode, will pass.

"Don't worry. You'll find another girlfriend." Mom—the optimist. Me—the depressed. Abandonment is my most painful emotional schema, patterns of thoughts and behaviours ingrained in me since childhood. Dad leaves, I'm a year old. Mom drops me in the laps of sketchy babysitters when I'm a preschooler because: single working mom. I'm six... or maybe seven, alone in a rowboat with *him,* alone in the pine-needle forest with *them.* Now it's the end of sixth grade, and my first girlfriend has unceremoniously dumped me.

Please don't leave me.

My dad? The man who walks out the door when I'm a toddler is never truly my father. He's a distant "uncle" my mom protects me from for the rest of my childhood. She does what she thinks is best for me. She puts my safety before a child's need to have a father. She uses her fear of losing me to obscure the paternal wonder in my eyes.

Mom manages a local pub/strip club, and her unstoppable worth ethic makes me a latchkey kid by default, riding my tricked-out, banana seat bike into the crosshairs of injury.

"Don't go on the hill. Just stay on our road, and you'll be safe," she tells me repeatedly while rushing out the door in bell bottom jeans so tight she zips them up with a coat hanger. I watch her do it every day.

Please don't leave me.

One afternoon, she comes home to find me lying bleeding on the trailer park's hill, knocked clean out, my bike a crumpled mess beside me. I come home from the hospital with stitches in my forehead shaped like an upside down cross. My mom's sworn duty is to protect me and boy does she try, but she can't do it all. She can't erase the trauma—what he hissed in my ear in the bottom of the boat. She can't help me un-smell the musk of teenage boys that permeated the forest.

I adopt a hidden sadness. It manifests as physical sickness—allergy flare-ups, asthma attacks, headaches. I become intimately acquainted with oxygen tents and grotty hospital food during three bouts of pneumonia. From inside clear, bendable plastic, I lie awake, thinking about my bike, my toys, my favourite Saturday morning cartoons, and my black Labrador retriever Princess.

I only visit Grandma and Grandpa Schreurs—my estranged dad's parents—when Aunt Mary and my mom remind each other that it's important I stay in contact with them, and that they only live five minutes away. My blonde bangs hang over my eyes, hiding the shy, 10-year-old me. I sit cross-legged on their shaggy carpet and my grandma holds out a shoebox, not wrapped but ribboned in spindly twine. Inside, a pair of wooden clogs from their homeland. I'm not sure if they're decorative or functional.

"You wear them..." my grandma says from behind her grandma glasses and pushes the clogs toward me with Nivea hands. I look down at my sneakers—ripped, unlaced, filthy, broken in spirit, sad. I force the clogs onto my feet, embarrassed at how uncomfortable they are. I picture my dad, who had only a back and no face, wearing the same wooden shoes when he was a child.

An angsty teen shadow walks alongside my traumatized child counterpart. Together, they embody my abandonment. The shadow clings to my bright purple and orange Airwalks and hides the secrets I can't speak aloud. It only lets go in darkness, so I walk through trails behind my house at night. In expansive black, with my Sony Walkman as loud as it will go, I find unexpected freedom in dangerous, haunted paths. I navigate the pitch dark to the hyper-blast of Christ on Parade's *A Mind Is a Terrible Thing*, pounding my fist and headbanging down a dirt road behind my junior high school and into zig-zagging trails that connect to the streets that lead me home. I'm fearless.

Dragging my feet and kicking at innocent pebbles on the way to school the next morning, the shadow's intrusive thoughts glom onto me for another day. I crank Dirty Rotten Imbeciles to scare it off and hope the sheer volume will bring me back to the here and now. Minute-long speed-punk tunes lift me from the doldrums, kick me in the ass, and prod me to carry on. But the shadow always catches up. Beneath my skin, abandonment's tendrils wind toward my heart, hog my chest cavity, and fester. When I stop moving, I leak self-defeat from my pores, and it pools at my feet. The shadow licks the spoils.

My unkempt, greying hair has been masquerading as dirty blonde since I strode headlong into middle age. White patches of post-stubble cover my steady jaw and chin dimple. Closer to the big 5-0 than the big 4-0, I'm too old to be working in a prep kitchen.

A year ago—an eternity—I surfaced from the muck of my bipolar diagnosis like Martin Sheen in *Apocalypse Now*. It was clear that I couldn't work a high-pressure job again because the one at the newspaper almost killed me. A job at my friends' cafe, sure, I can do that, even with a ticking depression bomb strapped to my back.

At 4 pm, my tradition while assembling enough breakfast wraps for the next morning is to put on Spanish Love Songs' *Giant Sings the Blues*. I need that extra push, and the album's lively, melodic punk keeps me moving as I drag hour seven of eight behind me on the grimy kitchen floor. I finger finicky ingredients and pinch tortillas with unsteady thumbs and index fingers, concentrating on folding them exactly right with Spanish Love Songs as my cheerleader. I'm not sure what I'd do without this day-end listening ritual. Most days, I question if I will even make it through, and by late afternoon I'm begging the prep-cook gods for mercy. Spanish Love Songs is my final push to another night at home where my body is meat-grinded into sleep before the next morning gives way to more food-prep doom.

The cafe's beginning-of-day checklist plunges me wrist-deep in red mix, a gloppy combination of slimy roasted red peppers and clumsily hydrated sundried tomatoes. I check perpetual, mind-numbing kitchen tasks off a laminated list covered in food specks and delinquent permanent ink. My thoughts are soulless and miserable. Anxiety, paranoia, existential crisis, despair, suicidal ideation. I plot ways to run away and never come back, and that adage about your problems following you wherever you go doesn't apply to me, because I want to sizzle and stew in my problems anywhere else but here.

The dish pit provides a strange solace as my hands slosh around in hot, soapy water that's turning greyish brown. I clean the drain trap and fling what my friend calls "sink snacks" into a trash can shit-mix of veggie peels and congealed pork grease. I pile food-processor paraphernalia higher than the sink basin allows and juices spill down its side as I turn Ziploc bags outside-in and watch unidentified globs plop out. Remnants of scrambled eggs flap around in a Teflon frying pan like soggy Kombucha SCOBYs. As I scrub burnt bits off soup-stained pots, my hands pass under scalding water, and I snap out of ruminating on exiting my life stage left.

Hours drag excruciatingly. Listening to Spanish Love Songs is crucial for my final push toward yet another 5 pm finish. I'm roused by guitarist Dylan Slocum's raspy screams and pumped with endorphins via flashy chord changes and the horse gallop of the band's rhythm section. At 4:45, pushing a mop around on the food-caked, un-mop-able floor, it dawns on me. I've listened to *Giant Sings the Blues* enough times to memorize every word and harmony, and somehow the album's fundamental purpose has been passing me by.

Shift's over. I change out of my clothes, drop them to the bathroom floor, and consider following them onto the reeking pile and assuming the fetal position. I pry off my skateboard shoes, the ones I sacrifice for minimum wage, so stained and crusty with food bits I can't tell what colour they are anymore. A fresh set of clothes immediately absorbs my food-prep stink. Out in the kitchen, Dylan sing-shouts "Bad Day," and I unclog my eustachian tubes, clearing the way for his words.

Hilltops covered in smog
And I can't breathe for what's felt like weeks
Held together with duct tape
But soggy like papier mache
I'll smile and say that I know everything's okay
I can't shake this feeling like I'm gonna die today

My cheeks turn wet and sting. Of the thousands of albums on my phone, I choose this one over and over. I know why now. Dylan's bleak lyrics keep me from disappearing. He sees me. I can name my depression. He can too.

I hate the way I live indoors
I hate that no one listens
I hate the way that I don't care
But I hate everything
It's a bright day
It's such a bright day

I flick off the kitchen lights and sag downstairs to write down my hours. In the months to come, as I lose my will to live daily, Spanish Love Songs always reminds me I'm never alone.

The Hex from Victoria instigates its live set with "Love's Old Curse," a song that's equal parts swamp punk and shrieking banshee. The number of local yokels in the queue for drinks triples the ones watching the band. The band's unholy wailing is the backdrop to cheap whiskey and tequila shots chased by the shittiest beer on tap.

I hate bars. Music venues should be inclusive for everyone, young and old, and sober folks need safer spaces to see bands. I used to only promote all-ages punk shows, but I caved. The sad fact is not enough people showed up to pay the bands what they deserved without a bar to feed the machine. Some of my friends who came to the all-ages shows just snuck booze into the venue or drank in the parking lot.

I don't drink. My alcoholic dad cautioned me with his absence, but 19+ bar gigs have become necessary evils. I'm able to pay the bands—albeit with dirty money—and the shady atmosphere is suited to drunk people who enjoy their sauce and don't have to sneak it in. Promoting bar shows is a painful compromise. Even if people are genuinely there to enjoy the music, it always seems like boozing is the focus.

Tonight will be pure torture, and not just because of slobbering drunks. During soundcheck, I watch greasy burger juice run over my wrist and drip down my arm as blood-raw patty chunks plop onto my plate. I glaze over and stare straight through my friends in the Hex, a monolithic heaviness overwhelming the posi-energy and hyperactivity I'm usually known for. Nodding off in my French fries, Megan nudges me with her elbow and whispers behind her hand, "Are you okay?" I can't shake a headache from hell that's threatening to staple my eyes shut. I wish someone would pry them open with metal pins like they did to Alex in *A Clockwork Orange*. I slump over and Doc Martens trample me in an internal mosh pit. I feel myself sink into a hole under the table and depression kicks the ladder from under me as I try to claw back up.

Come on. I can do this. It's a punk show.

I've never been one to hang back during a band's set. I like to be up where the excitement is—right in the fray. Tonight, as the Hex reaches its auditory climax with a warped cover of "Bette Davis Eyes," I huddle in the corner by the door, and all I want is to be home in bed. I'm at a punk show with my friends, and I'm miserable. If one of the things I love most can't make me happy, what can?

Why am I so fucking depressed?

Then comes the unthinkable.

"They found Adam. He's gone..."

What Megan is saying, it doesn't make sense.

They found Adam and then lost him again? What?

Then the word "gone" sucker punches me. I want to drop to my knees but steady myself and nod robotically. "Yeah, I thought he might be..." I say with a resigned half-smile. It's shock.

For the past three days I've been explaining away the possibility that Adam could be dead, shoving it into a hidden file registry labelled No Fucking Way. It's fitting that they find him while I'm creating cacophony with my friend Mel, blowing hair dryers into guitar pickups, pulling frayed drumsticks across worn-down strings. Adam loved noise. Making it with Mel was stopping me from fixating on where he could be. The forest? An abandoned building? On his way out of town on a one-way ferry?

The previous afternoon, Luke and I embarked on an epic, two-person search party—another one of our bushwhacks—and came damn close to the mountainside spot where they found Adam. Luke and I agreed we're glad we didn't find him. We wanted to find him alive. Not like that.

A few of us are headed down to the beach to pay tribute to Adam.

I ignore Luke's text and stay affixed to my couch. I can't bring myself to see Adam's warm face conjured in brilliant flames, his mourning friends huddled around the fire for one last look. The next morning, I rock on throbbing feet, staring at Adam's three-foot by nine-foot painting, *Under Pressure*, hanging in my basement jam room. This has become its home, where it was meant to be. Before it adorned its current wall space, it hung in my former newspaper office. Adam sold it to me for $100 and wouldn't take a penny more. My corporate boss winced the first time he saw it. "Why would you want to put that on your wall?" He should have seen the piece that Adam gifted me after I quit. It's hanging above the jam room's communal drum kit—a giant middle finger in dayglo oranges and pinks, splotched onto a broadsheet comics page from the *Vancouver Sun*. Fuck you, media corporations. You've been sucking journalists dry for decades.

Adam lived life his way, a prolific artist who painted in a style I was convinced people wouldn't or couldn't appreciate. He used salvaged wood for canvases, creating skewed shapes and sharp edges to match the kineticism of fringe characters with shocking, unsettling colours, trouble peeking from behind bubbling paint. Corporate bosses aside, I was off base about people not liking Adam's art, and pieces like "Love," depicting Satan with a crimson lipsticked grin, are mainstays at Powell River house parties.

Luke circulated a Tidal playlist with all the songs Adam posted on social media in 2020, the year he died. I balanced pangs of sorrow and flashes of respect when I saw bands like Black Flag, Sonic Youth, Hüsker Dü, Babes in Toyland, Suicidal Tendencies, Fugazi, and Melvins on the list.

I've known Adam lived with mental health issues since I met him in high school. His weirdo, esoteric vibe endeared itself to me. Ignorant people said he was too strange, but I disagree. One can never be too strange.

I wonder if Adam found the support that he needed all those years. Coping tools as simple as listening to music or as complicated as self-medication always have a tipping point. Sometimes the only way out... is out. To varying degrees, we're all lemmings walking off the cliff of a sick world. Those who live beyond the capitalist system's expectations, like Adam did, may feel trapped and hopeless, but still have a certain clarity—lemmings aware of an ever-impeding plummet.

One of the myths about suicide is that people want to die. Often, they just want their suffering to end, and they wish their life could somehow change. I can't begin to understand the unimaginable pain Adam's family and friends are experiencing, but I selfishly wonder if Adam's death brought him peace. And I know it's not my place to ask.

I hate the sentiment that memories last forever. Eternity is a shell game. The times Adam and I shared will fade like the Metallica back patch sewn on the acid-wash jean jacket I wore the first time we met in high school. He rolled up in his ride, popped his trunk, pulled out a saxophone, and serenaded a group of us with a punk version of "Careless Whisper." The conversations Adam and I had through the years, about living life outside the grasps of commercialism and government mind control (yes, he went cerebral), the bands we saw together, our thrill-ride trip to Vancouver for the Sparkmarker reunion in 2012, it will all fade away. Adam's infectious smile will fuzz and blur over time. The sound of his voice will muffle. I will lose grasp on the kindness in his eyes.

One thing I will never forget. Through and through, Adam was a punk.

A year and a half before I lose my gentle friend and three months after my bipolar diagnosis, I reach my lowest point and suicidal thoughts consume me. They push, and push, and keep pushing. Penetrative earworms even Napalm Death won't drown out.

I take a cognitive behavioural therapy course at the hospital, and I'm told my thoughts, emotions, and actions are connected. That's all my exhausted brain can absorb as I slump over a table along with 12 other depressed people—half with eyes to shoes, the others with heads to table. During one session, the psychologist teaching the course offers us a wellness nugget that finally sticks with me. One way to cope with suicidal ideation is to make a list of positive affirmations. I usually can't stand lists, and affirmations, and all that shit. They always make me think of those cheesy Stuart Smalley skits from *Saturday Night Live*. But when our kitchen knives start taunting me as I put away the dishes, I'm willing to give positive affirmations a go.

The crucial part about my list is I need to write it when I'm not depressed, an arduous task because I haven't had many sunny days lately. Reading the list out loud during my darkest times, I'm told, will reinforce my true beliefs about myself. That's the idea, anyway. Could reading a stupid list pull me out of depression when I'm convinced life is a steaming pile of Red Hot Chili Peppers CDs? All around me, people are going about their perfect lives with their cooing babies and cute dogs—laughing, joking, flipping their hair this way and that, chirping, "Hey, did you see what so-and-so posted online?"

Fuuuuuck. Why can't they see I'm suffering? No one can. No one ever will. I don't deserve affirmations... I don't deserve to live.

One day when Megan's at work, I put on *Left and Leaving* by the Weakerthans, a rare mellow choice in my musical canon, and I sit on the couch with my notebook. I stare at it until the lines on the pages blur. My rigor mortis writing hand pleads for a semblance of inspiration—for my internal naysayer to stop torturing me.

This is useless, you're so useless.

I focus on John K Samson's smooth voice, and my pen moves. The tip flows—red ink. I call my list Read When Depressed.

I'm safe

My family and friends love me

I'm not broken

I'm not cursed

It's not my fault

I'm not a failure

I'm a good writer

I'm a good person

I'm strong

I don't deserve to die

I have a life worth living

Sometimes I want to vanish completely
Call in sick from life
I woke up and didn't feel better
Don't know why I'd act surprised
At least each year is getting shorter
And the ocean's on the rise
Spanish Love Songs - "Brave Faces, Everyone"

At his most depressed, Dylan Slocum took 45 steps a day in his Los Angeles apartment, from couch, to bathroom, to kitchen, to couch. So say the lyrics of "Beer & Nyquil (Hold It Together)" from Spanish Love Songs' second album, *Schmaltz*. Dylan's written more songs about depression than any other punk musician I know. It's not the kind of thing he'd want to brag about, but his songs have helped countless people, including me.

I was hating life, grunting away in a grubby cafe kitchen. The self-destructive voices in my head convinced me I was a one-of-a-kind loser going nowhere, and I should escape my life, roll over, and die. Dylan's no-bullshit lyrics, his openness to sing about horrible, shitty, internal despair, poked a hole in my chest and shouted straight into my heart.

It's Halloween weekend, 2019. The Atlantic Nightspot in Gainesville, Florida is usually at half capacity on most weekends of the year. During Fest, the annual festival that brings more than 250 bands and 3,000 attendees to the university city, punks pack the Atlantic. Dylan and Spanish Love Songs are playing a Fest mystery set—a secret show announced that morning. The line-up for the show is up the block and around the corner. As for the chances of anyone else getting into the Atlantic, shit looks bleak. Punks shuffle their feet, talk nervously with their Fest pals, and hold out hope. The 200 lucky ones inside the club bellow their approval as Dylan slings his guitar over his shoulder and switches on his Orange Amplifier. He shoulder-checks his drummer and looks side-to-side at the rest of the band to make sure they're ready. The crowd is getting rowdy. It's time.

"Hey, what's going on you guys?" Dylan says.

"We're Spanish Love Songs."

The band launches into "Bad Day" and a rumble of bass and drums high in the mix threatens to overpower the guitars. Dylan's cranky yell cuts through the muddy sound.

I can't shake this feeling like I'm gonna diiiiieee today.

Every mouth in the venue is open to the ceiling. This is a party, a celebration. A celebration of facing depression.

A "heaviness" is how I and other people living with depression describe it. An intolerable pressure in the forehead and where the neck meets the spine. A bowling ball in the gut. Lifeless extremities. Sometimes people won't leave their beds, as if strapped down and held captive. A toothbrush is a 20-pound weight. Weight... oh, the weight.

More than 260 million people worldwide live with clinical depression, according to the World Health Organization. The original word for depression was melancholia, which dates back to Ancient Greece. Melancholy implies sad and uninspired, mopey even. That's not depression. Depression is being cold cocked with a cinder block. The blunt impact, the constant throb. Depression is closer to catatonia than melancholia, in my lived experience.

But punk can help. According to the American Music Therapy Association, music is valid therapy to reduce depression and anxiety, as well as improve mood, self-esteem, and quality of life, and I doubt many music fans, no matter their chosen genre, are surprised by this. Gerry Rafferty, a psychiatrist in a Dublin mental health facility for under-18s, creates playlists for his patients that begin with sombre music and gradually move to styles like punk and metal. According to Rafferty, his patients' self-hating, intrusive thoughts subside, and they begin to process external—what he calls "productive"—emotions. "Their moods rise as the playlists become more energetic," he tells me, motioning over his shoulder down the hall to the youth psych ward from his plain white office at Linn Dara Inpatient Unit.

Other studies, like the one published in the *Emotion* journal in 2020, show that listening to sad music as a calming technique can also help with depression. Although most people wouldn't think of punk rock as particularly calming, on days when I'm deep in depression, bands that embrace sadness and frustration, like Spanish Love Songs, lift me and settle my system so I don't have to wallow in self-pity. Couple that with other bands like Hot Water Music, which preach positivity and pull me from a smothering fog, and it's the perfect combo. The pleasure I receive from listening to my favourite bands produces a dopamine hit, which improves my mood. This explains why I listen to their albums over, and over, and over, and....

The Atlantic crowd is sweat-soaked. Dylan Slocum throws his guitar down, grabs the mic with both hands, and leans into the audience so Fest-ers can clamour with him.

We're gonna both die alone

If you can't get happy

Spanish Love Songs' "Concrete" ends with an extended drum roll, a fret-run up the bass, and a final, coordinated crash. Dylan bashfully waves his arms at the crowd to signal there will be no encore tonight because Fest runs a tight ship. He's already soaked through the towel around his neck, and the water bottle in his hand is empty. He humble-smiles on his way off stage as Fest attendees give each other sloppy hugs. A chorus of "that was awesome" echoes through the bar.

The next day, I bump into Dylan and his band on my way to see Against Me! at Bo Diddley Plaza, and I'm compelled to pull him aside. "Hey Dylan. I wanted to tell you how much I appreciate your music," I say. "I've been having a hard time, and your songs have been really important to me the past couple years." It's really awkward. "Thanks, I appreciate it," he says nervously, and we part ways.

Five months later, I'm interviewing him for the *Scream Therapy* podcast on the night before he leaves for the road. I can tell he's battling pre-tour anxiety. I'm in podcast-host mode, a contrast to the uncomfortable fan-to-band exchange we had at Fest, and I ask, "Is your modus operandi to write about sad and depressing topics, but stay hopeful?"

"Yeah, absolutely," he replies. He leans back and pauses, scratching his neatly trimmed beard and pushing his black-rimmed glasses up the bridge of his nose. He could be a psychologist. He's already nailed the look. "Well, I think our MO is to help people realize they're not alone in these feelings." His modest smile melts me a little. "Because that's a very powerful realization."

Mike Friedman, also known as Dr. Mike, is shaking his head methodically, perhaps easing a stiff neck. As a clinical psychologist, therapist, and health coach, he has over 30 years' experience helping folks in the New York area with their mental health issues. Mike tells me it took him until his 30s to find connection and purpose through punk rock and heavy metal. Before that he was depressed, anxious, and lost.

"I was a clinical psychologist. I should have known in theory how to deal with emptiness, or loneliness, or depression." He raises his warm eyes, and in them I see self-forgiveness.

Mike has loved loud music since he was young and thought singing in a band might give him a sense of purpose and raise his spirits. It was clear after a couple of lessons that he couldn't carry a tune. Unphased, he went on Craigslist and came across an ad for an alternative rock band looking for a singer. We both cringe at the words "alternative rock." For us punks, they're a death knell. "I'm not really sure why I thought that would work out okay," he chuckles.

Predictably, the jam session was a mess as Mike struggled to match his monotone voice with the talented band. I assure him I've been there, frozen behind the mic, searching for a pocket in the music to launch into a killer scream, only to hear my froggy voice croak out of the PA.

"It was so upsetting that I almost started crying," he says, and he's not being dramatic. "At some point, I just started screaming into the microphone. I was convinced I blew it and walked out. They left me a message the next day. 'Hey, we were gonna do an alternative band, but with your voice we're thinking of more a hardcore or thrash band....'" Mike smirks, and I sense a punchline coming. "I told them, 'Well, this is awkward. I actually don't know what the words 'hardcore' and 'thrash' mean.'"

The other guys played Mike songs by punk and hardcore bands from the New York scene, and having never screamed before, hearing other singers doing it floored him. Against the odds, his aptly named band Odd Zero has been thrashing for a decade.

Mike and his wife Aylin are the founders of Hardcore Humanism, which encompasses his therapy and coaching practice, a music and mental health podcast, and a blog. He tells me his humanistic and holistic approach helps clients identify their goals, overcome obstacles, and build an authentic, fulfilling life. In layperson's terms, humanism is about living the life you want to live, and Mike has been following his own advice in recent years. He says before punk and metal animated him, he wasted his days away and never had enough time to do anything of true meaning outside his work.

"This community came along, this whole art medium and culture, and it completely changed my life, and I didn't even know I was missing it. When I read about people who had created a life around it, I was, like, 'Wow, this is how I want to live.'" Life-affirming bands like Cro-Mags and Sheer Terror became conduits for Mike to tap into an internal intensity he didn't have a language for. The music didn't change him; it let him figure out who he always was. "Honestly, I don't know how it would have gone otherwise," he says. "I don't think it would have gone well."

Mike sometimes sees clients who are punks, tipped off by their tattoos, coloured hair, band t-shirts, and a distaste for authority. With them in mind, he challenges everyone who comes through his office door to enter environments and approach situations they're a little uncomfortable with. "I tell people to think for yourself, what your confrontation with the world is, the things that make you think outside the box, and be willing to go toward them, and that's what I learned from punk rock." Not judging people, openness, exploring passions, and creating a healthy community are part of what define the punk mindset, he says. "This kind of community can embolden people, and it can invigorate people," he says. "I know it did for me, and it certainly has been the backbone for my mental health for a long time."

Mike is shaking his head again. Maybe finishing his neck exercises? This time, his back-and-forth motions are smoother, like a hinge sprayed with WD-40. "I can't believe I lived the first 30-something years of my life having no knowledge or understanding of this music or its community... especially considering how important it is to me now."

Freshly showered punks huddle around steaming plates of grilled veggies and smashed potatoes. Rachel Taft smiles maternally. Her bustling kitchen is her happy place—the epicentre of her community contribution.

Since 2011, Feed the Scene, a "band and breakfast," has been filling punk bellies and fluffing punk pillows as bands roll through Baltimore. To date, Rachel's brainchild has hosted more than 1,200 bands from 28 countries.

I first met Rachel at Fest in Gainesville, Florida. She was all grins, handing out cupcakes to people waiting in line to pick up festival wristbands. I thought, *how fucking cool is that?* The cupcake was amazing. Double chocolate with sprinkles, if I recall correctly.

Rachel's warm personality and generous spirit hide a sadness behind her glittering blue eyes and round, upturned cheeks. Like pogo-dancing in the pit, feeding people is therapeutic for her. The joy she receives from going to shows and contributing to the scene is medicine for what she calls her "persistent depression."

Volunteering is one of the most effective ways to combat depression, according to Harvard Health Publishing. People who donate their time to a cause are more connected to their community, which curbs alienation, loneliness, and worthlessness.

After I had to quit my newspaper job, my counsellor at the time kept pestering me to volunteer. I didn't understand. If I couldn't help myself, how the fuck could I help others?

Since my diagnosis, I've trained to be a bipolar support group facilitator, crisis responder, and mental health coach. I hoped like hell it would help, and it does.

Feed the Scene was a way for Rachel to cope and find belonging, and her volunteer efforts went beyond giving bands a place to crash. For most punk bands, lack of food and lodging are the most anxiety-inducing aspect of touring. Feed the Scene became a full-fledged hostel, festival promoter, and volunteer-run non-profit society with Rachel at the helm. I'd be remiss not to mention that the meals and lodging at Feed the Scene are free.

Rachel has lived with depression for as long as she can remember and has had attention deficit hyperactivity since the age of two. Like, toddler two. A health team monitored her childhood symptoms and learning patterns and held off on medicating her until third grade.

"The first day I took the pills, I went into an antique store with my parents, and I didn't break anything. I almost cried." Rachel flips her flowing strawberry blonde hair over her shoulders with authority. "It was the first time I was able to concentrate."

After a family tragedy when she was 28, Rachel fell into the worst depression of her life. "Yay!" Rachel says, her sense of humour raw as she disguises hurt with a bubbly laugh. "My mom was 59 when she died in 30 seconds of natural causes, and we were not expecting it... at all. She was just gone. And I didn't know what to do with myself...." The lightness drains from her face, and she falls silent. Rachel's darkest times had her stuck in bed for days. She made a pact with herself to attend as many festivals and shows as soon as she could. She hoped it would lift her from depression. It worked.

"There's nothing like piling on top of 47 people and screaming at the top of your lungs," she says, her eyes finding their twinkle as her voice rises. "It's not something we can do in 'polite society' and it be acceptable, but it's 100 percent acceptable in our community to run into a room and scream with your friends."

Rachel and I were in those same dogpiles. We scooted past each other on the streets of Gainesville during Fest, rushing to the next venue. I'm sure we high-fived more times than we can count fingers. If Rachel wanted to inject happiness into her life, Fest was the perfect place to do it. What she didn't expect to find was something that would shape her future. During the infamous Fest afterparties, Rachel listened to band members share their tour stories gone wrong. Sleeping bags on dirty floors. All-night house parties. Shitty (or no) coffee in the morning. And the list goes on. Feed the Scene started to brew in her mind. Rachel could help bands by welcoming them into her home and, in turn, they would help her by keeping her accountable.

"Feed the Scene helped ground me back in reality." Her voice escalates, a self-soothing motivational speaker. "I had to bathe today. I had to eat today. I couldn't have cupcakes and cheese for dinner, because we had a band coming over, and I was making them dinner. I had to do laundry because someone had to clean the sheets. And I had to clean the house because someone was going to see it."

It's common for Rachel to plop down beside a band member who's sitting alone on her porch after a show and offer a set of ears. The rigours of touring requires musicians to deal with loneliness, alienation, and depression. It takes extreme effort to keep energy levels high enough to kick ass at every show. By the end of the night, band members have been known to melt into an emo puddle.

"I always tell people I'm their family. Do you hate your mother? I'm your mom. I've 'adopted' several adults who don't talk to their parents anymore. I text them on their birthday, and I make sure they're okay." Rachel's wide smile reveals glimmering teeth. She busts out the old saying... wait for it... "a family is chosen."

Rachel tells me her mom was an amazing caretaker and phenomenal cook, and I'm not the least bit surprised. Would her mom be proud of what she's doing for the scene? It will be nice to hear Rachel's answer, even though I think it's a given. She rocks forward and runs her fingers through her hair again.

"I feel really close to her when I'm feeding people because she always fed everybody," she says. "In the beginning my mom would have said, 'What the hell are you doing with yourself?' but the fact that we've accomplished so much with Feed the Scene, despite whatever mental issues I was dealing with, I think she'd be very proud of me."

INTERMISSION
PARKSVILLE, BC
RATHTREVOR PARK CAMPSITE
MONDAY, AUGUST 13, AND TUESDAY, AUGUST 14, 2018

The moment you pull the Toyota Corolla into the campsite your shoulder blades unhinge from your ears and drop to where they're supposed to live. Last night's show in Nanaimo has your body reeling and exhausted, from your pounding skull to your gnarled toes.

Two days camping with your best friend Greg and his family won't remedy five days of pure adrenaline pumping through you, but it should help. Cute kids, games around a campfire, shitty comfort food, and obligatory pleasantries with other campers—this has all the makings of relaxation time. If you could wind down, this would be the place to do it, but you just can't sit still.

You flop into the nearest camping chair and force yourself to stop fidgeting as Greg's wife reintroduces you to their two kids. "Remember your uncle..." she says, which melts you a little and pumps your brakes. The kids look up at you, glowing. They're so fucking cute you can hardly stand it. Watching them all pouty-faced, bike-ready, sugar-craving, superhero-obsessed, and scrap-happy, you pine for the happy parts of your childhood. You join the kids' goofy games and petty teasing, a big kid yourself. You want them to laugh at your uncle jokes and, sure enough, they do. As darkness descends, campfire flames lick your face. The kids giggle at your cheesy ghost stories. At bedtime, you promise you'll take them to bumper boats tomorrow. Excited, the kids dive into their tents. In time, they settle.

You're not ready for an early night. You wonder if you'll ever be. Skirting past the campground gates, you and Greg trudge up a ridiculous hill to the corner store, as if pulled by an unseen force. You catch up on each other's lives, and it's the perfect opportunity to tell the friend you trust most that you're slipping—that you've already slipped—but you don't know how to explain to him that your brain is skittering like soft-rot bacteria under a microscope. Instead, you badger him about making a documentary film about Propagandhi, one of your favourite bands. It's a project you've been talking about for years, and you're convinced this is an idea you guys need to run with, and now. You're blabbering like it's already filmed, edited, and ready for Netflix.

"I just don't have time for it right now, with the kids and work..." Greg says, then falls quiet. Roadside, a renegade cricket chirps.

Your life is at a crossroads, under construction, detoured, and you only have one way to go. More tours, more projects, more distractions, more escapes.

You're staving off sleep amongst campfire smoke, ass deep in your camping chair. The smell of burnt marshmallows hangs in the air, and the smoky, sugary deliciousness climbs your nostrils. It's the first near moment of calm you've had in weeks. Even the mosquitos are comforting.

Is this what it feels like to relax?

You pry yourself from the chair, drag your body to your tent, drop horizontal, and toss around on the unforgiving ground where a Therm-a-Rest should be. Intrusive tour thoughts are back—promo, meals, soundchecks, lodging. You plead with yourself to shift down a gear and push aside logistics for the next four shows. You coil up on the petrified dirt, and the adrenaline trickles out. Yes, your system's slowing, but you're uncomfortable as fuck. Like a not-yet-dead sardine jammed into a can, you donkey-kick with each muscle spasm, tossing and flipping in staggered fits with your regrettable camping gear. You abandon the tent and try the Corolla's passenger seat, where you furiously promote the tour on Facebook. Willing yourself to stash your phone in the glove compartment, you shove your face into that dreaded gap between car seat and car door. Digits, then appendages, lose circulation. Semi-conscious disturbances count as sleep, a precious and rare commodity on this tour—your dwindling life fuel.

Dreaming. The living room of a family member you can't place. Your unbuttoned red onesie reveals bite marks down your front. A crowd crams into the room, chortling and jostling family photos on the walls. Muddy boots leave naughty prints. Everyone points and eggs you on, making fun of your prepubescent body. Its hairlessness. You bolt to a bedroom, dive into the bed, and wrap yourself in the blankets like a toddler ready to roll down a hill. Someone creeps into the room, to the bedside, and the blankets scald you.

You're burning alive.

The sizzling morning sun has been piercing your car windows and slow cooking you since dawn. You wipe sweat from your face with a grubby t-shirt that's ripe with your body odour and shake off your nightmare.

It's time to take stock. The night off tour has massaged your aches, and the vice grips on your temples have loosened. You do a quick tour recap using a convoluted sports analogy. Walking out of the dugout on day one of the tour, you took a baseball bat to the head for five nights straight. Camping puts you on the injured reserve list for two days, but you'll be back up to the plate for the final four shows. Today, as promised, bumper boats with the kids. Tomorrow night, another baseball bat to the head.

WTF IS SLEEP?

I can't sleep. I'm manic. My brain is drowning in thoughts, ideas, plans, schemes. My back and neck feel like a gorilla is banging them with a coconut. Dawn provokes me through rumpled window blinds. The hum of what was once the world's largest pulp mill reverberates off our turn-of-the-century pine floors, and I try to focus on the ceiling's cracked plaster. Megan's untouched pillow is propped against the headboard, and I twist and fret in tangled sheets. I fumble for my phone on the bedside table and comb Facebook until the feeds repeat themselves. I'm so far back on people's walls, I'm unearthing time capsules. Almost 5,000 "friends"—the Facebook limit—can't satiate my need for a high. I toss my phone into the laundry basket where I can't reach it.

Please let me sleep.

Mind over matter is the snake oil of motivational speakers and new-age counsellors. My mania tricks me with a compulsive anti-therapy program, and I buy in. I swing my legs over the side of the bed to fish through the dirty clothes and find my phone under my Against Me! hoodie. I go back to bed, fall into the mess of sheets, roll onto my back, and return to the blue light of Facebook. The "suggested friends" function placates my desperate longing for connection.

Anyone in a punk band is an automatic target.

Stop it. Enough.

I chuck my phone back in the laundry basket.

Come find me, come find me, it coaxes.

If I continue my friend-request spree through the night, I'll have dozens of new feeds to excavate by morning. I stumble back to my phone in a trance, my mosh-pit plantar fasciitis barking at me. Hovering over the basket, there's a glimmer of hesitation, but it passes.

Scroll.

Friend request.

Scroll.

Friend request.

My social media use fuels my anxiety and amplifies an uncertain future. At the beckoning call of my phone, I'm important. People need me, and I need them. My screen time and mental health are at loggerheads.

Half a year prior, on my morning drive to my prison sentence as the publisher/editor of my hometown newspaper, it's like 24-grit sandpaper is scratching my insides. Either a torn muscle or I'm flirting with a heart attack. The closer to work, the worse the chest pains. I'm trying an alternate route today, and the same tightness as yesterday is Velcro-ed to my innards. I pull the work van into my reserved parking spot, kill the motor, try to catch my breath, and give myself the daily pep talk.

I can do this. I'm not dying. I can do this.

I walk through the front doors, straighten my posture, force out a "good morning" to unsuspecting Erika at the front desk, close my office door behind me, and tear the Velcro off, so I can start another workday. By 10 am, my morning routine throat-punches me. I alternate between struggling over the yearly budget to maximize profits and monitoring the newspaper's social media accounts—a story about the City of Powell River culling geese has 523 comments and counting. Moderating online bickering is a thankless, soul-crushing job. I can't think of anything less punk.

The sandpaper sensation is back, scouring the inside of my ribcage as I filter through the newspaper's Facebook account. I should talk to a doctor about my chest pains, but I don't. As is the case with my ailments, the way I figure, if it's minor, I don't need to deal with it, and if it's major, I'm going to die anyway.

How long has this been happening? A year?

Something else troublesome rears its head when I wake up the next day. Morning sickness. Not that kind, of course, although the symptoms are similar. Dizziness as I climb out of bed. Nausea as I pull myself out of the bath. Vomiting on occasion. Like the chest pains weren't enough.

I'm locked to the newspaper's social media all hours of the day, seven days a week. Not because I have to, not because I need to, because I'm compelled to. I always take my work home with me. Hell, I feed it dinner and tuck it into bed.

Work stress devours another weekend, and on a Monday morning the same as any other, I sit behind the wheel of the work van—a.k.a. the anxiety mobile. The van's defroster is making a comeback in its battle with the frozen windows, and I shift into drive. Halfway to work, a vice-like constriction attacks my chest again, and I pull off the road, gasping. It doesn't occur to me to breathe my way through the pain. No one's ever taught me how to breathe. My arms flap around like there's a garter snake in my lap, and the tightness lets off enough for me to finish the dreaded drive. Nearing the office, I flick the signal and hesitate. Muscle memory tells me to turn, my hands tremble on the steering wheel, and I force myself to drive around the block. I'm in work-transit purgatory. In a parking spot a block from my office, chest heaving, I know I need to quit my job or I'm going to die.

Two paydays later, I'm standing in front of my unsettled staff on lunch break with the corporate president at my side. We're making the announcement that I'm leaving my position as publisher/editor, a decision my psychologist and I agree might be life and death.

"Working with you has been a pleasure, but I will be leaving my position on March 14," I tell the staff in a full body shake and rattle. "I've just really been suffering at this job lately..."

"Well, not suffering..." the president offers, doing damage control.

I steady myself, fingernails digging into my palms.

"Yes, suffering... I've been suffering."

In time, I learn that the tearing in my chest is a false alarm, an overeager smoke detector with no fire—no smoke. The sandpaper didn't come out of nowhere one morning on the drive to work. It's been my lifelong passenger.

I'm outside Boca Fiesta's outdoor venue at Fest 17, soaked in my juices, the aftereffects of witnessing Gainesville, Florida speed-punks Post Teens crank through a 10-song set in 18 minutes. My arms are reeling from holding up the same three dudes who had their crowd surfs on repeat. I've already crafted a clever Facebook post about it.

Why are 90 percent of crowd surfers such huge dudes?

I catch my breath and wait for an attention hit. Notifications pop up instantly. Three likes. A comment from someone at Fest.

Hey wasn't that you that just stage dived at Post Teens and knocked my friend down?

Anxiety with bear claws, icy daggers down my spine. I'm called out on social media for what I'm sure thousands of my friends will see, and shame rushes through my body like a CT scan injection. As my friend network carries on unphased, lost in endless chatter, the words "wasn't that you" and "knocked my friend down" play on repeat as I mind-check a laundry list of my misguided posts from the past few months. This latest one is peanuts in comparison. How many people witnessed my increasingly alarming thread with my ex-bandmates about a rape joke one of their friends made—a fiery exchange that ignited October 2018, my month from hell? Facebook's endless tentacles hooked into me and fuelled a hypervigilance that overpowered me, threw me into psychosis, and landed me in the hospital.

I'm finally able to kick social media a year after my diagnosis and withdrawal symptoms worsen my anxiety—the sandpaper chest, the full-body flushes, and the misplaced panic ranging from the horrible (*someone in my family is*

going to die today) to the absurd (*something bad's going to happen today if I don't organize my CDs chronologically instead of alphabetically*).

My pleasure sensors conjure a phantom hand that itches to post something clever on Facebook—all those likes and comments within reach. I want so badly to share my poignant observations, band recommendations, and witty quips. I'm the funniest, most charming, smartest guy I know. Just one click can reactivate my account and satisfy my cravings. I consider replacing the social media high with another vice, maybe drinking again, but alcohol almost ruined my life too, so going back to the bottle isn't an option. I have to sweat it out.

With time, the phone cravings dampen. Space slowly clears in my head, and I have a longer attention span. Less scattered. The same question I asked myself the day my mom confiscated my phone in the psychiatrist's office is back.

Am I free?

Wrestled loose from my drug of choice, a chunk of time opens to address my anxiety and its connected emotions—fear, jealousy, shame, sadness. Breathing helps. Not having to obsess over the second-by-second happenings of thousands of "friends" helps. I sacrifice social status, whatever that even means anymore, to spend time with a handful of people I truly connect with. Real people, real friends.

During quiet times when my fingers still crave mindless scrolling, the punk scene is a healthy place to connect to the outside world. I discover deeper meaning and understanding in screams, feedback, and low-end rumbles. I have the concentration to pay attention to song lyrics again, like when I was a kid first discovering punk's positive messages. Rather than anxiety-inducing social media feeds bombarding me with corporate-driven algorithms, I focus on the music and people that enrich me. My social circle shrinks from thousands online to my chosen family.

Am I free?

In the age of smartphones, freedom is an endangered species.

Set no alarm 'cause I am totally guaranteed to
Wake to my chest beating for miles ahead of me
I lie awake as sleep escapes me
Beating to an infinite hum of anxiety
Worriers - "WTF Is Sleep?"

Unchoreographed guitar squeals fill the room as Gared O'Donnell's face contorts and spastic salutes shoot from his guitar-picked fingers. It's Halloween weekend, 2019, and I'm watching Gared's band Planes Mistaken for Stars at Fest in Gainesville, Florida. From the moment he hits the stage, I can tell he's on "Team Mental Health." The way he's channelling... something.

In February 2008, 11 years prior to me standing in front of him, entranced, Gared and his Denver-by-way-of-Peoria emotional hardcore/punk band played its final show before an indefinite hiatus. Fans, friends, and family packed the Marquis Theatre in Denver and prepared themselves for bitter-sweet fury. Would it be the band's last show?

Had I also been at that show in 2008, I would've screamed along extra hard, just in case. If a band I love goes on hiatus or breaks up, I spiral on their albums. Recorded music is a timeless triumph, but nothing compares to seeing a band live, urgency coursing through veins, sharp as the devil's tongue.

Gared was in a weird headspace that sub-zero night in Denver. What the edgy crowd didn't know was that a panic attack was about to clothesline him—an anxiety so terrifying he would have to throw down his guitar and sprint toward the venue's exit.

"We got 30 seconds into our first song, and everything in my life changed," Gared tells me a decade and a half later. "I didn't know what it was going to mean for the future. I didn't know anything except I was certain I was dying right then, and I could not get out of my skin quick enough." Gared tells me he understands now that he was having a full-on panic attack, and his crisis-riddled body laser-pointed at the quickest way out. "I needed to be gone," he says.

At the time, Gared was struggling through a divorce, drinking daily, and riddled with uncertainty—a tempest of stressors I was acutely familiar with in my 30s as my own mental health deteriorated. The band that kept Gared grounded for so many years was going AWOL, and life was crashing down around him. To make matters worse, in the bustle of final-show preparations it was one of the rare times, possibly the only time, where Gared took the stage without having a drink first.

In 20/20 reflection, Gared realizes playing what could be his band's farewell show made everything sink in. Two-and-a-half decades of playing gigs and touring the world with bandmates who were like brothers to him were about to be in the rear-view. Planes Mistaken for Stars, composed of four musicians who always found hope in dark audio pathways, was going away, potentially forever.

As Gared fled the stage that night in front of a flummoxed audience, his band's manager intercepted him. Gared told her that he couldn't breathe. With residual fear still clutching his husky voice, he tells me the word "terrifying" doesn't even begin to describe the feeling. One of Gared's friends massaged him to calm him down, and somehow, he made it back to the stage and finished the show.

Gared's panic attack was an encounter with a condition affecting almost five percent of American adults at least one point in their lives, according to the National Institute of Mental Health. Severe panic attacks cause chest pains and heart palpitations so intense they can mimic a major heart attack. For some people, even the thought of having a panic attack can bring on an actual attack. Impromptu attacks can happen in a grocery store line-up, the middle of a workday, or, in Gared's case, while playing guitar and screaming in front of a sweaty crowd of rowdy punks. "I thought it was an isolated incident, but over the years it just happened more and more," he tells me.

Gared always drives the routes closest to the nearest hospital. If he's going to have an attack behind the wheel, he wants paramedics to respond as fast as possible. In the years following his band's hiatus, Gared worked hard to get the panic attacks under control. He hadn't had a severe one in six years, his domestic life was stable, and then a violent incident in the alley behind his house beat him down. Literally.

"The band was getting ready to do stuff again. My wife and I had just bought our house. Everything was fucking great, and I was really feeling on the mend," he says. One Sunday night, a group of young men were causing a ruckus in the alley, and Gared went out to ask them to keep it down because his family was sleeping. He walked around the corner in his bedtime wear, consisting of jorts and flip flops, and came face to face with about 15 dudes. Gared told them he didn't want any trouble, but could they please turn down their music? He spun around to walk back to his house, felt what he calls "a static," and knew he was in trouble. One of the men cold-cocked Gared and some more piled on to boot-stomp him. He called out to his wife, and the men scattered. Gared pulls on his jean-vest of armour and tells me how the altercation put him back to square one with his panic attacks. "It really made me feel... fucking vulnerable. And then all the anxiety came back to the point where I couldn't leave my house because I didn't want to leave my wife and kids." Gared entered a constant state of hypervigilance. "I'd never sit with my back to the door. I had eyes on all the exits and was fucking sizing people up. I just couldn't fucking rest."

Talking about hypervigilance makes my own anxiety flare up. I used to go into a high-alert, superhero mode so often it was unreasonable and unstainable. I understand now it's not my responsibility to keep everyone safe. That's not to say I won't fight for the people I love, but Gared and I need to pick our battles and take care of ourselves too. Even though he's spent a substantial part of his life touring, he tells me when he's home and his wife leaves for work trips, he's a wreck, and that resonates with me—hard. Gared and I commiserate on our abandonment issues from childhood and how they fuel our anxiety. Staying well on those days our loved ones are away from home is a daunting task at best and dangerous loneliness at worst. In those solitary times that can turn to panic, Gared has the support of his brothers in Planes Mistaken for Stars, who thankfully reformed in 2016, and a worldwide network of punks he's met over the years.

"We're lucky to have punk," he says. I nod, and he nods, and look at that, we're nodding together. "You and I are talking to each other right now about how we deal with this mental health shit and how we get past the stigma of it. Nobody wants to admit they're weak, or they're flawed, or they have problems. But because of the way we were reared on punk rock, we understand that being able to own yourself is fucking punk rock." Gared is one of the most impassioned people I know. My conversation with him affects me deeply.

I email Gared a month later to ask him about the song "One Fucked Pony," one of my go-to distorto-anthems, and the possible meaning behind the lyrics, *We fell so hard to the fighting side, I fear that it quickened the fight in us to die*, which I link to anxiety, but he doesn't respond. I follow up with him, but I don't hear back.

A year after seeing Gared play at Fest, I Google his name to see what he's been up to. "Planes Mistaken for Stars Singer Gared O'Donnell Diagnosed with Stage 3 Oesophageal Cancer," reported *Exclaim!*, a music publication I contributed to for years before diving into the shallow end of community media. The band's manager, Emily Francis, the same person who intercepted Gared on his panicked beeline from the stage 12 years prior, had launched a GoFundMe page. "As of now the cancer is inoperable," Emily wrote. Oesophageal cancer is a treatable disease, but not a curable one. Whether doctors could save Gared's gravelly howl was secondary to his survival. Now it made sense why he hadn't responded to my emails—I'm sure he was fielding an outpouring of support. I checked the *Exclaim!* site for months, but no updates.

COVID postponed Fest 19 in 2020, but the festival returned in 2021. When Fest organizer Tony Weinbender and his crew announced the line-up, I scanned through the bands playing. Hot Water Music, Samiam, The Lawrence Arms, Spanish Love Songs, and the 300-band list scrolled on. As I reached the second half of the list, I thought my strained eyes were tricking me. I shook my head, squinted, and there it was, clear as a Florida sky in October. Planes Mistaken for Stars.

Unfortunately, Gared's band ended up cancelling a month before Fest 19, like dozens of bands did that year. "It is with deep regret that Planes Mistaken for Stars must cancel our show at Fest 19. This was a difficult decision to make," the band posted on social media. I assumed it was COVID-related. On November 24, 2021, Planes Mistaken for Stars posted again: "It is impossible to express the depth of sorrow in which we must announce that our brother, our leader, our captain, who has done more to cultivate love and light in this world than any of us can understand, has moved on from his physical form here with us and crossed the rainbow bridge into the eternal ether. In his final days/hours, he was surrounded by the love of his family, his friends, his bandmates, and many others from afar... May the light of our collective love carry Gared onto his next journey."

Six months before *Exclaim!* first reported Gared's cancer diagnosis, I was asking him a question that instinctively crawled off my tongue—a journalist's question I hoped wouldn't sting. "What does survival mean to you?" He repeated the question back to me. Not because he didn't understand it. It was as if he wanted the question to pass through his body before he answered. "What does survival mean? At this point, it means everything," he said, "because I want to be here to make what little shred of the world that I'm part of better, in any little way that I can."

Gared O'Donnell died at the age of 44.

During the past two decades, anxiety has become a buzzword, a catch-all for unease, stress, and worry. People throw the word "anxiety" around to explain reactions to distressing situations, but for the millions who live with full-fledged, clinical anxiety, life can be unmanageable. Anxiety is the most common mental health condition, according to the World Health Organization, and nearly four percent of the world's population is diagnosed with some form of it.

A 2016 study conducted by the University of Westminster and now-defunct UK non-profit MusicTank found that more than 70 percent of 2,211 musicians surveyed had experienced severe anxiety or panic attacks. The most common drivers were fear of failure, financial instability, pressure to succeed, and loneliness. In addition, more studies are finding that social media use increases anxiety. This may be obvious in our digital landscape, but it's important to note the overwhelming role social media plays in promoting indie bands. While the Green Days of the world have marketing teams, smaller bands go the do-it-yourself route. Punk musicians often tell me social media is one of the most stressful parts of being in a band.

Alicia Bognanno's anxiety got to the point where she had to hand off all of her online accounts to her manager. The singer/guitarist of Bully tells me social media is one of the worst requirements of being in a band, and it often puts her in a vulnerable, unsafe state. "I remember being up until 5 am, deleting five years of Bully's social media on every platform... just out of pure paranoia."

Ryan Patterson has found a life-hack to stabilize his anxiety and overall mental health. Exercise. After Ryan reached a body-image breaking point in his mid-30s, the Louisville, Kentucky scene mainstay tells me in his deep baritone how anxiety trapped him in existential crises and a specific phobia of death and dying. Every 10 years or so, Ryan's anxiety reared its hydra head, too many serpents to cut off at the neck. This time a death in the family sent him spiralling into panic attacks and agoraphobia. He rarely left the house.

It was around this time that Ryan started his darkwave solo entity Fotocrime. It was different than anything he'd done before, venturing away from the distorted fury of his former metalled-up punk band Coliseum. In the studio and onstage, Ryan faced his fears in a musical project that put him front and centre.

As his confidence grew, Ryan's focus turned to his physical health. He'd reached a pinnacle of 310 pounds from binging on food and a lack of exercise. Approximately three percent of Americans suffer from binge eating, according to the National Eating Disorders Association, and it's linked to negative body image, low self-esteem, emotional dysregulation, and trauma. Binge eating affects three times more people than anorexia and bulimia combined, and anxiety intertwines all three.

Talking to Ryan about eating disorders triggers me. One night over a decade ago, I laid beside my sister, literally a skeleton of her former self, her organs threatening to shut down, and offered myself as a sacrifice to the nearest grim reaper in exchange for her being alive in the morning. When the sun came up, we both opened our eyes. I decide not to mention my sister to Ryan—triggering topics are difficult to measure—as he reflects on what binge eating represented for him and the pivotal steps he took.

"Emotion and insecurity are tied up with that feeling of binging, and feeling full and satiated, and having your mouth full and your stomach full," he says. "All of those are clearly filling voids in your life."

In 2017, Ryan hired a personal trainer who created a plan for him that included weightlifting, cardio, and healthier food choices. As Ryan's body became healthier, so did his mental state, and he was able to wean off anxiety meds. "The one thing that doctors never told me is just how much exercise corrects your brain. I'm not on medication now. I have very, very little anxiety. I feel better every day about everything, and not just how I look. I feel like a cult member about it." His voice is entrancing and I inch closer. "It's so amazing how this has changed me," he tells me, "in every single way."

I fight the urge to become a junior member in Ryan's cult, someone in holding pattern for full initiation, flinching at the hazing to come. Compared to Ryan's, my exercise regime is limited—daily walks, sporadic hikes, and racquet sports if my feet can handle them. Chalk it up to too much time punishing my body in mosh pits and onstage over the years. As smug fitness trainers with masochistic grins would say, "You gotta keep moving—move, move, move!" I don't need indoctrination to understand exercise is a crucial part of my treatment plan.

Lauren Denitzio recalls times when a minor setback or stressful incident would derail their entire day, and they wouldn't want to leave their house. Living in Los Angeles by way of Brooklyn, the vocalist/guitarist for melodic punk band Worriers tells me songwriting and graphic design are huge parts of their life.

So is anxiety. After years of adjusting to the right combo of anti-anxiety meds, they still dread going out sometimes.

People living with anxiety and depression tend to isolate. They can view themselves as outcasts, not belonging in social circles. Those with anxiety, in particular social anxiety, avoid gatherings they find to be unsafe or uncomfortable. They fear these situations will increase their anxious feelings, potentially to unmanageable levels, further alienating them from the "in crowd." Punks, living with anxiety or not, may already find it tough to mesh with non-punks.

I have a vivid memory of going to a dinner party shortly after my bipolar diagnosis where my anxiety skyrocketed the moment I walked through the door. Conversation topics—social media, politics, pop culture, alcohol—triggered me, and I was paranoid about side-eye from the guests. Negative self-talk hammered home the skewed message that they all thought I was "crazy." My catastrophic thoughts were very convincing. As my vision narrowed and nausea gurgled in my stomach, I faked a bathroom break and ghosted the party.

I don't feel anxious or judged walking into a punk show. This includes the time I showed up with a set of salvaged jumper cables around my neck after my car burst into flames—another story for another time.

Andy from Submission Hold was working the door and joked that the cables were the latest punk fashion accessory. I chuckled, paid my five bucks, and dumped the cables in the nearest corner to pick up after the show.

Social trappings fall away the moment my friends and I bellow along to the lyrics when a band like Worriers hits the stage. Pointing skyward to sound a clarion call for communal inclusion, anxiety washes away. Punks have deeper connections to make than trading cocktail recipes and Netflix binge recommendations.

Despite our quest for individualism and rejecting the status quo, punks need to coexist with the outside world. Insularity breeds alienation, isolation, and eventual withdrawal. Lauren's song "WTF Is Sleep?" from Worriers' third album *Survival Pop* is a note to self, reminding them that going out to social events outside the comfortable container of the punk scene can be healing and, more importantly, a form of distress tolerance.

You'll feel better if you leave the house
It's too easy to be hard on yourself
Miss out on energy you get somewhere else
You'll feel better if you leave the house
And it's only the things you don't do that you regret

Distress tolerance is one of the four pillars of Dialectical Behaviour Therapy—the others being mindfulness, emotional regulation, and interpersonal effectiveness. It's a coping mechanism during a perceived or real crisis and can ease short- or long-term pain. According to DBT teachings, exposing oneself to anxiety-inducing situations, starting small and rising in intensity, can lessen anxiety over time. "Every time I would end up going out, 99 percent of the time I would have a good time and be glad that I did," Lauren tells me.

Members of punk bands that tour regularly are prone to enter a hyperactive state that isn't sustainable after they come home. The adjustment period after being on the road without reliable food, lodging, and transportation can sometimes linger until it's time to go on tour again.

After Worriers spends weeks or months playing all-ages show spaces and dingy bars, Lauren comes home extremely stressed out and they crash. They tell me touring affects their anxiety and general mental health, so they've cut back on time away. Personal space is also important on tour, like a quiet place to chill, or watching bands from the side of the stage. They recall earlier days when Worriers and their earlier band The Measure (SA) hit the road for weeks, even months, with no tour manager or anyone to sell merch. "It gets more stressful when you can't ever turn off," Lauren says. "When I didn't have help for long stretches of time, it got very overwhelming. I'd be an anxious stress-case by the end of the tour." With more control over their surroundings now, Lauren knows how to stay well on the road.

I can't imagine being away for weeks or months like the tours Lauren does with Worriers. The longest one I've gone on is a nine-show jaunt, and I came home a self-destructing wreck. Combine the lack of sleep, food, and routine with my mental health conditions, and any tour longer than an adrenaline-packed weekend getaway can put me at risk. Thankfully, Lauren has tons of practice. In addition to taking care of themself, Lauren assumes a parental role with their bandmates and friends. This serves two purposes—keeping their people safe and easing their own worries. Cue their band name: Worriers. After a show, Lauren texts four seemingly sarcastic but entirely serious words of caution to their bandmates and friends who are heading out to party.

Have fun, don't die.

It's a punk motto if I've ever heard one.

SHOW 6
DUNCAN, BC
THE HUB AT COWICHAN STATION
WEDNESDAY, AUGUST 15, 2018

You thought you'd have time to think, but you haven't had time to think. Camping in Parksville was your chance to recharge, but despite your best efforts to relax, the two days off defaulted to a gathering of your gumption—a mid-tour war room.

Your system shifts back into overdrive as soon as you leave the campsite, and tonight's show in Duncan has snuck up on you. The tour you've planned and planned for months and months is heading into its final leg, and DOA is joining the party for the next four nights, so you need to focus on logistics. DOA is a legendary punk band, one of the originals, and has played thousands of shows over the past 40 years. That counts for more than you can fathom right now. Band leader Joey Shithead and his DOA gang need food, lodging, and the agreed-upon payment. DOA needs professionalism.

Except for the dream show on Cortes Island, this one in Duncan has you the most hyped. The all-ages community hall holds 175-plus, and Punk Jams' first show with DOA is looking to be the tour's grandest spectacle to date. Duncan's only 45 minutes away from Victoria, and you've recruited a Garden City contingent for the show—five more miscreants, bolstering the Punk Jams line-up to 10 members, including a spoken word poet, noise artist, and burlesque dancer. Drue, a hirsute guitarist who will be hopping on for the rest of the tour, walks into the hall with a smile so big it must hurt his face. It's a gonna-be-the-night-of-my-life expression. You predict the prickling excitement in the room will amplify by 100 when Punk Jams hits the stage.

Not yet. Put a lid on it.

Your first impression was they were the type of people you should veer away from without raising suspicion. You watched them discreetly as they gyrated to Nanaimo psych-weirdos Moths & Locusts on the blackened makeshift dance floor on your friend Carlos' goat farm. The man's slicked-back hair had shaken loose like a lazy vampire's, generous globs of Brylcreem glinting in the moonlight. His counterpart, a woman 10 inches shorter, had coin-sized, earthy-brown eyes that seemed to say, "Keep your distance." As they slinked around on the dirt into the wee hours with blissed-out weirdos, you envisioned them scurrying into a couple's sarcophagus as the sun, threatening to burn a hole in their mysteriousness, peeked over the horizon and caressed the farm. At the time, you never imagined the figures in black would become such dear friends. The man: your most trusted tourmate and planning partner Mike, the mad scientist behind Crashing Into Things. The woman: his partner Tara. This is why you never trust first impressions.

You've been oblivious to a dent in the Punk Jams tour's armour. Sickness has plagued Mike in the weeks leading up to the tour, and his sinus infection overpowers enough antibiotics to choke a stallion. After every show, Mike flops down in his campervan like a human garbage heap, guts churning, and tries to sleep off the rottenness. Walking past the camper before tonight's show, you overhear Mike and Tara talking about her heading back to Victoria for three days. They'll reunite in Ucluelet for the tour's final show. Through the camper's tin-can walls, you can hear the desperation in Mike's baritone.

"I just wish I didn't feel so shitty."

"I know, love," Tara says, trying to comfort him.

Hearing Mike in this sad state, it dawns on you that you can't be the tour's ringmaster, clown, acrobat, lion tamer, and tightrope walker all jammed into one. You're hobbled; a self-propelling husk with four more punishing shows to go, but the others have made sacrifices too, and they're helping you make this tour happen—driving, hauling gear, selling merch, and taking care of each other. Taking care of you.

Look around.

Without your tourmates, circus elephants would be stomping you into the dirt.

The crowd scatters as you creep-crawl through their dodging legs and wave adult diapers around, flinging them into people's faces. Punks of all stripes—small-town emo kids, spiked crusties, metal bangers, goths, aging punk parents and their kids—look on in horror, scanning the diapers for brown stains as nappies bounce off their neighbours' heads. You spring to your feet, try to mosh, and butt up against unwelcoming bodies. Offering more diapers from your dwindling supply, you can't find any takers. You're not sure what everyone's problem is. You're presenting the poop pants as party-time peace offerings.

Everyone grab a diaper. Let's get this party started.

People have accused you of being performative, dramatic for the sake of drama. Performative implies that you're preconceiving or faking, and nothing could be further from the truth. For you, performing is about searing with excitement and losing all inhibitions for the latest, greatest performance of your life.

How far can you go?

You climb back on the stage, fire up your hair clippers, and have a hell of a time shaving off the chunks sticking out from the shredded underwear you're using as a skull cap. The clippers won't work on your grizzled facial hair either, a 10 o'clock shadow, neglected and bristly. Anguish twists your face into a Leatherface grimace, and you throw the clippers across the stage as tonight's Punk Jams band makes a muddy time-change into a dirtier, grimier riff. The layers of tonight's costume pin you down, trapping you in their tangles. You tear at your clothes and skin. You've been trying to shed layers since Punk Jams' inception. You've been trying to shed layers your whole life.

Get off. Get the fuck off.

You tear your costume apart piece by piece. A red bra tied around your face that you've turned into bug's eyes. A too-small windbreaker, upside down and backwards. An oversized studded belt because you're the heavy-weight champion of the world. A jockstrap flossing your ass, mere threads away from incident exposure. The love-print pyjamas you wore in Campbell River a week ago hang around your ankles like a toddler rushing to the potty. You leap onto the bass drum, turn around, and slap your butt cheeks while 175 sets of eyes look on in varying states of disbelief. You've ripped your self-control filter wide open. You spin and launch a final "yeeeaaaah" into the mic as this evening's drummer of choice, Scott, takes the full brunt of your undercarriage. It doesn't stop him leaping up into a celebratory stance, Punk Jams' own Lars Ulrich, his drumsticks in the air.

Your glistening arms shoot to the sky in a final salute to mark the end of another life-affirming shitshow, and you jump down from the bass drum and lumber off stage. You've made it through to the other side again. The crowd hoots and claps, and your exhilarated bandmates swarm around the stage like bees drunk on Red Bull, chortling as they coil up messes of patch cords. Chuckles of disbelief shake your chest as you look down at your near-naked body. You peek through the stage curtains and a mess of ripped clothes and diapers litter the hall floor.

Those were supposed to be souvenirs.

Tonight's performance began with adult diapers and ended with your bare ass. You burst out laughing. What a glorious mess, a show for the ages—all ages. An utter disaster in every best way possible.

"Did you see the review of the show?"

You can't tell whether Mike's voice is peaking with excitement or anxiety.

Oh god, what does it say? What did you do?

Embarrassment. Shame. Impending doom.

"Um, did they hate it?" You flinch.

"Hang on. I'll text you a link..." Mike says, shuffling around. The review pops up on your cell.

"Punk Jams was joined by various members of the previous bands and was also the most pure punk show I have ever seen... there was this dude who showered old underwear on everyone out of garbage bags and was wearing jammies and old shopping bags and a jock, which he stripped down to while writhing around being a major fuckin' punk. Underwear wrapped around his head and attacking his scalp with an electric razor, all the while screaming into a dead mic. He was throwing stuff around and generally dancing with a punk abandon that is the purest form of punk. The slack-jawed yokels had never seen anything like this and truth be told me either."

The writer is clearly an enthusiastic concertgoer. Opening for the legendary DOA, Punk Jams put on the "most pure punk show" he's ever seen?

Pure?

Pure chaos.

MANIC DEPRESSION

October 12, 2018.

I left out an important detail about the day I'm diagnosed with bipolar.

Near the end of my psychiatrist appointment, as my pounding melon embarks on a quest for what the rest of my life might look like, my brain catches a snag.

I turn to Megan. "What about..." She sees the word forming on my quivering lips. "...Fest? I can't miss it."

I try to form proper sentences to make the psychiatrist understand why I need to—have to—go on a trip three time zones away to another country. In two weeks.

"What's Fest?"

She looks to Megan for a coherent explanation. I butt in and blabber. I tell her Fest is my yearly obsession, my annual punk rock vacation in Florida, and I'll miss all my friends if I don't go, and it means the world to me, and, and, and.... I can tell the psychiatrist thinks Fest is a rave or something.

Held in Gainesville since 2001, Fest is a music festival specifically designed for punks. Fest has become a family reunion for thousands worldwide who take to the streets on Halloween weekend with pizza-eating grins, wearing black band t-shirts, and sporting thigh tattoos. With more than 300 bands playing in a dozen venues over 72 hours, it's a punk rock bonanza and DIY cardio workout rolled into one. That's how I explain it in my head. What my mouth says in the psychiatrist's office is jumbled nonsense.

Her concerned look should be enough for me to understand the risks of going this year. I could easily slip into a full-scale manic episode, go psychotic again, end up in a hospital in another country, or worse. But nothing's stopping me.

October 25, 2018.

Riding euphoric highs with mood stabilizers running through my bloodstream, I'm on a plane to Florida. Sitting beside me is an elderly man tapping his fingers to the beat in his headphones. "What are you listening to?" I'm one of those annoying people who insists on striking up conversations on airplanes. "Classical music," he says.

I tell my seat neighbour I'm on my annual trip to a punk rock festival in Florida, and he perks up and shuffles in his seat, interest piqued. "Punk? I've never listened to it," he says. I hold out my phone and make a proposition. "How about we trade music?" He's into it.

We pull our headphones out of their respective jacks and swap phones, but I'm not as fired up as he is. I'm not a big classical fan. I prefer my music to sound like a woodchipper with a guitar amp jammed into it. It's not long before my new buddy delivers his verdict.

He's shouting over Converge's "Thousands of Miles Between Us" and motioning wildly. "Oh, I love this!" The other passengers stare at him like he's a religious freak. I nudge him and glance at the seats around us, and he looks around the cabin, turns a flaming shade of red, puts his hand over his mouth, and removes his headphones. "I knew you'd like it," I say, quietly. "For me, punk is my classical music." He ponders this, and a look of understanding softens his wrinkles. "It hypes me up," I tell him, eyes flickering.

On my way to Fest, more than 5,000 kms from home, I pray to the punk gods I won't be flying too high when I get there.

Fest 11. Halloween weekend, 2012.

I stop mid-scream and look around the venue, grinning wildly. More than 900 people pack the Florida Theatre and sing along to the Menzingers, a melodic punk band from Scranton, Pennsylvania. We're all bellowing the same words and it's monumental. The next song begins, and Greg Barnett's lilting voice joins his jangly guitar chords. He sounds like he's creeping from the fog of a weekend-long hangover as he sings the bummed-out opening lines of "Good Things."

I've been having a horrible time
Pulling myself together
I've been closing my eyes to find
The old, familiar failures

Despite Greg's doldrums, the joy in the room is overwhelming. If we celebrate our misfortunes together, propelling them out the venue's doors and into the streets of Gainesville, everything will be okay. To my left, a woman in a leg cast thrusts her crutch up and down to the beat. To my right, a bunch of burly, bearded dudes are bear hugging. Everyone in the audience shouts along like jolly soccer hooligans, and we're all out of tune, but fuck it. Barnett and his Menzingers cohort Tom May abandon their mics and head to the front of the stage to pump up the crowd. I yell at the tall guy beside me to lift me up, so I can crowd surf.

I'm 39 years old, going on 24.

Nine years and eight Fests later, I'm perched at my dining room chair (my office chair) at my dining room table (my desk). The ergonomic gods are ready to strike me down. I look across the water in the direction of the Comox Valley Airport, the starting point of my first Fest, grind my teeth, and try to reclaim the excitement I had on that maiden voyage to Gainesville.

How the hell am I going to do this justice?

I find footage on YouTube of the same Menzingers show from Fest 11. Greg's strumming that old, familiar chord from the Florida Theatre stage. His throat-lozenged voice sends a warm flush of memories down my now-48-year-old spine.

I've been having a horrible time

Pulling myself together
I've been closing my eyes to find
The old, familiar failures

I study the video and see my Fest friends wailing along. Is that my head bobbing at the centre of the floor? I inhale for five seconds, exhale for eight, always let more tension out than you pull in, one of my counsellors taught me. My eyelids drop, and I'm back at Fest.

A guy I've never met is grabbing my shirt and shouting, "I love you, dude," in my face, then bouncing off into the mass of roughhousers. My moment—our moment—is coming. I push my way to the front. Someone hoists me onstage, and I see one of my buddies already standing there, grinning like a kid who got a drum kit for Christmas. Right as the band yells "1-2-3-4," we both stage dive and end up in a tandem crowd surf, raising our fists in triumph, throats hollering at the ceiling. Someone cradles me and lowers me to the floor as tears run over my cheekbones and onto my drenched Minor Threat t-shirt. In a blissed-out crowd of rowdies, in this incomparable moment, me and my new friends are the happiest people alive, and I never want this to end.

Another long exhale.... I bring myself back to the room, back at my desk, back on my unforgiving wooden chair. In the YouTube video, Greg is shout-singing the chorus.

I've been closing my eyes to find...
Why all good things should fall apart
Why all good things should fall apart
Yeah! Yeah! Yeah!

Fest 12. Halloween weekend, 2013.

I'm partying, running high on adrenaline. Somehow, I've been able to convince my hotel neighbours to lend me the ironing board from their closet. Prediction: their damage deposit, gone. I sprint out of their room to the stairwell with the board tucked under my arm.

"Dare me to surf down the stairs on this ironing board?" I holler. The look on my Fest friend Shannon's face says, "Yeah, do it. I'm next."

I position the board on the top stair and jump on. Its folded metal legs screech against the concrete stairs like a pickaxe on a chalkboard, I smash onto the stairwell's third-floor landing pad, and the unholy echo makes me want to do it all over again. Shannon and I do a couple more runs each, like in my skateboarding days, and we bolt when a hotel security guard shows up. This is the same security guard a group of us crowd surf down the hotel hallway late that night. With his permission, of course, after 3 a.m. negotiations.

"We promise to shut down our party if you let us do it," I say, offering my most convincing *come on, please, please* eyes. He's quizzical and says, "Heck, why not?"

Fest 13. Halloween weekend, 2014.

Gainesville Regional Airport. Six a.m. departure. Security. Boarding. *Oooof.* I slump into my seat on the plane, and my system crashes. I pretzel myself against the window, prepare for unconsciousness, and yank down the plastic shade. I'm not ready to see Gainesville, the hometown of Fest, shrink away again.

Twelve hours and four flights later, I'm home in my bed in Powell River. Whenever I roll over, my body sends me the pain sensors of a bulldozer dragging me down a gravel road. I'm a nightmare of bruises and scrapes from Fest mosh pits. My arms, legs, back, and chest are like runaway ink blots. I'm covered in badges of honour, and they hurt like hell, but my head hurts more. I always crash and burn in the first week of November when I'm back from Gainesville, and I've come down with "Fest Flu" again, a cleverly alliterated term of non-endearment used for the post-Fest depression some of my friends experience when the fun is over for another year, and it's back to real life. Fest Flu isn't the same for me. Real life implies going back to so-called "normal," and I don't know how to do that. My depression isn't just the post-Fest kind. A Jason four years from the future could explain it in two words: manic depression. Or one word: bipolar. Mania is my enabler and rewarder every year as I touch down for my punk rock family reunion in Gainesville. Depression is my punishment when I come home. If I want to keep going to Fest and reap its punk energy and inspiration, I'll need to find a balance.

Fest 14. Halloween weekend, 2015.

"Meet Jason. He parties harder than anyone!"

This is my friend Harry's stock introduction for me at a hotel room party, which is already raging at 3 p.m. before Fest 14's night two. Harry's a jovial Irish dude who we found passed out in his hotel room closet this morning, one leg dangling out. Harry's proclamation of my ability to party hard is 100 percent correct. I'm at my fourth Fest, and I'll be trying my hardest to abstain this year. I want to ditch the booze, but I'm still riding high on mania, so the party will rage on, and Fest is the perfect place to do it.

Staggering off my midnight arrival at Gainesville's airport last night, I notice an immediate shift in mood on my cab ride to the Central Florida city's University Avenue and Main Street epicentre. On the same weekend as Fest, gaggles of locals travel to the Florida/Georgia football game in nearby Jacksonville, where they've cheered on the University of Florida since the '40s. With a solid chunk of the city's 130,000 population away at the big game, Gainesville is taken over by punks, and it's always a steaming slice of utopia.

Fest is Christmastime without the family obligations—late-night pizza and high fives for everyone. It's the nonstop hyper-twinkle in everyone's eyes and the buzz I get from making countless new Fest buddies in the bustling lineups outside the venues. It's a friendly nod on the street from Laura Jane Grace of Against Me! and a quick chat with Chris Wollard from Hot Water Music. At Fest, pretension is a foreign word.

We've converged from around the world, walking down the sweltering streets with bags of records held proudly under our inked arms. Anticipation escalates as we hear soundchecks from inside the venues, and then—go!—dozens of bands go bananas every half hour. Thousands of punks run rampant between jacked-up performances and dance in unison to stagger-step revelations at 200 BPM. I'm sure Deadheads, Phishers, Juggalos, and whatever they call fans of the String Cheese Incident (Stringers?) can justify their obsession with the (in their case, horrible) bands they love, but Fest bands are different, and they cram more energy into one three-minute song than Dave Matthews has into his entire bloated career. No jam bands at Fest, just an unlimited amount of speed merchants and round after round of happy brain candy for all.

Among other amenities, such as the best $6 burrito I've ever had, king cans of Pabst Blue Ribbon cost only $3. For most attendees, Fest goes fist-in-fist with copious amounts of shitty beer and bottom-shelf liquor. It's also a place well-suited to rambunctious tomfoolery and hijinks. Like that time way too many punks crammed into the Holiday Inn elevator. The party didn't stop when they got stuck between floors and, in a drunken singalong, spilled into the lobby 20 minutes later like circus clowns from a tiny, polka dot car. My first year at Fest, my pal Bobby got drunk, climbed a palm tree, and found out the hard way that coming down is drastically more painful than going up. The deep scratches on his legs and chest made him look like he'd wrestled an alligator—a warped Florida initiation?

There's a difference between having fun at Fest and having waaaay too much fun at Fest (that's me). Like previous years, I run on three hours of sleep a night, but I feel completely rested in the morning as if I'd nailed 8-10 hours. My limbs could fly off my trunk in the mosh pit, and it would be the best thing ever. I launch myself in, ready to burst like a water balloon, knowing full well I'll be wearing a bruise bodysuit in the morning. It's next to impossible to talk me down from a bad idea, like diving into the audience from a hand railing during Crusades' set. I escalate as the night goes on, mania compromises my prefrontal cortex, my filter keeps dropping, and my brain tells me, *do it, do it, DO IT.*

Many punks frown upon stage diving because of the risk to heads, necks, and backs. Not scoping out your landing pad is a terrible idea, and most people stage dive at the right times in the right zones. I can't be trusted. During a breakdown in Modern Life Is War's first song, the band that provided the soundtrack to my mental health crisis three years later, I overshoot a spectacular dive and take out

some poor soul in a Dead Ramones t-shirt who's just trying to watch her favour-
ite band. Crowd surfing is an accepted activity at punk shows, but crowd-surfing
in only my sweat-soaked underwear? On my inaugural trip to Gainesville in 2012
for Fest 11, at the pinnacle of Mixtapes' set at 8 Seconds, the festival's second
largest venue, my editor at *Alternative Press* tweets at me from the venue balcony.

Is that one of our staff writers crowd surfing in his boxers?

At my first three Fests, hypomanic behaviour like this was a badge of
honour, but if I keep this up my conscience might end up smashing that badge
against a wall of shame. To cap off Fest 14, on night three of the best weekend of
2015, I'm in a bathroom stall at Loosey's Pub and find a full cup of beer perched
on the toilet paper dispenser. Perhaps it's a hoppy, citrusy IPA. A little warm.
Devilish mania perches on my left shoulder and pokes at my temple.

DO IT... Come on... fuck sobriety... down the hatch...

It's not beer.

Fest 15. Halloween weekend, 2016.

I'm planted in an open area of grass trimmed so neatly it could be Astro
Turf under my thrumming feet. I'm rigid with anticipation and edge toward
the beckoning circle in Bo Diddley Plaza that will soon fill with bodies
when the mosh pit erupts.

Rocking back and forth, my vision goes black, my neck stretches upwards,
and my face presents itself to the sky. With a siren call, the music swells. I lean
forward and jump from one leg to the other, a slalom skier in 28-degree heat.
The first chorus overpowers the air raid, my jumps turn projectile, side to side
as far as my legs will carry me, and my eyes lock shut. Inside them, I see myself
dancing alone in the middle of the grass. Only me.

Drums snap from snare, to tom, to bass drum, and back. Guitar scales
creep up fretboards like ants cresting their hill, carrying food 20 times their
size. Bass lines hop and skip, marbles plunking down a Plinko board. The band
drops into jazzed-up sweet oblivion, then an unknown, welcome force cranks
the volume knob...

The answer's there
Right before your eyes
Rise

...the song explodes. Bodies crash into me, and I'm flattened to the ground, but my eyelids stay glued. I hit the ground, and they pop open from the force. I'm back. A friendly face in a Bouncing Souls t-shirt blocks my retinas from the oppressive Florida sun, digs his arms under my pits, and pulls me up.

"Man, where did you go just now?" He shakes me around. "You all good?"

I'm better than good. Propagandhi's "Note to Self," a song I've only heard on album, came alive inside my eyes.

Rise.

Fest 16. Halloween weekend, 2017.

I'm sobbing in the middle of the Vancouver airport. In typical Jason fashion, I have nowhere to sleep the night before my trip. It's only 8 pm, and my flight to Gainesville leaves at 5 am tomorrow morning. I scope the airport for a place to crash, but I can't find any spots to punish my body for the night.

Work was ultra-stressful before I embarked on my latest incredible journey to the greatest place on earth. No, not Disneyworld—Fest. Two hours ago, I went straight from my office to the Powell River airport—the first of five flights in the next 24 hours—after a week of catch-up-before-I-leave chaos, knowing full well that piles of work would bury me when I returned. Months of being depressed, then snapping out of it, dangerously rejuvenated, then crashing again, has lodged a chisel in my ribs. I'm ready to crumble. To make things worse, I'm wandering aimlessly in YVR with nowhere to sleep. I'm in limbo hell. Depression comes in waves of nausea, and I'm sure I'm going to pass out in the middle of the airport. I call Megan and fall apart.

"I don't know where to go," I sob. "I can't find anywhere to sleep. I can't do this. I can't go on this trip."

"Get on the first hotel shuttle you see and book a room," she says, the voice of reason.

"I don't want to waste $150 on a room," I say through hot tears. My phone shakes in my hand as I pace in circles. I regret bringing her into this.

"Sorry for calling you. I feel so stupid that my trip is starting like this. Sorry. I'm such an idiot."

"No, you're not." Her voice holds steady. "Just get on the next shuttle."

Fest 17. Halloween weekend, 2018.

Whether he wants it or not, my best Fest buddy and long-time Fest roommate Malcolm has the important assignment of being my nurse in Gainesville for Fest 17. It's a clause in a contract between me and Megan. To go to Fest this year, it's required that someone watch over me. It's only been two weeks since my psychiatrist scribbled me a prescription that might as well have been in an alien language, and I'm only beginning to adjust to my meds. The most important one is the antipsychotic to knock me out at night and stop me from surging into mania again.

Megan and I create a safety plan to follow while I'm frantically running from venue to venue, seeing 15 bands a day for three days, and cramming Cuban sandwiches and gator tacos in my face. Malcolm's job is to do a general watch over me and make sure I take my meds while he's also frantically running from venue to venue, seeing 15 bands a day for three days, and cramming Cuban sandwiches and gator tacos in his face. Our zig-zagged Fest paths overlap here and there, although with 350 bands to choose from this year, we're not hanging out much. Even at the cottage we stay at, it's mostly a "good morning, dude," "good night, dude" arrangement.

Whenever we converge, it's golden. We sprint past the block-long Five Star Pizza lineup to High Dive where Massachusetts band A Wilhelm Scream is about to hit the stage. Malcolm, an upper New Yorker, has followed the band around the East Coast for years and more than 100 shows. We make it right up front in time for me to marvel at how Malcolm knows every speed-piston lyric, guitar riff, bass line, and drum beat, inside and out. The next day at the Civic Media Centre, a non-profit infoshop and library, we fall silent as Shawna Potter and Brooks Harlan from War on Women play a sobering acoustic set, including a heart-wrenching cover of Slant 6's "What Kind of Monster Are You?" In the 15-minute windows until the next band, Malcolm and I have excited chats over Flaco's legendary empanadas, vibrating about what to see later tonight.

Nurse Malcolm is supposed to make sure I take my meds in the morning when I wake up and at night before I go to sleep. Fest friends will do anything for each other—that's been established—but on Fest's second day, Malcolm makes it clear he doesn't need to take care of me. Given the internal chaos I've experienced the past three weeks since teetering on the edge of complete personal disaster, I thought trusting myself was a miniscule dot in the distant future. Fest had been a mania-inducing environment in the past and would be the easiest place to relapse.

And then what?

I'm guessing the psych hospital in Gainesville isn't the best environment for a fun-loving Canadian like me.

Malcolm trusts me. I can do this.

Fest 18. Halloween weekend, 2019.

I walk the streets of Gainesville with clarity for the first time. I don't try to convince myself I should set up camp here and never go home. I don't have delusions of jumping into the nearest cram-packed band van to keep the party going on a cross-continental tour. I don't loiter near the *Independent Florida Alligator* newspaper office and fantasize about an editor job in Gainesville and begin planning a coast-to-coast, country-to-country move and likely a one-way ticket to another crisis. Fest isn't my escape anymore, and it's not in competition with home.

This year, I revel in seeing bands like Jawbreaker, Planes Mistaken for Stars, Screaming Females, Torche, and the Casket Lottery, and appreciating quality time with my multinational friends. I gather these experiences knowing the memories will be hard to hold onto as the years pass. But I'm here. I'm present. I'm Festing.

Fest 19. 2021. Cancelled.

COVID puts a halt on Fest 19, and I'm bummed, to say the least. The cancellation stings all Halloween weekend as I binge on mini candy bars and hunker down with friends to cringe at a so-terrible-it's-good horror movie.

Fest is my happy place, and I hope like hell I'll return when this whole virus mess fucks off. If Fest 18 turns out to be my last Fest, I'll need to find my yearly boost of adrenaline and creative inspiration somewhere else. I'll start with the noise blaring in my headphones and creating a racket with my band buds. Fest's spirit lives on in my basement jam space with show flyers plastered on the walls and my cheap Fender Strat with the "Make Racists Afraid Again" sticker on it, beckoning me to inject it with all the nice things I can call my own, like the Menzingers said. Of course, I plan on doing Fest Friend check-ins with virtual limitations, and when I long for the feeling of euphoria—albeit controlled euphoria now—I'll be transported back to Gainesville, arms around my buddies as we holler to the punk heavens.

Fest is a rallying cry against those uncontrollable, manic times that have thankfully subsided and will always be part of my history. No matter how out-of-control my Gainesville adventures were, and no matter how bad the depression was when I got home, I find peace in them now. At the time, those Fest adventures meant hope and happiness. They meant everything.

Fest 19 redux. Halloween weekend, 2021.

After surfing swells of anxiety for weeks, I book my flight to Gainesville, feel a rush of panic, and check the numbers of new COVID cases in Florida's Alachua County. Almost 300 that day alone.

SCREAM THERAPY | 179

Six months later, after constantly fretting about the cases and trying to find a PCR test in Gainesville, Megan—eternally the voice of reason—points out that a positive test means quarantining for 14 days in Florida with nowhere to stay. My fingers dig into my desk and throb, but I lift them onto my keyboard like lead pipes and cancel my flights. Lowering the boom on my Fest BFF Malcolm is going to be painful for us both, but I need to break the news, and the sooner the better. I want to soften the blow, but my fingers are way ahead of me.

Hey bud. So, bad news. I can't come to Fest. Still can't find
    a fucking COVID test in Gainesville. If I get stuck at the
    airport or get COVID down there, I'm fucked. GODDAMNIT. I'll
        be there in spirit, I guess. Sorry. This sucks.

He responds instantly.

                        Wow, man. That fucking sucks.
                            I know… I reply.
                    Fuck that sucks, he repeats.
                            I know… I repeat.

Our phones go quiet.

Next is Kate. I've arranged for her crew to stay at our—shit, I mean Malcolm's—cottage five minutes away from Bo Diddley Plaza. I explain my dilemma and wish her an amazing Fest.

I'm glad I connected you with Malcolm. He's an amazing person
        and you'll love the cottage. Take a picture of Hot Water
                            Music for me.

Kate responds with a typical Fest-friends-are-best-friends response.

    I'm grateful you connected us with Malcolm. I want to do
whatever is possible to help you still be able to come? Like
if there was a place outside Gainesville for the test, we'd
                figure out how to get you to it?

I downplay my defeat.

        Thank you. I appreciate it. I'm bummed, but I guess it
                        wasn't meant to be this year.

Then Kate hits me right in the feels.

I really hope there's something that can still feel good and bring you some joy that weekend. You will be sorely missed.

I dig deep for my stock answer—thanks, I'll be there in spirit—watch her heart emoji pop up, and power down my phone.

I'll be there in spirit.

Fest 20, Halloween weekend, 2022.

I'm here. *In spirit. In mind, body, and spirit.* The words sound comical in my head, but here they are as I slide into a taxi with two Festers from Atlanta, Georgia who I just met getting off the plane. On the 15-minute ride downtown, we compare our band schedules for the next three days with outright glee. "See you soon," I say, jumping out of the cab and planting my feet on familiar Gainesville ground, 100% positive I'll cross paths with the Atlantans again this weekend, grinning triumphantly at each other during Hot Water Music's set, or nodding knowingly at the steaming Flaco's $6 burritos in our mitts.

At our cottage, I dump my stuff on the four-post bed—because I guess we're Fest royalty now—and check my messages. Malcolm's already Festing.

At Bo Diddley get over here

My first instincts are to run out the door, sprint to the nearest venue, and jump into a mosh pit—any mosh pit. But I pull myself back, take a deep breath, and type letters on my phone that would have been foreign at previous Fests.

Gonna rest. Wanna meet for food after? Boca Fiesta?

And so, Fest 20 begins. Rest, food, and another three days in punk rock paradise, in that particular order.

Turn me upside down
Otherwise, I'm gonna drink and drink and drink
'Cause I can't help what my head is telling me
I can't stop myself from listening
Manic depression
Endless obsessions
Laura Jane Grace - "Manic Depression"

I know the best way to describe living with bipolar. I'm eating a Navel orange, and it's the most amazing, perfect orange I've ever tasted. The peels come off easy and clean. The fruit inside, crisp and juicy. The taste? As if someone picked it in California in late May and it magically appeared in my hand. Two weeks later, I'm transported back, eating the same Navel orange from the same tree. This time it's gross, dry, and flavourless. I gag and hork it on the ground. Disgusting.

The orange hasn't changed. My mood episode has. And that's bipolar, formerly known as manic depression, a mental health condition that affects more than 45 million people, according to the World Health Organization.

Bella Vanek is all-too-familiar with the head-fucking, morphing orange—how it made her want to die.

It's Kill Rock Stars publicist Sydney Christensen who connects me with Bella and her surfy punk band Foxx Bodies. "Bella would be a great fit for your podcast," says Sydney in an email. "She wears her mental health on her sleeve, and Foxx Bodies is an important outlet for her."

A week later, Bella and I are Zooming. Sitting cross-legged and composed on her bed, she tells me her and the other members of Foxx Bodies were ready to relocate from Tucson to Los Angeles when she began having such extreme mood episodes that she planned her suicide. She says she had the means to do it and the intention of following through. Bella is one of as many as 60 percent of bipolar folks who plan or attempt suicide at least once in their lives, according to a Hungary National Institute of Psychiatry and Addictions study. That's 10-30 times higher than the general population, and of those, up to 19 percent will die by suicide.

On her days off from 14-hour shifts at a group home, Bella crammed in more activities than most people do in a week. After her breakfast smoothie, she'd do a few hours of shopping, clean her whole house, do her and her room-mates' laundry, go for a run, hit the treadmill at the gym with an iced coffee, eat a protein bar or an egg on bread for dinner, drink straight vodka on her stationary bike, throw up, and go to bed. Then her mood would switch and she'd crash for 15 hours straight, convinced she was a burden on those around her and should just kill herself because it would do everyone a favour. It was this kind of distorted thinking that led to purging her food and self-harm. Sadness, hopelessness, anxiousness, and confusion—symptoms of bipolar and other forms of depression—can become so intense that people are unable to cope and may turn to self-injury such as cutting or burning themselves.

"One time, I got off the couch in the middle of a movie, went to the bathroom, and cut my leg open so badly that I went to bed with a sock tied around my leg to stop the bleeding," Bella tells me. Her composure makes it clear this isn't a war story, nor is it strictly a cautionary tale. She can relive her self-harm, but not wipe it away. Bella's cutting and purging continued as she began to seriously address the sexual abuse trauma she'd been downplaying as "just a shitty relationship I was in." Suddenly, she looks like she's swatting away a deadly wasp and adds, "It was actually abuse that was affecting all of my relationships... and my brain."

Yes, the shitty relationship. It's important that we back up. Bella was 14 when her teacher began grooming her to have sex with him. A year later, he succeeded. She was babysitting his young daughter (who eerily shared her name), and his wife, also one of her teachers, was pregnant. Bella didn't have a father figure or male support system growing up and craved the attention and validation her teacher gave her.

"I looooved the feeling I had when I was making him happy, or making him feel seen, or connected to me, or whatever." She looks frustrated, like she's not explaining it right. I know how easily personal questions can trigger sexual assault trauma, so I swallow my urge to pry. Unprompted, Bella reveals a missing puzzle piece. She tells me her teacher threatened to kill himself if she ever talked about their relationship, and the abuse continued until she left for college. Bella kept texting with her teacher, but with distance she began to see the abusive relationship for what it was. One night, she went to his house to end it, and he coaxed her inside, upstairs to his room, and raped her. Bella finally worked up the nerve to confide in one of her bandmates.

"She said if I didn't stop talking to him immediately, she was going to tell the police..." Staggered, I let a "wow" slip out, interrupting her story, and fumble over an apology. She flips me a "no problem" gesture. "Yeah, wow is right!" she says, stifling a laugh. Bella finds her place marker and continues. "It was a very intense and really amazing friend move on her part. I had a breakdown where I was scream-crying in my dorm. I didn't understand why this happened with my teacher and how I thought this was okay or normal. And then I just stopped talking to him."

Two years later, with support from the people she told, Bella reported her teacher to the authorities. Videos of her and the teacher having sex, filmed without her knowledge, were used in court as evidence, and he was sentenced to 12 years prison time.

Suffering from post-traumatic stress from the years of abuse, Bella continued cutting and forcing herself to throw up. A year of severe depression and suicidality led her to her doctor's office. Enter stage right: SSRIs, or selective serotonin reuptake inhibitors. Notoriously risky for those living with bipolar, these types of antidepressants have a 35 percent risk of bringing on a manic episode, resulting in a bipolar diagnosis, according to the peer-reviewed medical journal BMJ Open. Out of the hundreds of bipolar folks who have attended the support group I facilitate, I've heard the story repeated again and again—depression, misprescribed SSRIs, mania, hospital, or worse. It's my story as well.

Bella's doctor put her on two different SSRIs, and her day-to-day life became incredibly destructive. Self-harm and purging escalated to the point where she believed taking the 100 pills she'd squirrelled away and chasing them with vodka was an easier and quicker way out than punishing herself with a slow death. One day at work, Bella could barely function and knew she needed her boyfriend to rush her to the hospital. Riding in the passenger seat of his car, she put a cigarette out on her arm four times before they got to the emergency room.

"I was diagnosed with bipolar, which was my worst fear because my dad has bipolar," Bella tells me. "But I was grateful I was in the hospital because I very much wanted to die."

As is the case in most families, my lineage includes struggles with mental health and addiction. I've often wondered if my estranged, alcoholic dad, my scalding-tempered grandfather, or—please, no—one of my four kids had, has, or might have bipolar. It's a terrifying thought but a rational one. Bipolar is the most hereditary of all medical conditions, and those who have relatives living with it have 10 times the risk of developing it at some point in their lives. Stats like that knock the wind out of me.

A frisky feline rescues me and Bella from genetic speculations that could trigger massive mood bummers. The orange and white tabby hops onto Bella's lap and into my screen. "That's my cat," Bella giggles. Because I didn't ask its name, let's call it Heather (a name I use for neighbourhood cats, not sure why). Despite sharing painful memories, the lightness in our conversation (mine and Bella's, not mine and Heather's) doesn't surprise me. Hindsight is priceless. Four years after my diagnosis, crisis memories aren't as disturbing anymore. I can talk about my escalation to psychosis and emergency trip to the hospital without my mouth drying up and my gut lurching. As opposed to my brief visit to a psychiatrist who sent me home with a mitt full of meds, Bella spent 10 horrible days in the hospital. On her first day, she snapped a paintbrush in half to cut herself. Luckily, Bella's psychiatrist visited daily and was able to tweak her meds until she was stable enough to go home. Bipolar was Bella's new label, and it was comorbid with her post-traumatic stress and self-harm.

She says her bipolar diagnosis brought with it a clarity, all the way back to first grade. Her vocal inflection rises like it's a microphone "check, one, two," and she plucks an early memory from the shame bank. "I remember one of the first times I got in trouble. My brother was mad at me, and I started yelling, 'I'm sorry. I hate myself. I just wish I would die.' Now that I look back on my life, I can see it... bipolar...." Her optimistic veneer cracks, her eyes drop, and she tries to wipe away the why-did-I-not-notice-earlier regrets a lot of bipolar folks grapple with. In my case, bipolar was completely off my radar for 46 years. I'll forever beat myself up for not seeing such obvious traits in myself that were too painful to admit.

I slip into journalist mode—a new defence mechanism for my own triggers when I'm talking to other folks about their crises. Sexual abuse, childhood trauma, suicidal ideation. Cue my inner journalist. Check my ingrained list of questions and pick one. What comes out is, "So, how do you feel when you look back on those times?" Bella doesn't hesitate. "Grateful they are in the past," she says. "Grateful that I made the decision to dive into the freezing water, because there is no good time to deal with trauma."

It's the perfect place for a transition in conversation, so I change the topic to punk rock, a tried-and-true grounding technique. I ask Bella about Foxx Bodies releasing its second album on Kill Rock Stars, the breeding ground for two of the best feminist punk bands ever—Bikini Kill and Sleater-Kinney. Bella's face lights up at the mere mention of these bands, and an epic smile forms on her sideways-egg-shaped cheeks.

"The reason I started playing music is because I was freaking out, and being down in the dumps, and then manic," she says. On a much-deserved Sunday couch-slouch, Bella came across *The Punk Singer*, a documentary film about Bikini Kill's Kathleen Hanna, who has devoted her life to championing women in punk. "I was, like, 'Holy shit, this is so cool.' I didn't listen to anything but Bikini Kill and Sleater-Kinney for a full year. It totally changed my life."

Instrumental in the '90s riot grrrl scene, the two bands addressed sexual abuse and trauma in their songs, which supported Bella when she needed it most. Now, Foxx Bodies is Bella's turn to speak her own truth while empowering others.

Inspired by the infamous concert where proto-punkers the Velvet Underground played a New York psychiatric convention in January of 1966, psychiatric nurse practitioner Kellie Newsome and psychiatrist Chris Aiken dug into the topic of mania and punk on a May 2021 episode of their *Carlat Psychiatry Podcast*. In addition to talking about the Velvet Underground leader Lou Reed, who was diagnosed with bipolar and underwent electroshock therapy at age 15, the episode speculates that influential musicians such as Kurt Cobain and Joy Division's Ian Curtis also lived with the condition before dying by suicide.

Kellie works at the Mood Treatment Centre in Greensboro, North Carolina (by way of Australia) and jokes that Aiken wanted her as a co-host because of her Aussie accent. Her sharp vowel sounds and regular use of rhetorical questions supply perfect intonation for a podcast. Less than two minutes into our discussion, Kellie slathers me with butter, telling me bipolar folks are her "favourite population of people." Mmm, tell me more. She laughs and rocks in her office chair. "There's so many positive aspects of being bipolar that don't get mentioned or focused on," she says.

First, weirdo creativity. Bipolar folks are ingenious at tapping into it. Kellie says studies show that the same genes that give rise to bipolar do the same for artistic creativity. For musicians with bipolar, pounding out dizzying, distorted bass lines or weaving rhyming couplets condemning society's ills can come effortlessly during manic moods. They can ride the swells of mild manic episodes—rapid thoughts, euphoria, increased energy, and lack of sleep—to be productive, start new projects, and flaunt their charisma.

Ensuring moods don't become too elevated is crucial. Mania is dangerous if it escalates over a brief period and can lead to paranoid delusions, psychosis, suicide attempts, and hospitalization. Mania can also be a slow burn. Problematic behaviour, such as overspending, gambling, sexual promiscuity, unrealistic projects, and extreme irritability, can compound over months, years, and decades, leading to the erosion of relationships. Someone in a manic state often becomes impatient and irritable as life around them moves too slowly. "You're not letting me finish what I'm saying." If Megan says this, I know I'm trending toward mania. Once someone is in a full-blown manic episode, no one, including their loved ones, can talk them down or reign them in. Kellie looks me in the eye and pretends she's trying to stuff a cobra back into its wicker basket, a gesture more effective than words.

From her work in Greensboro, Kellie is acutely aware of what mania looks like, and she has seen it in the rock musicians she has treated. Mania replicates the effect of alcohol, she says, shutting down the frontal lobes, the part of our brain that makes judgement calls and filters our behaviour. If a musician becomes manic onstage, they may have what feels like a religious experience, which they can direct toward band members or the audience. This can be as harmless as showering people with sweat and hugs or as damaging as destructive behaviour or unleashing violence.

"They go to the extreme, you know?" Kellie lets one of her rhetorical questions hang before referencing a recent case study. "With one of the punk musicians that we take care of, his bandmates were calling it quits with him, and everything started to fall apart. The mania escalates and escalates until it just crashes into depression."

Fucking... bipolar... depression.... The type of mood episode we bipolar folks would rather not talk about. Kellie tells me mania is a protection from depression, and if you stay high, you'll avoid the lows. But mania only staves off depression until it can't anymore. When someone with bipolar reaches the top of the rollercoaster, and we always do, the plummet can be stomach-shattering. I've woken up in a depression after an amazing show the previous night, unable to get out of bed, and not just because of the punishment I inflicted on myself in the pit. On the days I do get my shit together, depressive episodes can backhand me to the ground by lunchtime without warning. One minute I'm listening to Fugazi, typing truth to power, pupils glistening blue with possibilities, and then, *blammo*, my forehead is on my desk and Circle Jerks' "Live Fast, Die Young" might as well be "Live Slow, Die Now."

I've spoken to punk musicians who say depression strips their creativity and will to write songs. Bella Vanek from Foxx Bodies talks about how music pours out of her if she's manic, but when depression inevitably hits, she's convinced she'll never write another song again. One hypothesis is mania increases creative productivity, while depression supplies the creative material. What's that saying: without suffering, there is no art? The stripping of output that depression brings often causes musicians and other artists to go off the bipolar meds that treat their mania. Problem is, some choose to remain unmedicated because they're afraid of losing their creative ebb and flow, and without meds they can skyrocket within days.

I sometimes worry that my mood stabilizers and antipsychotic meds have dulled the pleasures in my life—have dulled me. Am I still the charismatic, hilarious, talented, justice-seeking Jason I was all those unmedicated years, and does taking my pills just bring me back down from the stratosphere? I've grown to learn that, for me, medicated life is the safer, steadier option. Kellie joins me on Team Meds and stresses that medication is one of the most important pillars of a wellness plan. It's also key to maintaining long-term stability.

"Medication can bring the extreme down and the depression up, and it doesn't have to mean being less creative," she says, using the universal bipolar hand signal, a top and bottom hand squeezing their way into the stable area in the middle. "I believe mania exaggerates the positive traits that make us human, but it has to be harnessed properly."

Kellie busts out another go-to indicator of bipolar—the ol' index finger rollercoaster. The goal is to turn the extreme coaster into a kiddie coaster and knowing how to hold on for dear life when elevated moods climb the monster-sized coaster again. Taking mood stabilizers and other meds doesn't mean punks need to retire from jumping into drum kits and screaming their throats raw. But they best beware: allowing mania to get to the point where reputation-melting episodes are left to reign supreme is bound to leave behind some carnage.

I'm hyped. Today, I'm talking to another punk living with bipolar. Before my first few *Scream Therapy* podcast interviews, I was nervous about saying something weird or asking the wrong questions. Now, watching the minutes countdown before my call starts, a calmness coats me like liquid antacid. That weird Skype sound—*bloop*—snaps me out of my mini meditation and, hey, look, Regan Ashton and I stare at each other from Salt Lake City, Utah, USA to Powell River, BC, Canada. Two countries and one time zone connect a couple of dudes with bipolar. We share pleasantries that aren't necessary because we already understand something about each other. I joke that we're instant bipolar buddies, and he shows me his wide grin and flashes his white teeth.

Regan spent seven years between ages 10 and 16 in Spanish Fork, Utah, a hick town (as he calls it) not much bigger than my own, and he says it wasn't the best environment growing up. Regan's sister turned him on to punk rock when he was only six years old, dressing him up as a punk in second grade. He joined his first band at 12, his second at 15. Punk became something to hold onto, what he calls a "buoy."

Regan dabbled in typical teenage behaviour—toilet papering, egging houses. Soon, it was experimenting with drugs and alcohol. His school expelled him for being drunk in class, and his mom was pissed, to say the least. "She tried to ground me, but I didn't fucking care. I'd play guitar in my room, and who gives a fuck?" For punishment, she shipped Regan off to the Pioneer Trek, one state over in rural Wyoming, where he pulled a handcart eight hours a day. "And, motherfucker, I didn't drink again for two fucking years." Regan uses expletives like he's having a fuck-and-shit fire sale.

While other kids in Regan's junior high school were already doing crystal meth, music kept him busy and inspired. His comparatively innocent drinking and troublemaking continued, and his stepdad came to the rescue early on, buying Regan a guitar amp to play his first show in exchange for Regan's promise to stop fucking up—a promise he'd soon break. Regan used meth for the first time on Christmas Day when he was 18 years old. Not so Merry Christmas. Soon after, he was injecting heroin. Not so Happy New Year.

Regan's one of nearly 70 percent of people living with bipolar who "abuse or have abused" drugs and alcohol, according to the Journal of Clinical Psychiatry. Far exceeding the general population, those with bipolar often use substances to regulate spikes and dips in mood and energy, only to experience more intense symptoms, longer episodes of instability, and greater risk of suicide.

Now 31, Regan has spent years questioning the role substance use had in his mental health. Up until recently, Regan had never played a show sober, and it's one of the reasons he enjoyed touring so much. Over the years, his bandmates in the melodic punk band Problem Daughter have been more than patient with Regan. When they found out he was using heroin, they'd had enough of his unpredictable behaviour and erratic mood swings. "At first, they were concerned, but they said, 'Regan's a big boy, he can do what he wants.' It started getting to the point where they had to intervene." He pauses and scratches his beard nervously. "It was either break up the band, or I stop doing heroin."

Losing the band scared him enough that he knew his only choice. Regan and his friend, the one he first used heroin with, moved to Salt Lake City and began splitting withdrawal medication every night because Regan had no health insurance. Unlike those who spend years, decades, or even a lifetime struggling to stop using, he was off heroin just three months later. It's been more than 12 years and he still is. But life with bipolar since not drinking or doing drugs has been hellish at times. Some days, depression glues him to his bed like a fly on flypaper, and other days mania makes him talk a mile a minute and he can't sit still.

"Now when my bipolar kicks in it's either my crippling depression, like, 'You're a piece of shit, why even get out of bed?' Or it's my manic highs, like, 'Let's do it, let's do it, let's do it, let's just do something....'" Regan waves his hands around at Tasmanian Devil's speed, stops, and pushes his glasses up his nose. I can tell he's putting on a brave face. It's the same face I see in the mirror on the days when I beg for a mood episode to pass, and pass soon. He gives me a look that says, "Don't worry, I can handle it," as his glasses reflect off his computer screen. From behind thick frames, he pierces the lenses and convinces me he's got this—he can manage bipolar. And I know he can, first- and second-hand. During bipolar episodes, I hold tight to stability with blood-drained fingers. And I've listened to folks in my bipolar support group share that they've had positive results from doing all the right things, like meds, therapy, sleep, exercise, and reaching out for help.

Regan and I—the bipolar buddies—end our call and part ways to tackle our respective moods one day at a time. We don't stay in touch because that's how life is sometimes.

A year passes by in a cymbal crash, and I'm in a much more stable place than I was when Regan and I talked. I hope he is too. With fingers crossed, I decide to send an email to see how he's been doing.

"Hey Jason! It's good to hear from you!" In emails, Regan replaces his expletives with exclamation marks. "I've been going to therapy every week and continuing AA. I recently started taking a new mood stabilizer, which I think has been helping, but it's hard to tell sometimes."

Yes, it is. It's awfully hard to tell sometimes. Are we getting better? What is better, exactly? Folks living with bipolar can't bank on day-to-day stability. We can only manage our symptoms to ride the creativity that comes with our mania and leverage our depression into introspection and reflection. The key is using our moods to our advantage without jeopardizing what's most important—stable lives.

We're getting there. We are. We have to be.

SHOW 7

You're taking an overdue piss on the Quadra Island ferry and spot something jammed in a hole where the urinal pipes snake out of the ceiling. It's gleaming blue; a gelatinous, alien-looking blob housed in a sparkly cardboard tube.

What the fuck is that?

On tiptoes, straining your shoulder muscles to their limit, you pull the tube from its hidey-hole. Its sour perfume burns your nostrils and overpowers your acrid urine. A soapy, industrial smell masks your pungent body odour. This oversized air-freshening mutation could be a game changer.

Your Corolla is an open can of rotten smoked oysters on wheels, oozing a shellfish-like stink out its windows. Your bags of costumes are smelling more rank as the tour rolls on, and you're too nervous to ask any of your crash-pad hosts if you can throw on a load of laundry. Their washing machines would reek for weeks. Soiled clothes have been sopping up your juices for days and are moulding. By the hour: more stench. By the day: more fermentation. Your body odour has gotten so foul it trails behind you like the poof cloud behind Charlie Brown's filthy little friend Pig-Pen. Every time you get out of the Corolla, your waft of dirty punk follows. Let's be honest: you've ruined the car. You need to light it on fire and push it into the nearest gravel pit. By the time you reach the storied Quadra Island Legion, your ride is bordering on radioactive.

"As God is my witness, he's broken in half!"

If the 1998 Hell in the Cell wrestling match has a signature sound, it's the sickening thud of Mankind smashing through a table after the Undertaker hurls him from a 16-foot-high steel cage. The Undertaker looms above Mankind, as if he's considering what style of coffin will be most appropriate. Mankind's skull is buried underneath the shattered table, legs pinned by a crowd barrier, body mangled. His hands twitch and his eyes flutter. Mankind's not dead, but will Mankind get up? Mankind always does.

Inspired by Mankind inexplicably climbing back up the cage to have his revenge on the Undertaker, you've branded your tour-worn body with a wrestling persona—the Punk Screamer. You have no wrestling opponent to grapple with and no steel cage to plummet from, but you're amped to shadowbox imaginary opponents. Audiences have seen your wrestler persona before—abrasive, larger-than-life, uncontrollable—a character who can do, say, and scream whatever you want. Tonight, at the Quadra Legion, you lean into your wrestling fantasies and use Punk Jams' wall of noise as your ring entrance music, your costume as flamboyant as ever with a ratty maroon cape trailing behind.

Your latest pieced-together band ramps up its assault as you fashion a wrestling ring around the poles that frame the dance floor, exhausting your arsenal of packing tape to create makeshift ropes and turnbuckles. Punk Jams pukes hardening sludge that slugs the eager audience square in the chest. The faux ring ropes might as well be police tape deterring looky-loos at a crime scene, but a small group of keeners break through the tape and smash into each other. You leap down from the stage like it's the top rope. It's the moment you've been waiting for—fresh, willing meat to tenderize.

You're the Punk Screamer, and you want a Royal Rumble, so you rip down the tape ropes as the band culminates in a dark, chugging force. Other audience members creep forward and approach with caution as if they're inching toward a compromised grizzly bear cage. Still stinging from the ambivalence of the Gabriola patio dwellers four (five?) days ago, you sprint into the

Legion's bar and patio area, lock in with the audio demolition in the other room, and your mouth explodes.

Why the fuck... aren't you... inside!? You're missing... the beginning... of the rest of your liiiiiife!

With rage as your co-conspirator, you rip cushions off an empty booth and hurl them into the parking lot below. Shock and confusion permeate the room, the bar staff shoot you hate-lasers, and you spin and run back to the stage, shrieking. The bellows of the Hell in the Cell announcer flood your head.

As the punk gods are your witness, you're still screaming.

Show 7 on Quadra is your own little Hell in the Cell.

"That was a great show, but you need some repeated phrases here and there. Something for people to sing along to."

Most punks would cream their ripped jeans to receive unsolicited advice from Joey "Shithead" Keithley, leader of DOA. The man is a legend, a four-decade-long touring machine with more DIY know-how than everyone else on this tour combined. Yet, you're the formidable Punk Screamer, shrugging Joey off after the show for not understanding the point of Punk Jams.

Punk Jams doesn't write songs. Punk Jams makes noise.

Four years earlier, opening for DOA in another one of your bands—one that wrote songs about getting beat up by jocks in big-wheeled trucks—wearing two-sizes-too-small long johns, you flailed around your hometown dive bar like a squid in a bathtub. Joey sat at the merch table beside the stage, his jaw hanging. After the set, Joey told you, "That was one of the best live performances I've seen." This coming from someone who's spent a half-century touring the punk circuit and sharing the stage with thousands of bands. But Joey's definition of a "performance" isn't the same as yours—for you, performing is fighting for your life and having the time of your life all wrapped into one.

Waiting for the Quadra ferry back to Vancouver Island the next morning, Punk Jams guitarist Drue pretends not to notice the car's disgusting fragrance. Occupying the passenger seat since the Duncan show, Drue is a grounding presence, a much-needed reprieve from your incessant self-chatter. Drue is a very patient listener.

Before crossing paths at recent shows, it had been 20-plus years since you and Drue had any in-person contact. You were never particularly close to him when you first met in 1999, connected through similar tastes in bands. Just casual scene acquaintances, really. Over the next three days, you'll become inseparable. Sometimes 20 years flash by, then pick up right where they left off. Acquaintances grow to be friends. Friends build to something beyond friends. And those beyond-friends evolve into lifelong friends. Bang. Chosen family for life. Very rarely does this happen within 72 hours. Ah, Drue. You bond at exactly the right time, because without him with you on this leg of the tour, well... it's best to leave that line of thinking alone.

Your future looms. Your viable post-tour life options are shrivelling. The elephant in the car is starting to pitch a fit, and it's trumpeting a question with no plausible answer.

Two more shows. Then what?

"Last night sounded great," Drue says to break the silence. "We had more of a Jesus Lizard sound going on. Very dark and chuggy." Drue tells you he had an epiphany onstage with Punk Jams last night. Mid-set, in front of the packed crowd, he understood it was time to seriously dive back into playing music and follow his passion. "I realized I can still play guitar," he says. "That I still *want* to play guitar."

"As for you..." Drue shifts in his seat, "...you were a wild creature up there." You want to dissect who this creature Drue's talking about—this Punk Screamer—really is and what its true motivations are. Offstage, after daylong travel and during late-night comedowns, you dodge ruminations about the shit-pile of stress and worries at home, make jokes with your tourmates, and fish for details about what happened the night before. Behind the wheel, on these long drives, you fantasize about never going home. Never, ever going home.

What's your end game?

You board the ferry, hands on the 10 and two, and Drue shuffles sideways in the passenger seat and tries to make eye contact.

"Don't take this the wrong way," he offers, a little skittish, "but it's like you're trying to get as close to the edge of destruction without falling off. It's like you're purging all that anger and hate. But I can also see the love and joy in your eyes. Like you've found your family."

SAVE YOUR GENERATION

Words fight to bust through cement. Matter over mind.

Fuck. Come on. I can do this.

Powell River's Historic Patricia Theatre is the scene of my 46th birthday. I've gathered my friends to watch the Fugazi documentary film *Instrument*, a much-deserved present to myself. I'm still reeling from my psychotic break, and it hinders my ability for thoughts, ideas, and fingertips to flow freely. Like a head injury, my psychiatrist told me. I shift between my feet at the front of the theatre, look down at the crumpled paper in my shaking hands, and the words I typed earlier that day eke out.

Fugazi is a band that plays music for the marginalized, the disenfranchised, and the disillusioned. Fugazi is a band for the people. But Fugazi isn't just a band. Fugazi is love. Fugazi is life. Fugazi is a glimmer of hope in a desolate world. Fugazi is an eternal pocket of joy. Fugazi's music is alive and ever-changing. It takes on new forms of brilliance every time I listen, and it's always in my heart and in my head.

The first words from my fingertips since my bipolar diagnosis are about the Washington, DC band that, more than any other band, has helped shape my life. I'm not satisfied with what I wrote. To say I'm rusty is a massive understatement, and my lack of confidence morphs to self-defeat. In the coming weeks, like a marathon runner's false start, my hands begin to seize, and my words follow. I spend intolerable months—two, or three, or maybe six—in a depression that burrows the idea into my skull that I can't write for shit.

I'm the worst. I should just give up now.

Fugazi never leaves my side.

Pause tape. Freeze time. Rewind. Winter 1991. Contemplative, strummed F sharp chords introduce "Blueprint" from Fugazi's *Repeater* cassette, and they squeak into the Simon Fraser University concourse from a tiny, mono speaker mounted outside CJIV, the campus radio station I deejay at. Guy Picciotto's piercing voice hits on the 16th bar—*I'm not playing with you, I'm not playing with you, I'm not playing with you, yeah you*—and my anticipation is set to stun, waiting for the rhythm section to join in. On cue, Joe Lally's silky bassline effortlessly intertwines with Brendan Canty's snare/hi-hat stagger step. My best friend, roommate, and radio show co-host Bill mocks a sinister grin and cranks the volume. Fugazi fills the studio.

We'll draw a blueprint
It must be easy
It's just a matter
Of knowing when to say no or yes

Ian MacKaye's Gibson SG guitar knives through the silence and hangs in the balance.

Pause tape. Freeze time. Fast forward. Halloween weekend, 2018. Fest 17. I've locked myself to the front row as Brooks from War on Women revives those same strummed F sharp chords. The feminist punk band's cover of "Blueprint" is unexpected, perhaps the result of an inspired decision between Baltimore and Gainesville in the group's rickety van, but it makes perfect sense given the two bands' headstrong lyrics and heart-lurching music. Shawna, the band's vocalist, spots me and pushes the mic into my face at the pristine moment. I've had these lyrics ingrained in me for 30 years and counting.

Never mind what's been selling
It's what you're buying
And receiving undefiled

Time's a gift, and as the world slowed down, I spent countless hours listening to the Fugazi Live Series, an ongoing documentation of almost 900 shows the band recorded, where its members use improvisation to connect threads of audio freedom. Studying Fugazi and playing my own rudimentarily inspired music, I've become intimately connected with spontaneity's role in the creative process. To experiment beyond boundaries is to be in control. Boxed in, it's impossible to thrive. Creativity shrivels and souls deteriorate.

It's easy to buy into what surrounds us—the learned behaviours that repeat themselves endlessly.

While the world progressively becomes the stomping grounds for misguided minions, Fugazi reminds me to be respectful, empathic, caring, and supportive—how to educate myself by listening to others and nourish the roots of my own perspective and beliefs. Fugazi taught me that the personal is the political.

I admire Fugazi's dedication to breaking the cycle of aggression at its shows and encouraging everyone to respect each other's space and stay safe.

After decades of finding comfort in slam dancing, I've come to terms with the fact that I don't always have to rely on the mosh pit—its communal congregations of pounded flesh, someone always waiting to pick me up—to feel safe anymore. I can pick myself up now. It's time to give the grubby, beer-stained, pit-worn Chuck Taylors a rest. It's time to add new dances to the mix.

Fugazi was always about positive action and community involvement—every one of its DC shows was a benefit for a local organization. Fugazi helps me remember how important it is for us to take care of each other. Fugazi reminds me to appreciate what life has to offer and never, ever take it for granted.

Fugazi isn't just a band.

Fugazi is love.

Fugazi is life.

I wish the words I wrote on my birthday were more eloquent, more meaningful. I wish my friends in the audience that night had cheered, held their hands to their chests, and swooned over every word, because I desperately needed the ego boost. Instead, my words came out stilted, mere fragments of what they could have been.

Still, they were my words, and they came from my fingers. In the months and years to come, more times than I can count, Fugazi would clip jumper cables to my chest and kickstart my heart.

I've been waiting for this moment for 27 years.

I'm at Fest 18, Sunday, November 3, 2019, smooshed against the stage barrier in communion with thousands of punks at Bo Diddley Plaza in Gainesville, Florida. It's redemption time. I'm finally seeing Jawbreaker.

Not yet. Vancouver, 1992. Two years out of high school. I've been really depressed lately, prying my eyes open with my thumb and forefinger in morning journalism classes at Langara College. It's just burnout, I tell myself. I have an early Sunday shift working at a fucking Costco, so I shove breakfast into my face and brace myself for another day of irate customers, like the muscley dude who beat me up in the toilet paper aisle one time, but I'm trying to block that day out. My shift is drrraaaaggging. I lean against my till and beg my comically oversized splatter-paint Swatch to run double time.

Home by 3 pm, I drag my pre-comatose body through the apartment building lobby, slouch against the elevator wall until I hear the "ding," lumber down the hallway, fumble with my keys, nudge the door open, kick my shoes into the closet, hit the bed face down, and pass out. I jerk awake at 5:30 with a startling realization.

Fuck, Jawbreaker is playing today.

I scramble out of bed to check the show flyer that's been strategically magnet-ed to the fridge for weeks. "Jawbreaker. All-ages! No booze, no fights, no jerks. Sunday, May 17, 4 pm." A hot flash turns me to ice. *Fuck! No! I missed Jawbreaker!* My heart might as well have fallen out of my chest and splattered on the floor.

Three decades later, me, my ratty Amygdala t-shirt, and the punk parishioners are moments away from seeing Jawbreaker hit the stage at Fest. I'm full-body buzzing. The band members walk out, all smiles, and count into their first song. It's gruff, melodic, and sharp as a diamond drill bit. I'm honest-togoodness euphoric, not my unfiltered manic euphoria, and everyone around me is dancing and swaying. Our mouths open to the sky like we're in Charlie Brown's choir. Hearing the bridge hook of "Save Your Generation" in concert is a life-defining moment.

You have to learn to learn from your mistakes
You can afford to lose a little face
The things you break, some can't be replaced
A simple rule: every day be sure you wake

People I've never met pull me into a group hug. We understand the gravity of this experience, how watching a cherished band play live can meet our basic need to belong in the world. How, in this moment, life stands still, problems and worries subside, and hope prevails. My cheek-to-cheek grin squeezes my tear ducts. I look around at my new friends, clutching me and crying. I never want to let go.

Blackberry Fest, 1997. We stand out like mangled thumbs, two high school students and 20-something-year-old me wearing ripped clothes with patches sewn on them. The three of us scream our throats hoarse while hammering our frustrations out on patched-up instruments.

My three sisters, ages seven, 10, and 12, are horrified. They're running in every direction and crying. Our guitarist's mom, a bank manager: also crying. Dudes in camouflage jackets walk by, yell at us to fuck off, and threaten to kill us. The more respectful onlookers are in varying states of shock and disbelief.

Return to Sender, my first serious punk band, is playing at Powell River's sacred summer street party on a makeshift stage made from wooden pallets. Around us, tacky booths overflow with bargain basement knick-knacks, tacky tie-dye smocks, unidentified knitted items for the older set, and sickly-sweet baked goods to satiate the oh-so-delightful church goers who gawk at us like we're the Antichrist incarnate.

We stare down the crowd. We spit condemnations of capitalism, racism, sexism, homophobia, the meat industry, and police violence through the lens of young men who use dial-up internet to voice our dissent on punk message boards—the late-'90s, carrier-pigeon version of social media.

My out-of-tune bass gurgles out of the rattling PA system and rumbles down the street into the ears of more unwilling listeners. Our bursts of noise are uninhibited, and they liberate us. The jocks, assholes, and authority figures that we've spent our youth rallying against will be forced to listen or leave. Lyrics like, *every cop's a bad cop, don't feel threatened by the fucking jocks*, and *that Nike swoosh is bigger than your head* are our small-town revolutions.

The seething mob is gathering, and we spot a lone dissenter. A drunk guy dances in circles with a Budweiser can foaming in his hand and shouts supportive obscenities at us. He's doing this amazing solo mosh like he's trying to body check and bust down an invisible door. I holler into my microphone that he's the only person in the crowd who "fucking gets it."

Two days prior, we held the closest we ever came to a band meeting to choose our 25-minute set list. I'm sure we were all wondering, *how do these band meeting things work?* Sitting in a circle, staring at each other blankly, I break a silence we're not known for.

"Maybe we should just play our mellower songs?"

Mellower songs for Return to Sender means ones that don't make people cry and run screaming. I leave my suggestion hanging, and we know it's the exact opposite of what we want to do. Our drummer Kelsey gives us his infamous, devious look, and I know what he's going to say. It's what I wanted to say to begin with.

"Let's play all of our fastest songs," he says.

"Fuck yeah! The ones with the most political lyrics and swearing," I say.

"Okay, let's do it," our guitarist Mike says.

Full consensus, and so it's to be. We will rattle the deeply rooted conservative cages in Powell River—the ones that mush our faces into the ground just for being who we are. If they're going to look down on us, let's give them a reason. Let's make people abhor us. Hundreds will witness our royal "fuck you" to a stifling town that already hates us.

If just one person gleans inspiration from what we're doing and realizes, just maybe, they're not alone in this godforsaken town, our work here is done.

We want to sound an alarm for the freaks, one that tells them it's okay to be an outcast—it's okay to be a punk. And that's exactly what we do.

On bad days, when the depression fog clogs my noggin, the last thing I want to do lately is play guitar in my new band. Remember notes. Remember riffs. Remember songs. Remember lyrics to those songs. Fuck that.

The members of my band Rifle Rafle (also known as Riff Raff), at a median age of 42, always hug each other before our jams. It's a cosy guarantee of imminent, welcome escape—an ultimate bond through music. On bad days, my hugs are frail and stiff, almost lifeless. My bandmates must see that I'm depressed. The shadowy bags drooping down my cheeks are a dead giveaway.

"How are you doing?" they ask, because that's what we as humans do to settle the balance. If I'm not well, and you're not well, who is well, and how do we, as humans, come to terms with such collective misery? We ask, "How are you today?" and, "How are things going?" and oftentimes we're not honest with each other. Instead, we huddle around the construct of mandatory wellness. But I trust that the members of my band genuinely want to know how I'm doing. They're aware that I live with bipolar and have always been empathic, but I'm not honest with them. I'm a wellness performer. I perform wellness when I'm not well.

"I'm okay," I lie, pretending I'm struggling to find an A on my A string with my shitty guitar tuner. I look around the jam space at my friends—my drummer, bassist, and guitarist at the ready—and I panic. I can't escape the negative self-talk that convinces me I have no right to be in this band. Any band.

Click, click, click, click.

Drumsticks signal our first song, and my heart muscles flex. My furrowed brow relaxes, and my pursed lips allow a half-smile, the kind my dialectical behavioural therapy course teaches me can turn a frown upside down. Life is instantly more tolerable once I'm immersed in making a racket with my friends, and two hours pass in moments. We wind our patch cords and pack up our gear, already stoked about the next jam. We hug each other goodbye, and their bodies warm me.

I don't want to let go of the comfort in our collective noise, but I always know it's inevitable. I help them load their amps to their cars, eke out a frail wave as they drive away, lock up the basement jam space, drop my butt onto the porch bench, and deep-sigh myself into oblivion.

On bad days, Rifle Rafle is much-needed therapy. On good days, Rifle Rafle is a celebration of forging healthier neural pathways—the ones I learn about in TED Talks done by neuropsychologists wearing Madonna headsets.

Standing across from each other in Mel's 120-year-old heritage house's music room, we fidget with excitement. I can't stop thinking, and I suspect she is too, *how is this going to go, exactly?* It's the first jam for our noise project, tentatively called Personal Work, alternately Audio Interface. We'll settle on the name Wise Mind, after a technique both of us learn in dialectical behavioural therapy—the sweet spot where the reasonable mind and emotional mind intersect. Yay, Team Mental Health!

Somehow, our noise just happens. Guitar feedback bounces off the walls and distorted samples of children's television commercials cut into the mix. Garbled radio frequencies share space with the celebratory beeps and chimes of kid's toys. A dumbbell plopped down on a keyboard holds an ominous tone and competes with a custom-made drone synth, handmade by another noise freak in California. Mel's haunting yet playful vocals puncture the mass of white noise, and my worries—depressed (the past) and anxious (the future)— dissipate. I pull air into my lungs until they overflow. I'm dreaming awake.

Thirty years prior. Fresh to Vancouver. Holding an electric guitar for the first time. My new buddy Punk Rock Andy is teaching me "House of the Rising Sun" (ouch) and "Blitzkrieg Bop" (better) on an electric guitar plastered with band stickers. I'm amazed at how punk rock can come out of me in a flash of sloppy barre chords. I experiment with playing instruments for decades. To make up for my lack of musical knowledge, I pound on guitars as if they're percussion instruments, and I feed off the spontaneity and freedom of an unconventional style. "Downpick Schreurs," they called me when I played bass in Return to Sender. To this day, I know little about guitar techniques other than, "Follow the beat (or don't), hit the strings, and go!"

My bands and noise projects over the years have always been an important part of my wellness plan, even as I was staving off a mental health crisis. Jamming and being creative inspires and excites me, and that's all I need, really. Everything else we do—the recordings, the live shows, the hand-screened t-shirts—is secondary. If someone else likes what we're doing, bonus, and if any of my bands over the years become the impetus for someone else to form one, or turn on their ignition for another creative interest, what an honour that is. Pure gravy.

Ultimately, playing and listening to punk rock, at its essence, has a higher purpose for me. It calms me when life's pressure cooker threatens to blow chunks of me all over the ceiling. Being in punk bands places me entirely in the moment. Tiny guitar-string ridges rubbing against my index and ring finger, such simple movements to cause such volume to explode from amplifiers. My upper lip pressed tight against microphone mesh, vibrations in my throat rising, then soaring. An arched back. A high-kicked leg. A gut full of validation.

Punk is a whole-body marvel. It's my meditation practice.

If you could save yourself, you could save us all
Go on living, prove us wrong
Your leap of faith could be a well-timed smile
Survival never goes out of style
Jawbreaker - "Save Your Generation"

The phrase "punk rock saved my life" is a recurring declaration in this book. The phrase "punk rock and the public library saved my life," not so much.

Kristin Belkofer, a licensed professional counsellor based in Milwaukee, Wisconsin, grew up in a Cathlotic community where the repression was so thick, she says she woke up feeling less and less human every day. Sexually abused as a child, Kristin tells me she can't put into words how she struggled in her life at home and school. I'm hesitant to push Kristin for details. In the support group I facilitate, we have an agreement to not ask questions when someone is sharing. People share what they're comfortable sharing at any given time, and questioning may lead them to areas they would rather not go (so says Group Agreement 8). Although my facilitator and journalist instincts often clash, I'm proud of my restraint.

Kristin settles in her seat and tells me she didn't like being at home as a teen. Instead, she would walk 10 minutes from her house to the public library and sigh with relief as the sliding glass doors left the outside world behind, even for a couple hours.

"I always tell people this story..." she stifles a laugh, the back of her hand coming up to her cherry-red lips. "I would read *Spin* voraciously. I would read about Courtney Love and the more mainstream riot grrrl stuff, and I'd think, 'This is not quite me.' I still had an outsider feeling." As Kristin grabbed the latest *Spin* off the rack one Saturday afternoon, what she had been looking for dropped into her lap. Literally. With a you're-not-gonna-believe-this look, she continues. "It was a photocopied zine with a bunch of bands I'd never heard of and a bunch of weird art." Her eyes sparkle, and in them I can see her clutching her new prized possession, straightening at attention in a plastic library chair. "I didn't know what it was, but I thought, 'This is it. This what I am.'"

Ah, yes. Zines. The sense of a whole new world opening. My first zines were the standard punk rock bibles (*Maximumrockandroll*, *HeartattaCk*, *Punk Planet*), which exposed me to a dizzying array of new bands. This led me to personal zines and making my own. People around the world were sharing their lives, scars and all, with an endless support network facilitated by self-addressed stamped envelopes, a concept so foreign now it might as well be from the Dark Ages.

Kristin's exposure to punk culture didn't end amongst the shelves of magazines and dusty book stacks. It spilled into the library parking lot where a group of skateboarders fist-pumped Kristin an olive branch, one she couldn't find anywhere else. Punks use special sonar, and they know one of their own when they spot her/them/him. Just because Kristin was a book nerd didn't mean she couldn't be a punk. In fact, her nerdiness was an advantage.

"The other guys at my school didn't give a shit. They just thought I was weird," Kristin says as she finesses a strand of hair behind her ear. "But these other guys had the punk radar, like, 'This girl is going to be into this kind of shit. We should let her into it. I bet she'd love it.'"

Formative moments. Opportunities to take our lives in whatever direction we choose. As she learned more about support networks and community through her youth and into adulthood, Kristin decided she wanted to be a therapist. She received her Master's in Community Psychology and opened a private practice called the Clara Healing Institute in 2021. She avoids what she refers to as "love and light" therapy and opts for a client-centred, integrative approach. "We don't have to be victims in society and the mental health world," she says.

Kristin's also the founder of Punk Rock Therapy, the online equivalent to the zines she grew up reading. The Facebook group brings together people from all over the world to support each other in wellness and healing. Kristin's group reminds me of one of the last positive things I did on social media before I yanked myself offline. Fest Mental Health was a group I formed where people who attended Fest in Gainesville could share their struggles around mental health leading up to and during the festival. The group only had around 100 members. Even so, it was inspiring to see them taking care of each other, mobile phone to mobile phone. Kristin's group grew from just her acquaintances to more than 1,000 punks worldwide. Punk Rock Therapy members help each other in an altruistic, non-hierarchical way, an approach she longs for in the therapist community. Working within a mental health industrial complex that overuses the biomedical model to explain mental suffering dropped Kristin right back into the kind of isolation she experienced as a teen.

"I would leave psychologists conferences and think, 'Damn, I'm never going to fit in anywhere in life.'" She looks down at the giant butterfly on her t-shirt, and her facial expression intensifies as if she's conjuring and holding space for psychologists who aren't content to dive under the capitalist umbrella—a space where people with mental health conditions are no longer treated like mere consumers. Kristin jokes she could have followed the standard, blonde, white lady counsellor path that was established by a bunch of other standard, blonde, white lady counsellors. "There's a rhetoric and, for lack of a better word, branding that surrounds the industry of therapy, and especially of female-identifying therapists," she says, stroking her black choker necklace.

Kristin is particularly interested in seeing her clients develop ecological systems, "which is just a fancy way to describe the different areas of thought and influence we're part of," she says. The human ecology theory was developed in the late '70s by Russian-born US psychologist Urie Bronfenbrenner, whose name should be scooped up by a fantasy metal band, and it suggests that quality of life and social environment are dependent on each other. She learned early on that finding the punk community, where she could behave, think, and feel how she wanted, was invaluable. For one, the Punk Rock Therapy online group offers her a support system that satisfies her core need to care for others in an environment where others care for her.

Our conversation turns to the visceral and embodying therapy of music and our mutual love for Against Me!, the anthemic Florida band who have raised so many spirits with albums like *Searching for a Former*

Clarity and *Transgender Dysphoria Blues*. The anthemic, piercing guitars; the rollicking rhythm section with its boppy bass lines and syncopated drums; the gut-wrench power of Laura Jane Grace's voice. The way songs like "Unconditional" and "Don't Lose Touch" envelope us. I can't always recall the specific details of hearing one of my favourite bands for the first time— the where, when, and how—but I remember the hairs on my arms standing up, the prickle on the back of my neck, and the thump-thump of my heart. The tingling anticipation for the next note, riff, or scream, and the ultimate payoff, because from visceral reactions comes the power to act, create, and overcome. Kristin's knowing nod tracks from ceiling to floor and shakes her hair loose again, her thumb and index finger at the ready.

"Punk rock is going to sustain me for the rest of my life, no matter what I do, because it's an ideology that I'm growing and developing myself from, personally and professionally. Bands like Against Me! 100 percent changed my life. When I heard them for the first time, something healed in me." Kristin's smile beams like a spotlight panning her face. "I don't know if there's anything anybody could have done to make me as healed and moved as that."

"Something in her clicked."

The word "clicked" smacks off Amanda Fillipelli's tongue like the snap on a leather handbag. Amanda worked in the mental healthcare system for 10 years, teaching adolescent trauma survivors how to find empowerment in their stories. These days, she's an author, editor, and book coach who teaches connection and healing through storytelling.

As a teen, Amanda spent her formative years in Pittsburgh's punk scene and found its positivity inspiring. She, in turn, became an inspiration to others when she started working as a counsellor at residential treatment facilities for youth. In her work, Amanda leaned into her punk upbringing to further her clients' therapeutic goals. One afternoon, she was driving a young woman who was living in a group home to an appointment and saw an opening.

"This girl was difficult to get through to. She'd been at the facility for a long time and struggled with addiction and self-harm." Amanda squares her shoulders. She tells me she also harmed herself as a youth.

What "clicked" for Amanda's passenger was a song Amanda played on the car stereo. "The Young Crazed Peeling" by The Distillers, a Los Angeles punk band fronted by the sneering, charismatic Brody Dalle, was one of Amanda's favourites as she struggled through teenhood and the pecking order of high school. Amanda tells me the young woman perked up as soon as the song's lyrics burst from the speakers.

Are you ready to be liberated
On this sad side city street?
Well, the birds have been freed from their cages
I got freedom and my youth

Amanda rests for a moment and swivels in her chair, basking in the thought of Brody's punkified contralto. One of the songs that protected her from high-school bullshit was now a pay-it-forward to a new generation—another punk circle completed.

"It made the girl understand it's okay to take this music and use it as an opportunity to lash out and express yourself, instead of lashing out against yourself," Amanda says, clasping her fingers together, "and it changed something in her." Noting the young woman's improvement, Amanda decided to incorporate punk rock and other music into her therapy sessions with other youth. Most were stuck in a broken system, cycling in and out of mental health facilities, and the music opened them up, she says. "So many of the things they were feeling—the frustrations, the rage, the sadness, the problems with self-image, even symptoms inherent with their diagnoses—were things I knew the music could help them express."

Eventually, staff allowed the young woman to go off grounds and take part in field trips because of good behaviour. Whenever Amanda drove the Distillers' newest fan around, loud bands were the soundtrack. "She always wanted to rock out in the car," Amanda tells me with a blooming smile. "It was a healing experience for both of us."

Eventually, Amanda became disgruntled working in the slow-to-adapt mental health sector. She was fed up with how much money was going to CEOs and psychiatrists instead of addressing the mental health epidemic. "I was so tired of hitting up against so much bureaucratic red tape. I have a liberal core that wants to buck the system," she says, throwing me a sly grin.

"A true punk!" I practically yell at her, and she just laughs. Looking back, Amanda realizes expressing her anger as a youth was a logical pathway to helping people later in life, whether it was the at-risk youth in her past jobs or the emerging writers she helps now.

"When I was first introduced to stereotypical punk like the Sex Pistols, the violence of it reflected something I understood," she says. "It didn't make me want to go out and hurt anyone. It made me understand my anger at the system, and society, and even the hierarchy in my high school. It made me understand that the feelings I had were normal."

Amanda gives me a rebel-with-a-cause chin dip. A true punk.

Transforming anger into stress relief and freedom of expression, like Amanda Fillipelli was able to do with at-risk youth, should be a "no-shit" shoulder-shrug, yet mental-health-establishment dinosaurs flash their decaying teeth.

An antiquated misconception, especially among conservatives and fundamentalists, is that listening to punk rock and heavy metal, so-called "angry music," will make listeners angrier, but studies show otherwise. Australian researchers have found that listening to "extreme" music helps to process and regulate emotions. Leah Sharman, a University of Queensland researcher, tells me her 2015 study revealed that pairing angry music with angry emotions can enhance mental health.

The impetus for the study was one of Leah's colleagues mentioning to her that they listened to loud, intense music at bedtime because it relaxed them and was a way to wind down at the end of the day. Been there. This is a tactic I've used for years if my mood is elevated before bed, and I can't... fucking... sleep.

"This was fascinating to me," Leah says. "I thought it would be interesting to see if there was an effect of relaxation from listening to these genres of music, rather than the more typical idea of this music making people more aggressive."

In the study, Leah and other researchers asked participants to describe an event that made them angry, such as work or a relationship, then had them choose between 10 minutes of their music or 10 minutes of silence. "Listening to 'angry' music is going to be more likely when you're already feeling angry," she says. Results showed when participants chose music to match their anger, it regulated their emotions more, and they felt more active and inspired in comparison to choosing silence.

Other studies have garnered related results. In 2019, researchers at Macquarie University in New South Wales found music with violent themes doesn't make fans more susceptible to violent imagery or desensitize them to violence. Macquarie conducted a separate study the same year that found that fans of death metal, a subgenre obsessed with guts and gore, used the music's emotional charge for motivation and to process anger and other emotions such as sadness.

Hardcore Humanism mental health therapist and coach Dr. Mike Friedman put it best when he and I talked recently. "We're here to heal wounds," he told me, "not cause wounds."

Simon Forsyth has picked his Minor Threat shirt with the band's infamous *Out of Step* black sheep on it to wear for our Zoom call. The moment I see it, I'm positive we'll hit it off. I pull out the ratty, stained Minor Threat t-shirt with the same design on it, still hanging in the closet that doubles as my podcast studio. The shirt is two sizes too small after all these years, but I've got something better to show him. I roll up my sleeve and reveal a Minor Threat black-sheep tattoo on the inside of my left bicep. With our matching boyish grins, we could be long-lost siblings reunited at a DC hardcore show.

Simon is a therapist based in Dublin, Ireland who discovered punk as an out-of-step (pun intended) teenager. He's another mental health professional who uses a humanistic approach—that we can all find belonging if we find the right environment. I notice Simon is holding a piece of paper in his lap, looking a bit sheepish (again, pun intended). He turns the paper over like a five-year-old showing off a drawing of a lopsided unicorn.

"I did something that I do in counselling with my clients—writing as therapy," Simon says. "See, I did a punk diagram." Sure enough, he's written the word "punk" inside a happy starburst shooting from the middle of a sheet of letter-sized paper turned sideways. Surrounding "punk" are about 50 words Simon associates with the music that informs his life. Resistance. Unapologetic. Free. Confidence. Unity. Transgressive. Self-belief. Experimental. Intelligent. Inclusive. Sexy. Supportive. Power. I could go on.

During his teen years, Simon was painfully aware that he wasn't being his authentic self. Huddled over his desk reading books about the refreshingly brash individualism of the New York Dolls and Iggy Pop, he saw life-changing doors opening. Simon recalls how inspired he was by the fearlessness of the punks he looked up to and the courage he found in the music's rebellion and freedom. He makes a direct correlation between discovering punk at 17 and coming out as gay a year later.

"Punk represented that huge possibility around doing things..." he snaps his fingers, "without even thinking. Without anxiety, without being scared. To this day, when there's anxiety in my life, I'll ask, 'What would Lux Interior of the Cramps do? What would Kathleen Hanna of Bikini Kill do?' Just knowing these people exist gives me that sense of 'just fucking go for it.'"

Society typecasts punks as extreme extroverts with zero-to-100 personalities. Simon is the opposite—an introvert who uses music to process his emotions. Someone who passed Simon walking to his office in Dublin City Centre wouldn't guess he listens to Minor Threat and Bad Brains unless their Spidey-punk senses were tingling. Then again, maybe they're punks themselves, just as unassuming as Simon, going back to their own offices after a plate of bangers and mash at the pub. Remember, punks are everywhere.

Punk is therapy. I and others I've talked to have proven this. We swear by the power of the music and its scene to help us through tough times and, in extreme cases, self-directed threats to our very existence. But Simon has a reminder for me. Yes, punk is therapy, but therapy is also punk. I find myself spacing out on Simon's diagram as I try to grasp the idea of punk as therapy turned on its head. Punk... is therapy. Therapy... is punk.

Approaches to psychotherapy fall into five broad categories—psychoanalysis, behavioural therapy, cognitive therapy, humanistic therapy, and integrative or holistic therapy. Different counsellors use specific forms of these, such as somatic, eye movement desensitization and reprocessing (EMDR), and family systems. I've had at least a dozen therapists in my life, and I've never thought of any of their approaches as punk by nature. Plus, therapy always seems like such a privilege, another thing for rich folks to throw money at when they're not vacationing in the Bahamas. Every time I need therapy, I conduct a cost-versus-benefit analysis under a rotating roster of Swiss-cheesed health insurance plans, but it hasn't been an issue until lately. For my past 48 counselling sessions, British Columbia's Crime Victim Assistance Program paid for me to address my childhood sexual abuse, then my coverage maxed out. Unfortunately, therapy is a form of self-care most people don't have access to, or can't afford, especially in countries with a lack of health care services.

For select clients, a sizable number of which Simon sees pro bono, he developed a therapeutic writing workbook called "This Workbook Is a Punk." The title gives me goosebumps. He bills the workbook as a "punk rock self-esteem, self-help therapy resource," and it asks three takeaway questions: "What am I resisting? How can I rebel against it? What might I (re)claim for myself through my efforts?"

"Your clients are so lucky to have you," I tell him, my gush aligning with his blush. No offence to any of my counsellors over the years, but I wish someone could have handed me a workbook like that, so I could be in touch with what Simon calls my "inner protestor."

"This is different from other internal voices many people are more accustomed to, such as the inner critic or saboteur. The inner protestor voice might be just as powerful, if it can just be given the space and encouragement to emerge," says Simon, raising his eyebrows from behind light-grey-framed glasses. Even though he uses the workbook sparingly, its messages stay top of mind during all his counselling sessions. He's pitched the idea to adapt the workbook for a UK organization specializing in creative writing for the queer community.

I originally found Simon through a blog post called "Punk Rock Doesn't Give a Shit About Your Inner Critic." In it, he lists ways in which punk challenges a person to be themselves. Reading the list, it was clear—first of all, he and I needed to talk—that it could benefit anyone.

"Punk challenges you to say NO," the post begins.

"Punk challenges you to identify a status quo that no longer serves you and stand up to it.

Punk challenges you to be and act and do in a way that feels right for you.

Punk challenges you to be visible and unashamed.

Punk challenges you to be friends with who you want.

Punk challenges you to be goofy and just go with it.

Punk challenges you to get angry and channel that feeling into creating something better for yourself.

Ultimately, punk challenges you to resist, rebel and reclaim."

Had Simon written his blog post and workbook in the early '80s, they would have been perfect fodder for Minor Threat lyrics.

"Punk and therapy have so much in common. Punk therapy is creative, but it's also an act of resistance," Simon says, illuminating our Zoom room. He tells me it's common for his clients to be angry, and that's okay.

We label anger a negative emotion—we're told to bury it, put on a smile. But punks own their anger and, unlike so many others in society, they have a healthy way to express it through music. Simon nods as I mouth the two words we know are coming. Scream therapy.

"Anger is perfectly valid, and it can channel resistance against that voice that says, 'Keep that to yourself,' or, 'Don't cause a scene,'" he says. "So, when these things come up in a session with one of my clients, I don't have to name it as being punk because there's this energy. It's like a fight." He raises his fist in a we-can-do-this-together salute and shakes it at the ceiling.

The concept of punk as therapy—and therapy as punk—begs the question: in a capitalist society with a top-down psychiatric model, why aren't more people screaming?

SHOW 8
PORT ALBERNI, BC
THE RAINBOW ROOM
FRIDAY, AUGUST 17, 2018

6:45 pm.

Port Alberni is a dump. A pulp-mill-spewing, big-trucked, dirty-jeans-wearing, multi-marijuana-dispensary shithole. Thank fuck this godforsaken place has an escape route through the towering Douglas Firs in Cathedral Grove on the way to Ucluelet, the scene of tomorrow night's planned fiasco—the tour's final show. But first, Port Alberni: Gateway to the Pacific West Coast.

Gateway? More like a glorified rest stop.

The cafe near the wharf sells one-dollar donuts, a smoking deal, except for the Costco box shamelessly placed on the back counter. The coffee looks like, well, best to not think about that, and the sandwiches in the display cooler are slices of white bread with defrosted lunchmeat crammed between them.

Tonight's venue is a bowling alley and strip club combo turned failed music venue, stripper poles intact. The owner/manager is an admitted Trump supporter, and the uninterested sound guy is a former glam rocker who says he's worked with DOA before, believe it or don't. Gaudy chandeliers cast a dreary ambience on a room that's—peek behind the MAGA man's red velvet curtains—in awful repair.

This is fucking embarrassing.

Before the show, hipsters at the craft brewery down the street sip beers with names too annoying to repeat while nibbling on $30 artisanal pizzas. The patio is a yuppie-magnet packed with way-too-happy couples and their sweatered dogs playing ironic board games. The couples, not the dogs.

Port Alberni is arguably the worst place on Earth to book a punk show. The crowd at the Rainbow Room is rough and tumble, and it's only 60 people, tops—a shamefully sparse turnout for a DOA show. One thunder-hungry headbanger in an Ozzy shirt hangs out at the side of the stage. Other audience members wearing strategically ripped jeans slouch in VIP booths with decades-old upholstery that's stained from bottomless vodka cranberries. The energy in the room is post-apocalyptic, real end-of-the-world-type shit.

"There's a buzz around town for the show," the slimy venue manager emailed you earlier that day.

Why did you book this fucking show?

10:45 pm.

The nightly purge.

You're ugly. Not worthy. It's all your fault.

Inner shit talk loops over a pickaxe-on-sheet-metal soundtrack. Your skin is crawling.

That's right. Slap your belly paunch. Slap it raw.

In threadbare Calvin Klein underwear hiked up into a Speedo, you rip off a strangling, canary yellow scarf, leave it in a pool of grime on the bar floor, and replace it with a Glad trash bag.

Yank it over your head. Asphyxiate yourself.

After a failed leap onto the stripper pole, plastic bag as head, your Punk Screamer morphs into a blood-hungry bat and hangs upside down from a cubby hole above the stage. The riffs crush. The room rumbles. Head-rushed anguish.

"Fuck this town," your Punk Screamer howls. The crowd recoils.

Keep howling. Keep howling at the bowels of hell.

2:45 am.

The Trump-loving venue owner is also a slumlord. His shabby, vacant, crash pad's history is unimaginable. In the backyard, broken patio chairs and a milk-crate coffee table sit precariously on a cracked concrete slab. Band members nurse three-quarter-finished beers, cigarettes balancing on bottom lips.

Go to bed. You have to sleep.

You find the nearest bedroom and zombify. Mould stains on the ceiling above the bed creep closer in Rorschach patterns.

4:45 am.

Shut up, brain. Brain will not shut up. *Shut up, brain.* Brain will not shut up. *Shut up, brain...*

6:45 am.

Time to rage.

You pop out of bed in a flash—crash and dash. Smashing the walls, punching the doors, thrashing down the halls, screaming obscenities. You stage dive onto your groggy tourmates' Hide-a-Bed, crushing their legs. Pores still leaking booze, they spring up and yell, "What the fuck?"

It's just a joke. You didn't mean it. It's just a joke.

8:45 am.

Driving. Exhausted.

Put down your phone. Eyes on the road.

Hairpin turns.

One more show. You're almost there.

NEVER GOING BACK

Today is October 12, 2022, the four-year anniversary of my mental health crisis and diagnosis. Four years from the day bipolar stormed my barricades wearing muddy combat boots and flashing a sinister sneer. In the 1,095 days since then, I've been desperately calling a truce between my depression and mania—ongoing negotiations for a mood-episode no-fly zone.

It will pass.

I used to want to punch someone in the kidneys when they said that to me.

Fuck you it will pass.

It wasn't passing in two miserable, life-swallowing weeks of depression. It wasn't passing in two unbearable, hyper-charged weeks of mania after that. Rinse and repeat. It just wasn't passing. But four years later, here I am, stable with fingers crossed, more stable than I've ever been, pre- or post-diagnosis.

The moods will pass, I tell myself, guarding my kidneys.

My life to this point has been an eternity and a blip. Decades of undiagnosed bipolar sparked a fuse that has weaved through my body since childhood and warped my perception of time—a blur of lost memories, pinpointed regrets, hazy adventures, and impenetrable bonds.

Has the joy outweighed the turmoil?

My internal voice often mimics my counsellor's. It's easier to hear someone else asking the tough questions. My actual counsellor (not my internal one) says I should be proud of myself for how far I've come in the past four years. I'm following my treatment plan. I'm taking care of myself. I'm not constantly pulling sticks from the bundle strapped to my back, ready to flog myself whenever I make a mistake.

"Can you give yourself permission to give yourself a hug?" my counsellor says, and I cringe. Self-care and self-compassion are concepts I didn't understand before and still don't feel comfortable with. But I can see my life more clearly now. I've been looking down the throat of a dragon without it scorching me to ashes, and in there I've found an abundance of introspection. My scared kid grew into a scared adult, and I stayed that way until middle age. It was always someone else's job to take care of me, love me, mother me. I couldn't uncurl from the fetal position, shielding myself from the ghosts of my abusers in the rowboat and the pine-needle forest. My constant fight or flight wasn't sustainable and, at 46, as I've well documented, I broke.

Much has changed for me since October 12, 2018. My abuse memories don't haunt me as much, and I know how to breathe to calm myself. I'm a more active listener, although less so if I'm trending toward mania. (Just ask Megan.) I don't completely withdraw when I'm depressed anymore, and I don't completely lose control when I'm manic. I'm aware of my shifting moods and how quickly they become dysregulated, and I have a handle on the symptoms and ramifications of living with bipolar.

What about the eternally pondered question of whether my bipolar diagnosis is a blessing or a curse? A curse is an easy out. *I'm cursed. Why me?* Wallowing in self-pity digs me into a mud pit with slick, clay sides. The only way is down. But calling it a blessing is also an easy out. *I'm blessed. Yay me!* Sailing the choppy waters of naivety can lead to the depths of disappointment. Again, the only way is down.

Turns out there's a third choice. My diagnosis is what it is, it's here for life, and I might as well embrace it. This sounds annoyingly zen, but the more I think about it, the more it fits with where I stand today. It's not a question of whether my diagnosis is good or bad, it's a matter of what I do with it and how I handle it. I'm not cursed or blessed. I just am.

Wake up. Morning walk. Speed-yoga. Smoothie and toast. Take meds. Foggy head. Fingers frozen in thought.

Four years? Has it been that long?

My shoulders lock and my temples pulse. I'm having trouble concentrating again. My recent diagnosis of attention deficit hyperactivity (comorbid with my bipolar) explains why I'm so scrambled every morning. The diagnosis has been validating and a way to parse out symptoms that don't fit with bipolar. For one, it explains why I've always had so much trouble concentrating, skittering around the house like a lost amoeba. Today, I hush my disjointed, internal chatter with the regularly rotating *Mouse Ear [Forget-Me-Not]* album by the vastly underrated Ottawa '90s emotional hardcore band Shotmaker. Turn it up; find the flow, and cue the magic wordmaker.

Routine is the key to my stability. Social rhythm therapy (a.k.a. Circadian rhythm therapy) has been my saviour since life for Megan and I quieted in March 2020, along with everyone else's. I wake up at the same time, go for a walk at the same time, take my pills at the same time (big shoutout to my current meds cocktail), eat meals at the same time, and in 12 hours and 45 minutes, I'll go to bed at the same time. Same, same, same. Stable life isn't boring. Really, it's not.

I play music. As of this moment, I'm in three bands—one noise project with Mel, one oddball punk band with Rin, Lindsay, and Cam (a.k.a. Little Pharmer) and one screamy, doomy metal trio with Darren and Sasha. And there's always another musical project in the works. I've also stayed connected with Fest friends from around the world and we talk about our favourite bands through Messenger because that's what keeps us stoked.

"Up the punx!" It's a fun thing to say, but I've always wondered what it means exactly. I looked it up on Urban Dictionary—an air-tight source if there ever was one—and what I found flabbergasted me. "Up the punx!" is defined as "to pull yourself together emotionally, physically, and mentally in order to raise the bar in your life, despite what's going on around you." Amazing. I always thought "up the punx!" was just something we yelled at each other when we high fived.

So, where do I go from here? What do I do now? Sometimes when people ask me what I do, as people often do, I'll jokingly say something like, "Get up in the morning and breathe." It's easier than explaining how I (barely) make a living. Ah yes, the subjects of money, and jobs, and careers, and financial stability—they're just not top of mind for me anymore. I've got more important things to focus on, like my health, Megan, my kids, my family, and my friends.

At this stage in my life, do I even need a resume? Well, okay, I'm a writer. It took me until recently to be able to say that again, even after running the deadline treadmill for 25 years as a journalist and music writer. These days, I write when I want, what I want, how often I want. Distorted thinking lies to me, tells me I'm a fraud—not "a real writer." When I'm stable, I've learned to respectfully tell my distorted thinking to redact itself from my CV.

I produce, edit, and host the *Scream Therapy* podcast about, yep, punk rock and mental health and its *Flex Your Head* spinoff podcast about classic punk albums. I love everything about podcasting, even the four-hour editing sessions that seize my back and fuse it to my chair. Also, I'm an editor on hiatus after two decades of obsessing over spelling, grammar, and sentence structure. I'd love to get back into it someday, in a non-soul-sucking, freelance kind of way.

In the outside world (like out of the house), I work a two-hour shift at the Patricia Theatre in the evening—the same Patricia Theatre where my nervous mouth spilled anxious words before the Fugazi documentary screening on my birthday. Side note: working at a movie theatre was one of Ian MacKaye from Fugazi and Henry Garfield a.k.a. Henry Rollins' first jobs as teens. (I'm a bit behind the times over here.) On afternoons, I deliver medication to people with mobility and mental health challenges. The pharmacy manager tells me I'll be "phased out" soon, so they can hire a corporate courier to do the job. The gig doesn't pay much, especially after the cost of gas and car maintenance, but I get to listen to podcasts and sometimes drive around with my youngest son and his 732-song thrash metal playlist, so that's pretty sweet. Once my pharmacy phaseout is complete, I'm hoping to pick up another odd job in the afternoons to break up my day. I really need to break up my day.

Over on the volunteer section of my resume, I'm a bipolar support group facilitator, crisis responder, and mental health coach. It's rewarding and enriching, exactly what volunteer work is supposed to be.

Interests and hobbies? I drag my mosh-pit-weary feet on hikes with Megan when I can. I play tennis with a farmer friend, have lost every match for as long as I can remember, and my body suffers for days afterward. Oh, there's Sunday pickleball—a racquet sport that's more my speed these days—in the same junior high gymnasium where I sold beer under the bleachers in Grade 8. Also, Saturday night poker with a group of oddballs who beat my two pairs with a three of a kind every time I go all-in. It's great fun.

That's all I've got. References available upon request.

I'm not sure what my livelihood will be tomorrow, next month, or in five years. What do I do with the MFA in Creative Nonfiction that I finished while writing this book? I haven't thought much about that either. And I'm not sure what I'll write after this book. Hopefully another one. Lately, I've been thinking about becoming more involved in the mental health community, but the last thing I want is to become another cog in the machine or risk relapse in a high-pressure environment.

Long story short: I don't know what I'm going to do, and that's okay. I've made it this far. It will all work out. Managing my mental health is my full-time job, and it always comes first.

We all know the Greek myth of the Flight of Icarus, the cautionary tale of a winged boy who flies too close to the sun. In my version, Icarus doesn't fall out of the sky at all. He soars through it.

The anthology *Live Through This: On Creativity and Self-Destruction* features an essay entitled *Cello Speak: Exploring New Languages for Madness* by Bonfire Madigan Shive, an avant-garde musician and long-time member of the activist mental health organization the Icarus Project. In her essay,

Bonfire writes about how the mental health establishment strips a person's self-empowerment and demonizes them in the process—how it pathologized and suppressed what she calls her "madness." As Bonfire shed the baggage piled on her, she saw how doctors labelled her inner voices as "psychotic episodes" to demean, criminalize, and overmedicate her. Bonfire's perspective is fascinating. In particular, the next part. In a section of her essay called *Voices*, she writes, "It was clear to me that moments of crisis, trauma, or 'breakdown' could also be opportunities for 'breakthrough.'" This thwacked me. Was my mental health crisis a breakthrough, the beginning of a better life? Were the past four years spent white-knuckling the bipolar roller coaster my hellride to someplace better? Like Rhode Island grindcore band Fucking Invincible named one of their albums, *It'll Get Worse Before It Gets Better*.

One of my kids' favourite books growing up was *We're Going on a Bear Hunt*. It's the goofball kind of story that, if read in just the right tone of dad, can bring pre-slumber joy to a bedtime routine. My 19-year-old daughter says it's "cringey" when I bring it up. Well, she better be ready to cringe because the lyrics to the song in the book are, and I quote:

We can't go over it, we can't go under it
We're just going to have go through it

Scream Therapy: the only punk book to quote a children's story and a radical essay in the same chapter. Take that, Jello Biafra. Take that, Raffi.

It's fall 2020, and I'm zeroing in on the bookshelf over my friend Drue's left shoulder as his voice passes through me, in one ear hole, out the other. He's dropping knowledge, but my brain is too muddled to comprehend what he's saying. His musings are the same ones I'll read in Bonfire Madigan Shive's essay two years later. If only I could rewind my cognition like a VHS tape. Fuck you, brain fog.

Drue had his own mental health crisis in 2018, just 14 days after mine. It's one of the reasons we've become such close friends.

"As much as it took me to recover from my breakdown, I'm kinda thankful it happened because I'm a better person for it," he tells me on our Zoom call.

Boom. Drue's describing his own "breakthrough," and it doesn't even register with me. Or what he tells me next. About me.

"You're a person who understands more of the world now," he says. "You're more caring and empathetic. And that's a lot to be thankful for."

If you rest, you rust
Trade sorrow in for trust
If you rest, you rust
Find your ground, and follow the light out
Hot Water Music - "Never Going Back"

David Meagher has been a psychiatrist for more than 30 years—a punk 10 years longer than that—and he's seen the benefits of the punk rock ethos in mental health recovery.

David spent his teens in Cavan County in the Northern Ireland province of Ulster after growing up in London. He came back to Ireland with a Cockney accent and, nicking Irish comedian Sean Hughes' joke, says he "spent the next two years in a headlock." David gives a chortling laugh that rattles my earbuds. Not long after moving back, he found a group of outsiders to hang out with, as punks always do. He and his new friends bonded over an allergic reaction to the way-too-traditional Irish music and terrible country and western that dominated the local radio waves. By the time early Irish bands such as the Undertones and the Boomtown Rats formed in the mid '70s, David's crew were starving for high-energy music that challenged conservatism.

"We listened to it and said, 'Wow, that's gotta be it!'" he says, and busts out another chortle.

Skip forward four decades, and I come across an article titled "Punk Rock Made Me a Psycho-therapissed" in the British Journal of Psychology. The author: Dr. David Meagher. The article references how mental health issues factored into the music of punks such as Joey Ramone and Mark E. Smith of The Fall. More to the point, David, who moonlights as guitarist in folk-blues-punk band Sons of Southern Ulster, makes the case that psychiatry is the "punk rock of medicine"— a bold claim.

In the piece, David writes, "The core tenets of recovery share considerable commonality with the ethos of punk rock—self-direction, respect and responsibility, person-centred, strengths-based, empowerment readily translating to the punk notions of DIY, positive action, self-efficacy, inclusiveness, and challenging misinformed convention via anti-hierarchical beliefs." It's an earful, so

I'll interject David's dissertation to take a deep breath... and continue.... "For those who enjoyed their formative years as psychiatrists to the tune of punk, the movement seared our brains with an indelible scar, providing permission to think outside of the box, to challenge convention, and to believe that everybody can make a useful contribution."

Nailed it, David.

In recent years, professionals in mainstream psychiatry are looking for alternative treatment plans to encourage self-empowerment in patients. Sometimes progress in the mental health system is so gradual it's hard to notice. David thrives on changes from within, and he's been head of teaching and research in psychiatry at the University of Limerick since 2007, an influential position that allows him to use unconventional interventions with his patients.

Sex Pistols' "Pretty Vacant" gurgles from a top-loading CD player that's straight out of the '90s. Belching out of overstrained speakers, it sounds as if guitarist Steve Jones is throwing his infamous distortion pedal against a wall. An esteemed psychiatrist is jumping around with a blow-up guitar, shredding a guitar solo as his fingers touch down on synthetic plastic at record speed. This therapeutic intervention for inpatients is the Air Guitar Project, developed by mister Psycho-therapissed himself, David Meagher.

"I make a fool of myself and I'm very happy to do that," David tells me with a shit-eating grin. "It gives everyone else permission to cut loose and say, 'Well, if he's doing it, I'm sure I can too.'" I look past the computer screen David and I occupy and eyeball the *Never Mind the Bollocks, Here's the Sex Pistols* cassette sitting on my tape shelf. My guitar-picking fingers twitch. Where do I sign up for this Air Guitar Project? Right, I'd have to book a trip to Ireland, but, luckily, air guitar is a global activity, so I demonstrate how it can be done over Zoom, and David growl-laughs his approval. The Air Guitar Project is a simple way for him to buck the system with encouraging results, and he's had multiple requests from patients to hold the rock-out sessions more frequently. "It's all about patients taking a break from their problems and connecting," he says. "On the ward, young people don't want to go to bingo, like me granny would do, and they don't always want to go to group therapy and talk about their feelings."

David tells me he's often thought of conventional psychiatry as a religious cult. A decade or so into his four-decade career, he realized that instead of trying to find all the answers, mental health professionals should leave room for people to find their own. My journey mirrors this approach. Although I can't picture anyone on my health team playing air guitar—"I don't like punk at all, but I'll read your book," my psychiatrist once told me—they helped me take control of my own care. Once a psychiatrist appointment, therapist session, mental health course, or support group ends, it's up to me. I, and I alone, am the person who can manage my symptoms and work toward living a fulfilling life. I must take ownership of that.

David addresses me, and I perk up, jogged out of my thoughts. "You know, Jason..." David rocks back in his chair for dramatic effect, his receding hairline mirroring mine. Seeing that he has my attention, he drills down his point. "To be honest, I mean, look, the common practice in psychiatry has been that patients aren't equal. It's all been very top-down. It's important to embrace right from the start that the outcome we're looking for is people realizing their potential and functionality. It's not just symptom control."

I'm sure David's "Punk Rock Made Me a Psycho-therapissed" had more than a few Sigmund Freud motherfuckers doing a double take and shaking their curmudgeon fists. At its core, the article is about folks striving to find their best selves and the places in their lives where they feel most alive. "The core of the punk ethos is recovery and being fearless," says David. "There's a determination to take control of things. That's a big advantage, really, isn't it? It's not the laid back 'hey man' hippy thing, is it? It's much more proactive and assertive."

If David's forward-thinking psychiatry has a soundtrack, it's punk rock played on an air guitar.

Living with a mental health condition is an ever-evolving learning experience. It's not enough that the journey is always changing, so is the language around it. I've been reflecting on something mental health activist Sascha DuBrul said to me near the end of our lengthy Zoom call two years ago. Words that, in retrospect, have altered my life. Remember, Sascha already dropped the mic and rocked my world when he suggested diagnosis might not be the beginning of my mental health journey.

In the days, weeks, months, and years following my diagnosis, when crossed wires between my mind and body threatened to snap under the weight of my history, my goal had been to recover. I wanted to punch bipolar in the face. I needed to overcome it. To win. Recovery meant getting better. It was my light—my way out. But the fear of living with bipolar for the rest of my life, and the terrifying possibility of relapsing into another manic episode, kept me from looking at the full scope of my mental health—the long game. One that didn't require a claim to swift victory but instead a steady, eventual recognition of stability. Two years my junior, Sascha also lives with bipolar and has been stable for more than a decade. He's one of a growing number of mental health advocates moving away from the language of recovery.

"Honestly, I'm not the biggest fan of the language of recovery," Sascha told me at the time. "So, what am I recovering from? Am I recovering and going back to the way I was before? Because that certainly is not the case." A low-watt light bulb hung over me as I stared at Sascha with a growing glimmer of understanding. *Wait... I don't want to recover... to go back to the way I was before... the damage I was doing.* The next words out of Sascha's mouth screwed a new, mega-watt bulb into my socket, creating a luminescent a-ha I'm still humming from.

"Transformation. I like to use the language of transformation," he said. "I'm not interested in a mental health recovery movement. I'm way more interested in a mental health transformation movement." My thought-pistons fired. *Transformation... transformation movement... through and out... not back.*

"You don't look at a caterpillar that forms a chrysalis and say, 'Oh, that caterpillar is in a state of recovery,'" Sascha continued. "And a chrysalis doesn't just stay a chrysalis—it becomes a butterfly." My jaw loosened and words dropped out: "Do you feel like a butterfly?" "Hmmm." He paused, for an awkwardly long time. "Yeah, sometimes." The issue with the metaphor, he explained, is we don't stay a butterfly either—it's a spectrum.

The American Psychiatric Association found that more than 50 percent of people who recover from a depressive episode will experience at least one more in their lifetime. An increasing number of health care professionals and members of the mental health community are encouraging the term "pathways to recovery" rather than recovery. I'm not sure this terminology cuts it anymore, now that Sascha has introduced me to the language of transformation.

"I have different stages of evolution and transformation," he told me. "No way have I ever felt like the word 'recovery' captures what I went through, because each time I went through one of those experiences I learned so much, and I gained so much."

I should have given Sascha another mic to drop.

Shortly after my diagnosis, I veered away from disordered and pathologized language such as "mental illness" toward person-first language like "living with a mental health condition." One thing that never occurred to me before talking to Sascha is we can also challenge the term "mental health." "We call it mental health," he told me, "but it's actually just liberation. Individual and collective liberation."

If those with lived experience use their own language—whatever helps them form their own identities—instead of what the medical system and societal conventions dictate, freedom and independence could be the focus. The Icarus Project, the social justice group Sascha co-founded in 2002, proposes that a person's mental state benefits from collective liberation. Sascha told me he prefers to look at mental states as "sensitivities" and "dangerous gifts."

"Rather than seeing ourselves as diseased or disordered, we see ourselves as having wings that you have to learn to use," Sascha told me at the time. "I really don't like talking about illness, or disease, or disorder, or dysfunction. I want to leave space open for people to figure out for themselves what it is they're struggling with."

One of the biggest myths in psychiatry is that a chemical imbalance in the brain is the root cause of mental health conditions such as clinical depression and generalized anxiety. Many mental health experts now claim the "broken brain" line of thinking is a Big Pharma marketing scheme to sell the idea that we can be fixed with little white pills. For me, with time, mood stabilizers and antipsychotics have helped tremendously to regulate my mood episodes, but I reject the common consensus that doctors prescribe meds to "fix" our brains. I can't stress the number of times I've heard this false narrative. Investigative journalist Johann Hari's book *Lost Connections: Why You're Depressed and How to Find Hope*—which I devoured in two three-hour sittings—reveals how most prominent scientists and doctors now debunk the long-held, "broken brain" belief.

Enter the bio-psycho-socio model. Biological is the body (such as physical functions and genetic factors), psychological is the mind (such as thinking patterns and stress response), and sociological is the environment (such as social and cultural factors). Under this model, the three overlap for the onset of a mental health condition. Of particular interest are the environmental factors. Not falling in line with status-quo expectations of behaviour can lead people into dangerous territory, even more so if they're predisposed to mental health issues. Sascha and I identified with this during our Zoom session. We—and countless punks—have often lived at odds with the environments around us.

"When I got my ass locked up in a psych hospital when I was 18, and they told me I had a biological brain disease, I was so embedded in punk rock and anarchism I said, 'Fuck you people.'" Sascha scoffed, paused, and busted out lyrics to Suicidal Tendencies' "Institutionalized," an old standby and infamous "screw you" to involuntary hospitalization, and we recited them together:

What are you trying to say, I'm crazy?

When I went to your schools, I went to your churches,
I went to your institutional learning facilities!
So how can you say I'm crazy?

Sascha moved on from The Icarus Project in 2014 to train as a mental health clinician and start Transformative Mental Health Practices where he helps people who want to use their "mad gifts" to better themselves. Before we ended our lengthy call, Sascha left me with another critical point to ponder.

"What if we flipped 'mental illness' around and said, 'Actually, the society we're living in is really sick'? Its foundations are based on genocide and slavery. Instead of just fitting ourselves into a society that's really broken, what if we use the fact that we're different from society to try and change society?" A content look washed over Sascha's face as he left me with simple yet life-defining words. "I got that outlook from where I came from," he said. "I got that from punk rock."

My magazine editors always hammered into me that writing based on email correspondences is a no-no. Impersonal, they said. Stilted, they complained. Lazy, they accused. Grumpy faces made grumpy demands because those are the demands they've always made. I mean, I've agreed in the past. How do we read body language in words? As an editor, I crammed the same rule down the throats of journalists and music writers for decades. Get people on the horn. If they're within driving distance, sit your ass behind the wheel. The Zoom videos kids are using these days? Holy fuck. What a revelation.

Following up with Bianca Cruz, screamer of the blazing-fast Amygdala, I go against my own advice and email her questions about her current mental health. This way she can reflect and answer on her own time. She responds within the hour.

"Hey Jason! I'm glad you reached out to me. I've actually been meaning to email you. After our conversation, I started to think about what specifically was affecting me," she writes. Bianca was managing borderline personality the best she could when we talked at the end of 2019. Family life was tough, and support was coming mostly from her bandmates. In her email, it's clear she's been through hell since I talked to her. Her emotions ooze from my Mac mail. I can almost see her sturdy herself and type her pain. "I reached my breaking point. I wanted to commit suicide," she writes, and I imagine her fingers clicking the keyboard fast and hard now. "I was crying daily and all my relationships were failing. I didn't enjoy anything."

Epic sigh over here. I'm tracing back the untraceable hours lying on my couch in near catatonia, a total lack of caring that, if it tries to hijack me these days, I need to wrestle from as soon as possible or it will consume me. The tone of Bianca's sentences transform into excitement, become less punctuated, more abbreviated, her turning points denoted by lack of paragraph breaks. "I've been on the right path. I'm now in therapy. I'm taking medications to manage my mental health. I realized I was having up to 10 panic attacks a day. I can't believe I survived like that for so long."

In addition to her borderline personality diagnosis, Bianca now has comorbid diagnoses—chronic depression, generalized anxiety, and panic attacks—and is thankful to her mental health team for helping her navigate them. In the past, Bianca's undiagnosed clinical anxiety and depression made life seem impossible when all she wanted was to get a handle on her symptoms and become stable. In her email, she shares that she's working consistent hours, has new responsibilities at her job, and, at age 26, she got her driving permit.

Researchers from Temple University in Philadelphia and Portland State University found that 33 percent of people with lifelong mental health conditions had been in recovery/remission for the past 12 months or more. The research study defined recovery/remission as being able to take part in everyday activities and community living while managing symptoms.

"I'm thriving!" writes Bianca. (Note to my inner editor: allow exclamation points from emails.) "I feel like I'm making up for lost time. However, I don't ever want to fall in that hole again." The word "however" shows up twice near the end of Bianca's email. It's a word I overuse, along with "but." During my depressive episodes, no matter how many lips I bite and tongues I hold, I cannot stop the word "but" from coming out of my mouth. If they're not beaten into the ground though, the words "however" and "but" don't have to be negative. Bianca seems to use "however" as a self-affirming word of caution. It's the anti-tidy-bow on a package never meant to be entirely wrapped and, punk willing, never ripped wide open and left in shambles. "However, I'm not completely out of the woods yet," she writes. "I don't think I'll ever be. I'm not afraid to say that I need to manage myself on the daily. I'm not ashamed to take medication I've been needing for so long. I finally feel at peace."

Talking to others about their lived experience is a responsibility I treat with seriousness and sincerity. These respectful, mutually beneficial conversations about punk and mental health define the *Scream Therapy* podcast and, in large part, this book. However (and there's that word again), allowing someone time to formulate thoughts in their own home, at their own desk, with the people they love close by, is another respectful way to understand their journey and sense their body language, outbox to inbox. By email, Bianca might have opened up to me in a way she never would have over another Zoom call, the awkwardness on our faces plopped onto screens using 5G.

To tell the story of Bianca's mental health journey toward transformation, I'm honoured she—and everyone else in this book, no matter what the communication mode—gifted me the words to do so.

"I Wish Upon a Shooting Star" is the last song on Amygdala's album, *Our Voices Will Soar Forever*. In the song, Bianca urges listeners going through their own transformation to honour the crucial act of reclamation.

Now we rise!

We will take back what's ours!

The lives we always deserved!

The lyrics define the crux of punk's approach to mental health. Speak our truths. Support those around us to speak theirs. The more we talk, the easier it is to scream.

As I began working on this book and the podcast, it was Bianca who was the first person to tell me, "Punk rock saved my life," and those who came after her repeated this mantra. At the time, the validation of her words welled my eyes with tears. The final words of her email bring them back.

"I hope your book can open the world up to the power of healing through music and storytelling."

Yeah... me too.

SHOW 9
UCLUELET
ARMY, NAVY, & AIRFORCE VETERANS CLUB
SATURDAY, AUGUST 18, 2018

You're straddling a ladder you found in the janitor's closet, screaming your face off. Because you need to. Because you have to. The ladder you're commandeering sits in the middle of the mosh pit, and ruffians crash into it from all angles. It wobbles from side to side as you try to steady it with your arms, a desperate tightrope walker. The force from the swirling pit knocks the ladder onto one leg, teetering, then crashing down, tangling you in aluminium, your appendages sticking out, your right hand pinched in the top step. You're trampled in spilled beer as you scramble to escape. Someone—a bastard—grabs the ladder and swings you around on the floor. The momentum pulls your body loose and leaves your pinkie fingernail behind.

"Um, you fell off the ladder yourself," Mike tells you later. "It was me who moved the ladder out of the way, and you just rolled around on the floor screaming."

Wait. What?

On day 11 of the nine-show tour, you finally break. Fantasy has become reality. You've become one with the Punk Screamer—alone, on the floor in the swampy beer, your squashed pinkie bleeding. A video on Mike's phone shows your face covered in duct tape, ear to ear, hairline to chin—a cross between Iron Man and Hannibal Lector. With the look of a vengeful ghost in a Japanese horror movie, a wispy black and white shawl drapes over your shoulders and covers your ground-beef torso. Your red onesie, a superstar on this tour, has made its return, and you've hitched it around your waist.

You drag a folding chair onstage, drop your full weight into it, and reach for your untrustworthy hair clippers. Tonight, you must finish the job. You bait the audience with the buzzing apparatus and wait for someone to step forward—someone who wants the chance to shave a bellowing beast. Back from Victoria, Tara is up to the task and grabs the clippers. Mike grimaces and holds his phone steady to film the shearing. After each pass of the clippers, you self-flagellate. Self-inflicted chest slaps that burn you red. Your fists pound your face, one after the other in rapid-fire furiosity. Tara finishes the worst haircut in history, takes two steps back, eyes her handiwork, and doubles over laughing. Finally, the days-long scalp mangling is over. She retreats right before you launch yourself from the chair and swing your microphone stand into the front row, narrowly missing innocent bystanders.

Your microphone is dead. At this point, you don't need a microphone. You dry heave from the heat radiating on your duct-taped face—your second skin. You're exhausted, a fractured marionette, a puddle of mud, a bloody stump, dust. You go limp and hit the floor. Over, finished, done, gone, out. It's the first time in Punk Jams' history you call for surrender before the band stops playing.

Is Ucluelet your final celebratory dance or the path that leads to your undoing? A warbled Munchkin singsong fills your head, but your mouth won't let it out.

Punk Jams is dead
Long live Punk Jams
Punk Jams is dead
Long live Punk Jams

AFTERMATH

OCTOBER 28, 2018

I need yr help. I fucked up big time. I'm having some dark
thoughts.

Middle-of-night texts always equal panic. This one's from Drue. Watching
his blinking Messenger dot... dot... dot... stop... start... is torture. I duck into
the bathroom of my Fest cottage in Gainesville, Florida—the other side of the
continent—and call him. Drue picks up before the first ring, voice instantly
cracking.

"Buddy... I'm in a bad spot."

Drue's tears practically drip through my phone from 3,000 miles away.

Wait, if it's 6:30 am here, that means... it's 3:30 am there...

I slam my ass down on the edge of the tub.

"Are you okay, Drue? What's going on?"

"I fucked up. I fucked up, man. Everything is fucked," he croaks.

"Where are you? Are you okay? Talk to me, buddy."

His silent pause is deafening. Agony in dot... dot... dots....

"I think I need to go to the hospital," Drue says, barely audible. "I'm not
right."

I snap into rescue mode and work out a plan—from another country on
another coast—to get Drue to the hospital in Victoria.

"Okay, I'm here for you. Just try to relax." I'm his breathing coach now.
"Take some deep breaths." His inhales sound like a wet vac at the end of a

wind tunnel. "Okay Drue, listen to me. Take another deep breath... now let it out... slow. You can do this. Now, tell me what happened." His mouth noises lurch forward, then back, like the jellied legs of a rookie cliff jumper. "I'm fucked," he sobs. "I was driving the work van home after a show at Logan's... I crashed it into a telephone pole, and it's all fucked. I'm fucked. I feel like I'm having a nervous breakdown."

Breathe. Slow. Both of us.

"Drue. Listen. You have to call Mike. He won't care that you're calling so late. He'll bring you to the hospital. Now tell me where you are."

"I'm at home," he says, a bit calmer now. "The cops brought me here. I thought about calling a suicide hotline, but then I remembered you might be awake there."

I direct traffic. "Okay Drue, call Mike. Please."

"...okay, I will. I will.... Thanks buddy. Love you."

"Love you too, Drue. You're going to get through this."

I text Mike.

`Drue's in trouble. He's going to call you. He needs to go to the hospital.`

More... dot... dot... dots.... This time from Mike. Drue's life could be hanging in the balance and those fucking... dots... taunt... me....

After what feels like an eternity crammed into moments, Mike lights up my screen.

`Okay, got it.`

I lift my butt from the tub and stumble back to bed in a daze. Malcolm, my trusty Fest roommate, springs up, roused from his chainsaw snores.

"What's going on, dude?"

"It's my friend back home," I say. "He's having... a nervous breakdown."

I fold into bed and wait for Mike's text telling me that Drue's going to be okay. I survived my crisis. He could too, right?

Live fast (but don't die young)
Slow down, but never, ever stop
Paint It Black - "The Beekeeper"

It's August 18, 2021, three years to the day since the final Punk Jams show in Ucluelet. Drue and I are eye-to-eye on our laptops, having a much-anticipated catch-up without the in-person extenda-hug it deserves. Near the end of our conversation, we get to talking about the tour. And the Punk Screamer.

That I was you, and you were me.

"It's like a monster was unleashed in you that just wasn't willing to go back into the box," Drue says. He notices I'm uncomfortable and eases off. "Don't get me wrong, it's just that something was eating away at you, and it needed to come out."

I have a favourite photo from the tour. It's not one of me as the Punk Screamer, the conductor of the beautiful mishmash that is Punk Jams. It's not the photo of me trying to scream-swallow a microphone, sweat stains creating unsightly patterns on my patented red onesie. It's not the photo where Drue is leaning back-to-back with me, throttling his guitar to tame feedback, his eyes sparkling, his hair a grizzled, finger-in-socket bouffant. It's not even the photo of my jockstrap-flossed ass mooning 175 perplexed punks at the Duncan show.

In my favourite photo, Drue and I sit on the bumper of the stinking Toyota Corolla. We've made a pit stop on the way back from the Ucluelet show—in Port Alberni of all places—so Drue can hop in the Crashing Into Things van and the two of us can go our separate ways. I've popped the Corolla's trunk, and peeking over my right shoulder, amongst all the music gear, are the garbage bags I hauled around, putrid garments spilling out. I see the shredded canary-yellow scarf. Pairs of underwear in ghastly shades of brown and orange. The rest, indistinguishable, smushed into red and pink. In the photo's foreground is my patchy, shaved head, that of a squirming dog in veterinary pre-op, and the manic, goofy look on my face. Drue has his arm around me, weariness hidden behind a pair of cheap pink sunglasses, face muscles relaxed, the antithesis of my lopsided, euphoric grin. Drue's smile is absent, but I know he's smiling inside. His scruffy, collarbone-length beard hangs with confidence, and he looks cool as a, well, fuck it... cool as a cucumber. Our torsos squeeze against each other as we jostle into the photo frame. I can almost hear the cell phone shutter noise commemorating a quintessential, tour-ending memory—a photo I can smile at when life feels hopeless again.

Drue's been doing better since his emergency trip to the hospital in October 2018, two weeks after my own. He's playing music that he loves, he's in a wonderful relationship, and he lives a relatively stable life. I've been doing better too. But stability is a tricky game, and I need to continue doing the daily work, because going back to who (or what) I was on that tour isn't an option. It's triggering to relive that 11-day trip. Certain stories bring smiles, others we give a proper burial with bowed heads, silence in the knowing.

After the whirlwind tour with Drue and the Punk Jammers ended, going home was my only logical choice. Knowing what I know now, the first thing I would have done—aside from kissing the welcome mat—was stuff the Punk Screamer back into the box that Drue talked about, lock it, and eat the key. I would have backed away in tiny steps, flinched, and prayed that that part of me wouldn't bust the lock open and spring out in a ridiculous costume like a suped-up jack-in-the-box, hellbent on dragging me to the next onstage debacle.

I've resolved to carry the tour's scars with honour. I've promised myself to celebrate the good parts and keep the bad parts locked in the box. When I came face to face with bipolar two months after returning home, I didn't have the Punk Screamer's masks to protect me anymore. I had to find a way to protect myself.

My legs drift in circles like a slow-motion Roadrunner escaping from Wile E. Coyote. He wants to catch and eat me. But I'm in control now, and I know how to get away.

Somatic therapy is quite the trip for processing trauma. I pay attention to my body and how its sensations connect to emotional pain and dysregulation.

My counsellor gives me the stereotypical prompt of, "When you're ready, bring yourself back to the room."

Right... I need to come back to the room. Okay, come back to the room.

I creak one eye open, then the other, and the fluorescent lighting, unsuccessfully filtered by a piece of floral bed sheet, pounds my pupils. My counsellor asks how I'm doing in that soothing voice all counsellors probably have to perfect before they get their Master's degree.

"I'm okay, I guess?"

My sexual abuse memories still come with the uncertainty of who, what, when, where, and why. Also, how.

"How do I know these things actually happened to me?"

"Let me ask you this," my counsellor says, "would you be having these memories if they weren't true?"

Hmmm. Good point. I slump in her turd-brown office chair, let my eyelids drop again, and my muscles twitch. My eternally restless knees stop knocking, and I'm momentarily lifted off the chair in a full-body jerk.

"That's good. You're doing some good work there. Check in with your body," she says. "What are you feeling right now? Where are you feeling it?"

I don't have to dig for answers. I tell her about a smothering weight on my tailbone that's poking through the front of my groin.

"Is it okay to just sit in the feeling for now? When was the last time you took a breath?" This is her go-to intervention. My shallow panicked breaths aren't helping me remain calm or stay present in my body. I need a deep one, so I claim it.

"That's a nice, big breath. That's good," she says. "Can you tell me what just came up?"

I'm never reluctant to reveal what I can remember of my abuse. I'm not ashamed or embarrassed to talk about it, and I've never thought it was my fault.

Another big breath.

He's pinning me down as he whispers those things to me in the rowboat, as he does those things to me. Click. Flash. I'm face down in the dry, sharp pine needles, pants around my ankles. They're all laughing, calling me names I don't understand.

"Okay. We talked about moving slowly with this," my counsellor says gently, "so I want you to take a pause and describe the sensations in your body."

Trauma has padlocked my neck and shoulder blades. My chest feels constricted and buzzy. I'm having trouble with my breath again.

"I'm here with you. You're safe. I want you to focus on those feelings for a minute," she says. "Can you do that?"

I can.

My breath normalizes, and my shoulders relax. "Now bring yourself slowly back to the room."

I do.

Once I'm settled, she asks me about music, as she often does, because she knows it pacifies me. She enjoys hearing about the punk subculture I cherish—the community and support it offers. She understands it's my safe place.

"How was the tour?"

Wild stories are on the tip of my tongue, and it hits me like a spiked 2X4.

Holy shit. I've never told her about my monster in the box. The Punk Screamer.

On tour, the places I went behind the masks and under the costumes were my joy and my rage bound together, timebomb coping strategies wrapped in unhinged protection mechanisms. I've learned to accept that the Punk Screamer was my only way to stave off the mental health crisis waiting for me back home. I hate thinking about what could have happened without that tour. If I'd stayed home, depression's bile could have eaten away at me. Without something to purge the acid, without Punk Jams as a creative outlet, no matter how chaotic it was, I'm not sure I would have survived.

When I was on stage—*when I was you*—I was able to keep from shattering, but it came at a cost. I put my body through the ringer. Beat it to hell. I broke myself, but I put myself back together just the same.

If I hadn't gone on that tour, a darker incarnation of the monster in the box could have dragged my inner child back to the pine-needle forest, taken me out in the rowboat and thrown me in the lake, the weight of my trauma sinking me to the bottom.

I always take the same route to the river. Walking down my neighbourhood alley is a treat because it's fun to scope out the junk in people's backyard. Old trucks with no wheels propped up on rotting wooden blocks. Kids' play forts made from tarps and ripped bedsheets. AC/DC flags hanging in laundry room windows.

Plunging into the river is my daily ritual, starting about mid-April until my birthday in early November, depending on how long I can withstand the cold. Every afternoon, huddling over my computer, eyes crossing from screen strain, the river's crispness pulls me out of my chair.

The alley is quiet today, but my earbuds are not. I'm listening to City of Caterpillar, an emo-hardcore band from Richmond, VA, and the volume on my phone won't go any louder. As always, the music is blocking my internal chatter. I'm focusing on the guitar feedback, distorted drums and bass, and noisescapes. Oh, and the screams, always the screams.

The second-to-last backyard before the river is my favourite. It's my friend Cam a.k.a. Little Pharmer's house. He's one of the few people in town who understands why punk is so important to me—how it's helped me heal. I hope he's in his backyard, elbow deep in the garden or playing a pacifist's version of Nerf guns with his radically adorable kids. I don't see any sign of Cam or the kids, but I need a pen and paper because I have an idea for another book, so I let myself in his backyard gate. City of Caterpillar's song "A Little Change Could Go a Long Ways" has sparked me. Rustling through half-finished art and kids' woodwork projects on Cam's lean-to porch, I find a blunt pencil and a scrap of a brown paper bag stained with pine-tree pitch. I cross the street with my dull writing tool and sticky scroll and walk down the path toward the river. Sitting on its bank with goose shit encircling me like I'm about to be willingly sacrificed to a punk deity, I scrawl words and diagrams that will be illegible by the time I'm home. Just scribbling them down helps.

I've done my thought-collecting for now. The river is beckoning. I'm out of my clothes at record speed and wade thigh deep. One huge breath, and I'm in, kicking under the surface as my central nervous system resets. My bipolar takes a breather, and I hear punk rock inside my head, clearer than the water I slice through. I surface and gulp a lungful of air—invigorated, transformed in the moment. One more dunk, and my body rebels. It's fucking freezing. I scramble out of the water, shake my arms and legs, and my feet burn cold. I shiver and sob.

Can I sit in that feeling for a moment? Yes, I can.

I towel myself off and jump into my underwear. My earbuds go back in before I put on the rest of my clothes, and City of Caterpillar is still creating a magnificent racket. The song is called "Fucking Hero." Every time I come out of the lake, I feel like one.

I never thought I could write a book—any book. After my diagnosis, I convinced myself I couldn't write another word, never mind 257 pages. My depressed moods fogged me out, poisoned my fingers, and tricked me into self-sabotage—*don't even fucking bother*, they snarled—that writing about punk rock and mental health was stupid, and it was all a waste of time. Then my mania went into overdrive, and I would become a creative raw nerve, jonesing to write an *Odyssey*-length manifesto (*ooh, ooh, look, look, another creative masterpiece*). Because of my mood dysregulation, punk and writing alternated between positive forces guiding me through life and useless burdens I was destined to fail at.

My mood episodes still set me back, of course they do, and, honestly, on my worst days I'd rather not be here. But those days are fewer and farther between. My weather is unpredictable. Some mornings, the sky dumps rain. By afternoon, it's clear. Other mornings, I crowbar myself from bed and open the blinds to find a harsh fog rolling in. When it finally burns off, I notice the swaying trees, the falling leaves, the chirping birds, and the buzzing bees. (I just wanted that to rhyme).

I've learned that when I wake up in the morning, I can check my weather, and as Ian MacKaye from Fugazi and Dischord Records so wisely says, "Dress accordingly." Sitting in front of my sunny window today, in my mainly sunny existence, I've found a better life.

Punk sustains me. Its positive impact was immediate when I first heard Blaine's *Thrasher Skate Rock* tapes. And Fugazi, and Minor Threat, and Heavens to Betsy, and Converge, and Black Flag, and Rites of Spring, and Spanish Love Songs, and Worriers, and Against Me!, and Jawbreaker, and Hot Water Music, and so many others. Almost 40 years into our history together, punk rock has given me—and the incomparable people in its scene—agency to scream. We scream because it helps us cope. We scream because it gives us hope.

Punk has saved us before, and it will save us again.

ACKNOWLEDGMENTS

Mental health team, for teaching me to advocate for myself. Dr. Bell, Dr. Ramirez, Shona, and all the counsellors along the way who have, with such care, listened to me ramble.

Meds, you little beauties, I'm glad I finally trusted you, and it's been comforting to check in with you twice a day.

Bipolar support group members, every Sunday it's my honour to be part of our community.

University of King's College MFA classmates, faculty, and writing group buds, let's stay in touch.

Susan, for your constant thoughtfulness and encouragement.

My MFA mentors, Cooper, for reminding me to keep my "skin in the game," and Wanda, for telling me to "put my foot in it."

Ryan from Anteism, for knowing shit about books. Ella, for also knowing shit about books.

Fest Friends Are Best Friends, especially Malcolm, my Fest roommate for life (A Wilhelm Scream, forever!), and I hope to see you all at Fest 30 when I'm 60.

My noise pals: Mel (Wise Mind); Rin, Lindsay, and Cam (Rifle Rafle a.k.a Riff Raff); Darren and Sascha (Con Man); Murray, Rin, and Lindsay (band name tbd); and Kim and Mel (band name tbd). All the members of Punk Jams, you know who you are. Thanks for letting me sweat on you.

My patron saints who walk and talk, and talk and walk, and spend time with me when I need it most: Mel, Mike I., Drue, Darren, Luke, Cam, Jeff, Mike S., Donald, and Adam H. I cherish every friend I have—near and far—more than I can say in words.

Hey Greg and Cruiser: Metal Mental Meltdown 'til death!

All the badass punks featured in this book, you were so generous and gracious with your stories. Eternal respect and thanks.

Family, please know how much you mean to me.

My kids, Lane, Lily, Max, and Oliver, I'm endlessly proud of you for doing what you want, not what you're expected to do.

My love, Megan, thanks for rescuing me from that aggro photographer dude at the Hot Snakes show in Portland on September 7, 2012. I love you more.

Myself, for sticking it out.

Come say hi at screamtherapyhq.com or email me
at screamtherapybook@gmail.com